A HISTORY OF

HUNGARIAN LITERATURE

BY

FREDERICK RIEDL, Ph.D.

PROFESSOR OF HUNGARIAN LITERATURE IN
THE UNIVERSITY OF BUDAPEST

NEW YORK
D. APPLETON AND COMPANY
1906

Published, October, 1906

PREFACE

'O mächtig ist der Trieb des Vaterlandes."

SOME years ago, when travelling in Hungary, I paid a visit to my friend Dr. Szily, then Secretary of the Royal Hungarian Academy in Budapest, and chanced to take up a volume of Mr. Gosse's " Literatures of the World" series, published by Mr. Heinemann, which was lying on his table. "Ah," I said, "we ought to have a book like that in England about Hungarian literature. Very few of us know anything of your literature, of the fine poetry it contains, of the many features which distinguish it from other European literatures." "Well," replied Dr. Szily, "if you can get the book published in Mr. Gosse's well-known series, the Hungarian Academy shall commission the ablest exponent of Hungarian literature in Hungary to write it, and present the manuscript to you as a gift."

"Your offer is very handsome," I said, "and as soon as I get back to England, I'll ask Mr. Heinemann if he will accept it."

That is the story of the origin of this history of Hungarian literature. The publisher and the editor alike expressed their willingness to accept the generous offer of the Hungarian Academy.

The choice of the Academy finally fell on Professor Riedl, Professor of Hungarian Literature in the University of Budapest, and the author of a biography of the

Hungarian poet, Arany, a book of remarkable power, which brought Professor Riedl into immediate prominence in his own country.

Competent translators were found in Mr. Ch. Arthur Ginever and his wife (born Ilona de Gjöry), a daughter of the Hungarian poet Gjöry, who have brought to the work all possible skill and care. I am also much indebted to Mr. and Mrs. Ginever for help and advice in translating and revising a few of the specimens of Hungarian poetry.

The book is unique in its kind in that it has been written entirely for the English public, and has never appeared in Hungarian ; indeed no such work exists in Hungary, and it will be as new to the Hungarian public as it is to the English. All honour is due to the Hungarian Academy for their generosity in thus spreading knowledge among the nations.

Hungarian literature makes, I think, special appeal to Englishmen. It is generally recognised how closely our literature is bound up with the country's religious life and political history. But in no country in the world is literature so much a part of its history, of its patriotic feelings, and of its struggles to preserve its liberties, as in Hungary. The epic and lyrical poetry, the drama, and the prose of every class, all alike sound those notes, and the melody is triumphant or despairing according to the period of the nation's history in which it was composed. Less perhaps than any other European literature has Hungarian literature been influenced by the literature of other lands. It mirrors throughout the simple, unsophisticated feelings and thoughts of men who loved their country wholly, sincerely, faithfully, and were ready to lay down their lives to preserve its freedom. Here, if ever, the soul of a people is revealed in its literature.

My sincere thanks are due to Mr. William N. Loew of New York, and to Mr. E. D. Butler, late of the British Museum, for their kind permission to reprint some of their translations of Hungarian poems.

The unacknowledged translations, including the extracts from the " Tragedy of Man," are renderings of my own. I have also revised the whole of the translations, with a view to bringing them as closely as possible to the letter as well as to the spirit of the original.

C. HAGBERG WRIGHT.

LONDON, *April* 1906.

CONTENTS

A HISTORY OF

HUNGARIAN LITERATURE

I

THE HUNGARIAN PEOPLE

A THOUSAND years ago, about the end of the ninth century, events, the results of which proved of great importance, took place in that part of Europe which is encircled by the Carpathians, and watered by the Danube and the Tisza. In that fertile district, known then as the Avar plain, in the very heart of Christian Europe, there suddenly appeared a tribe of wild, pagan horsemen, some one or two hundred thousand strong, who took possession of the country, settled upon it, and made it the centre for their predatory raids. It is astonishing how far those dreaded horsemen wandered in the course of their many campaigns. They poured unchecked over the whole of Europe. Marching northwards they reached Bremen, and reduced it to ashes. Southwards they penetrated as far as Athens, and in the west they camped before the walls of the Eternal City, which Attila himself never reached. They encamped beneath the gigantic arches of the aqueducts, and pitched their tents in Subiaco, in the gardens of Nero. They streamed eastwards, and knocked with their iron maces at the golden gate of Constantinople. They forced their way through the Pass of St. Bernard and through the Pyrenees, and wherever they went, they were as victorious on their steeds as the Vikings in their ships. But as soon as the predatory warriors, who had watered their horses in the Ilissus, Ebro, Elbe, and Tiber, settled down within the borders of Hungary, they founded there a strong and lasting state.

Many another race had from time to time inhabited the plains of the Danube and the Tisza before the Hungarians, but none of them had succeeded in creating a state. The Celts had found a home there, but disappeared thence as from most other regions. At the time of Augustus, the brass eagles of the Roman legions visited the virgin forests of Pannonia. It was there that the wisest and noblest of rulers, Marcus Aurelius, wrote the greater portion of his philosophical works. There, too, was born that unlucky successor of the great Augustus, Romulus Augustulus, the last ruler over the Empire founded by Romulus, and with the pitiable figure of that shadow-like emperor the Romans vanished altogether from Pannonia.

Then the blood-red waves of the migration flooded the country. The Huns came; their greatest leader, Attila, and his followers, built their wooden houses on the plain between the Danube and the Tisza, but they soon disappeared, to be followed for short periods by the Longobards, the Gepida, and the Jazyghiens. Next came the Avar race, but only to be overthrown by Charlemagne.

Last came the Hungarians, who alone succeeded in holding their own, and the state they founded became, through the excellence of its constitution, one of the most powerful in Europe. In the fourteenth and fifteenth

centuries the great countries of Europe had not yet attained
to real national unity ; Hungary, under her kings Louis
the Great and Matthias Hunyadi, took the lead in that
respect.   Every European people has its own special gift.
Greece and Italy have the gift of art ; Rome has law
England political liberty and the power of planting
colonies ; Germany has metaphysics and scientific
method ; while France is distinguished by good taste.
Hungary's endowment was a strong sense of nationality, that is to say, the desire to found and to maintain
a state which knitted the people into an organic
whole. Simultaneously with the growth of the national
spirit, and lending it strong support, arose the nation's
literature.   Henceforth Hungarian life and literature
developed in perfect sympathy with one another, and
kept pace so accurately together that, in the middle
of the nineteenth century, when new aims opened before
the people, and an ardent patriotism enthusiastically
welcomed the new ideals of democracy, the nation's
literature attained its zenith.

The principal motive of Hungarian poetry is to foster the
national idea in the hearts of the people. That powerful
racial element is revealed in the efforts of the Hungarians
to found a strong and enduring kingdom, and in their
continual struggles on behalf of their rights and unity.
Their first epic poet, Sebastian Tinódi, wrote his *Rhymed
Chronicles* after the battle of Mohács (1526), one of the
greatest catastrophes known to history. What could
his lays recount, save the downfall of his country,
and her desperate struggles for existence ? Valentine
Balassa, the most noteworthy Hungarian poet of the
sixteenth century, lived at the time when England saw
the wrecks of the Invincible Armada floating on the

ocean, the waves of which were now freed from the tyrant. But, in Hungary, alas! the poet and hero saw nothing but desolation, and went to meet his fate with a sad heart at the siege of Esztergom, fighting against the Turks. The chief Hungarian epic poet of the seventeenth century, Count Nicholas Zrinyi, happened to be travelling in Italy when Milton was there. Soon the return of each poet was claimed by his country, but the different parts which awaited them are characteristic of the fates of their respective lands. Milton left Italy, and with his pen helped to fight for, and to win, freedom under Cromwell's leadership.* Count Zrinyi devoted all his powers, both as general and as poet, to the great task of delivering Hungary from the Turkish yoke, but he did not live to see his aim fulfilled. The ideals of Zrinyi the leader were identical with those of Zrinyi the poet, and his literary work was like a trumpet-call to the nation, to awaken it from the torpor into which it had sunk under the "Turkish Opium," as he called the efforts of the Sultan to ingratiate himself with the subjugated Hungarians. Is it not natural that the leading theme of poets like Zrinyi should be the feeling of nationality?

After all danger from the Turk had passed away the Austrian influence threatened the national independence. At the time when Bishop Percy, in England, began to collect the treasures of ancient folk-lore, Hungarian popular poetry was just beginning to flourish. But by what sad events it was nourished. It sprang from the soil of the battlefield, during the wars of

---

* In his prose pamphlet, *Defensio Secunda*, Milton states that his mind was stronger than his body, and that therefore he did not court camps, where any common man could be as useful as himself.

Francis Rákóczy, Prince of Transylvania; its theme was the patriotic but vanquished Kuruc, or national army.

In the nineteenth century, while the poets of England were singing songs of triumph over the downfall of their country's foe, Napoleon, Hungary's sons trembled for their fatherland as they saw the signs of approaching danger, and foresaw a day when they might share the fate of Poland and be obliterated from among the nations. In the poem *Szózat* (Appeal), which became as popular a national song with the Hungarians as *Rule Britannia* with the English, the poet Vörösmarty drew the pathetic picture of a great day of burial when the nations of Europe would stand around the grave where the Hungarian nation had been entombed.

About the middle of the nineteenth century John Arany was Hungary's greatest poet. His dominant note, like that of Lord Byron, was one of profound melancholy, but how differently were the two poets circumstanced. Byron wrote after Waterloo, while on the heart of Arany was stamped the tragedy of Világos, where the Hungarian army was compelled to lay down its arms, after the whole country had been flooded by the Russian allies, called in by Austria to crush those who dared to struggle for liberty.

It must not be thought, however, that Hungarian literature is exclusively national in its contents and character. Just as the country itself is open to the waters of the Danube, rolling down from the west, so too, from the time of the Middle Ages, its literature received a stream of western ideas. Every epoch in Hungary's intellectual development was closely related to movements in Western Europe. Each new wave of impulse originating there—the asceticism of the Middle Ages, the Renaissance, the Reformation and Anti-Reformation, the Baroque style, rationalism, romanticism, and the new democratic ideals—reached the borders of Hungary, and left some mark upon its mental life.

II

THE HUNGARIAN LANGUAGE

IN studying a literature it is necessary to give some consideration to the language in which it is written.

At a first glance, Hungarian seems as much a stranger among all the other European languages, as the erratic blocks of the geologist amidst their foreign surroundings. It is not related to the language of any neighbouring nation, either Russian, German, or Wallachian. It is true we may find in it fragments from all these; the Hungarian word *harcz* (battle), for instance, is identical with the German *Hatz; fogoly* with *Vogel*. There are numerous Slavish words—*király* (king)—*kral;* and Latin ones as well—*muzsika*—*musica*. All these, however, are evidently borrowed words.

The origin of Hungarian has often been discussed by philologists; some thought it was derived from Hebrew; others that it was of Slavish origin; while some regarded it as an ancient speech having no relatives among modern tongues.

In the eighteenth century, however, an incident occurred which suddenly threw a ray of light upon the subject. In 1769 a Hungarian astronomer, a Jesuit, John Sajnovics, went to the north of Europe to observe the Transit of Venus. At Vardö, on the extreme north coast of Norway, he saw a great deal of the Laplanders

2

and it struck him how very similar their language was to his own. That discovery outweighed in importance all his astronomical investigations and he published a book maintaining the common origin of the two languages. (*Demonstratio Idioma Ungarorum et Lapponum idem esse.*) The work proved the origin of the Hungarian language, for it was well known that the Lapp idiom was akin to the Finnish, and to that of several of the small tribes living in the northern parts of Russia.

It had long been known in Hungary that there were a few scattered tribes related by race to the Hungarians, dwelling far away in north-eastern Russia. In the thirteenth century, Julian, an enthusiastic Franciscan monk, was told that a Hungarian tribe, the Baskirs, was still living somewhere on the frontier between Europe and Asia, and practising the old pagan religion. Julian at once resolved to go to these Asiatic kinsmen of his and convert them to Christianity. He accordingly went, and discovered them on the banks of the river Kama, and they understood his speech.

Towards the end of the fifteenth century, King Matthias Corvinus also heard, from travelling merchants, that far away in the east there were some tribes related to the Hungarians. He intended to open communication with them, but he died before effecting his purpose. Two hundred years later, Martin Fogel, a learned Hamburg physician, on reading the first Hungarian grammar, became convinced of the relation between Hungarian and Finnish, and wrote a book on the subject which served as a foundation for the theory of Leibniz concerning the kinship of the Hungarians, Finns, and Laplanders.

Sajnovics, the Jesuit, detected a similarity not only

between words but also between grammatical rules. We know now the names of several more related tribes living in northern and central Russia. There are the Ostyák, the Mordvinian, Cheremisz, Votyák, and Zürjén. There must have been a time when all those tribes lived in one land in common with the Hungarians, and spoke one common language. One of the proofs given by Sajnovics is that the similarity occurs in the most familiar words used in primitive life, such as numerals, names of parts of the body, pronouns, water, fire, sun, moon, wood, names of animals. Another proof is furnished by likeness in grammatical structure. Hungarian is a language of affixes. Many varieties of meaning which other nations express by means of prepositions with the article, or by various separate words, are expressed in Hungarian by a letter or syllable, either simply added on at the end of a word or fused with it. The Hungarian equivalent of the three words " I see thee," is " *Látlak.*" " For my father," is " *atyámért,*" the last syllable of which is composed of the affixes m—my, and ért—for.

According to the evidence of the oldest written fragment, a funeral speech (1200 A.D.), those affixes were originally separate substantives, which were merely placed beside the principal word, as though, for instance, instead of saying "within the house," we were to say "house, interior."

Another feature which distinguishes Hungarian from all the Indo-Germanic languages, but which we find in the language of the Ugrian tribes, is the assimilating of the vowel in the affix to that in the stem of a word. Just as in music the notes in a chord have to be in harmony with one another, so in a Hungarian word. If the stem contains the vowel, o, u, or a (the latter being pronounced like o in hot) the affix must contain a sound of the same kind. Not only are the words similar in the languages of the Ugrian race and the Hungarians, but also the grammatical rules. It is now proved that Hungarian is one of the Ugrian languages.

There are some scholars who do not accept this view of the origin of the Hungarian tongue, amongst others Arminius Vámbéry, the well-known Orientalist. His opinion is that Hungarian is derived from Turkish, and that the Ugrian elements in it are all of later date. It is true that the language contains a large number of important words, chiefly substantives, of Turkish origin, but they are borrowed words, and no more warrant our regarding Hungarian as a Turkish tongue than the considerable Romance element in English would justify us in calling it a Romance language.

III

THE MIDDLE AGES

It was in the tenth century that the Hungarians came from Asia, founded their state, and embraced Christianity, and were thus brought into contact with the Europe of the Middle Ages, and shared in its civilisation. Some features of that civilisation were common to every country. All the nations of Christendom possessed the two fundamental institutions of the Church and Chivalry. And community of religion in those days, when religion was the chief source of light for men, meant vastly more than it does now. The mass, the liturgy, and the majority of the legends were the same everywhere. Two stars shone in the sky during the long night of the Middle Ages : religion and the spirit of chivalry. The relics of Hungarian literature which have come down to us from that epoch reveal the influence of only one of those two great luminaries—religion. All the works inspired by the genius of chivalry have been lost. There is a whole library of legends in prose, laboriously inscribed on parchment and decorated with initials by pious monks and nuns ; but they all breathe a spirit of fervent piety, and are not concerned with chivalry.

The first brilliant figure of the later Renaissance was King Matthias Hunyadi, whose great name evoked the slumbering forces of the national poetic genius.

The religious spirit was undoubtedly the most prolific source of literature during the Middle Ages. Religion played a very large part in the life of the people. All that was noblest in them was derived from it; whatever knowledge they had was connected with it, indeed without it their minds would have been almost blank. Chivalry was for the few, but religion was the only luminary on the mental horizon of the multitude, and but for it they would have been almost in darkness. It is not surprising, therefore, that the literature which has come down to us from the Middle Ages is nearly all religious. If we wish to know what men were like in those days we must read their hymns, written on vellum, and bound in leather with brass clasps; their books of tales, adorned with elaborate initials; their chronicles, with their quaint coloured illustrations, in which certain stiff, meagre figures may be recognised by their crowns to be kings; or, perhaps, an occasional fragment of a song, scribbled by some enamoured notary or clerk on the margin of his account books, during the time of the carnival.

The greater part of what has come down to us consists of sacred tales or legends. The earliest Hungarian book (that is, the first large codex) contains the legends relating to St. Francis of Assisi. It is called the *Ehrenfeia Codex*, after its present owner. Many a legend gathered round the lives of the Hungarian national saints. The most notable came from the line of the Árpád kings (eleventh to thirteenth century). Among them were St. Stephen, who induced his people to embrace Christianity (died in 1038); his son, St. Imre, who died in his early youth; the chivalrous hero, St. Ladislas (eleventh century); St. Elizabeth, daughter of King Andrew II.; and St. Margaret, daughter of King Béla IV. The literature of legend is a vast forest, the trees of which are wrapt in a mystical moonlit haze. Let us for a moment enter the dense, tangled forest; we shall probably find no straight path, but above us we may see the stars of heaven shining through the leaves.

Every age has a different conception of space and time, of the place occupied in the Universe by Man, and of the changes which the whirligig of time brings to mankind and to the world in general. The man of the Middle Ages was convinced that his little Earth was the centre, and the chief concern of the Universe. Such a conception is entirely childish to our mind. He imagined Heaven to be so near the earth that "our world" and "the other world" might easily communicate with each other. The "other world" was the really important thing. Nature, as we understand it, had little interest for him.

Why pay careful heed to nature and her works? Whenever it should prove necessary or beneficial, the skies would open and a host of glorious spirits would descend upon the earth. In seeking for help against the many physical ills of earthly life, the man of those times never attempted to subjugate the powers of nature and make them serve his purposes, but tried instead to win the active benevolence of supernatural powers. There were no difficulties, no obstacles nor wants, with which miracles could not cope, and it was by miracles that vice was punished and virtue rewarded. Only hard experience in the school of life could correct those views, and bring the *lucidum intervallum* of truth.

Those conceptions are abundantly illustrated in the Hungarian legends. When the coachman falls asleep, the carriage tears on its way in perfect safety for the sake of St. Ladislas (1094) who is inside. When his army is perishing from lack of food in an uninhabited district, at the prayer of the saint-king, large herds of oxen and buffaloes rush out from the wood. When a poor blind girl goes to the tomb of St. Ladislas her blind eyes fall to the ground, and she sees them fall, for new eyes have been given her. The first Christian king, St. Stephen, heals every one of whom tidings are brought to him, by cutting a slice of his own loaf of bread and sending it to the sufferer.

St. Elizabeth is also helped by a benevolent miracle when once, in her embarrassment, she deviates from the strict truth. This miracle is narrated in the *Érdi Codex* with childish *naïveté*. " It came to pass on a day when it was very cold, that the lady St. Elizabeth, taking good care that nobody should see her, carried the crusts and remnants of dinner to the poor outside the gate, a thing she had been forbidden to do. And lo! her father, the King (Andrew II.) suddenly stood before her. He was astonished to see her all alone and walking so hurriedly, and said to her : " Whither goest thou, my child Elizabeth ? What art thou carrying ? " The King's noble daughter, being very timid and gentle, felt ashamed, and could not answer anything but " I carry roses." But her father, being a wise man, remembered on a sudden that it was not the time of the year for roses, so he called her to him and looked at what she was holding in her lap, when, oh! wonderful! the crusts had all become roses. Oh, immortal, blessed, immaculate purity! The ever blessed King of Heaven did not let the words of His beloved handmaid bring her to shame. And her father, filled with wonder, said : " If this maiden lives she will be great."

The forces of nature had not to be laboriously conquered as they are to-day ; they were all expected to be
at the service of morality, blessing or injuring, to enforce
her precepts. A bright star descended from Heaven and
shone above the tomb of St. Ladislas. The beasts of the
field either became tame domestic animals or performed
symbolical duties. When St. Benedict died a martyr's
death near the river Vág, an eagle hovered above the
water for a whole year. Over the death-bed of St.
Elizabeth there fluttered a bird, singing sweetly. Among
these legendary figures is St. Margaret, daughter of King
Béla IV., clad in a coarse, hairy garment, her tortured
body sore with self-inflicted wounds, around her waist
a hempen girdle studded with sharp nails, and in her
hand a scourge, while the tearful eyes are filled with a
look of pain and yet of exaltation. The nun, in that age,
was not less heroic than the knight.

What extremes religious fanaticism reached, and how
in its exaltation it trampled under foot everything which
we hold sacred in human life, is clearly reflected in the
mirror of these legends. When St. Elizabeth was
informed of the death of her husband, who had gone to
the Holy Land in accordance with her advice, the legend
tells how "she offered her fervent thanksgivings to
God." As soon as her neighbours were aware that she
had become a widow, alone and unprotected, they
turned against her and robbed her of all her estates.
"And then," says the narrative, "the noble daughter of
the king was driven to live in a pig-sty where she poured
out her thanks to God for all her trials and misery.
When morning came she rose and went to the monks,
who were named after St. Francis, and implored them to
sing a *Te Deum laudamus* for her. As she passed along

the street she was met by an old woman whom in former times she had loaded with charity. This old woman now thrust her into the mud. Elizabeth offered prayers of thanksgiving for this also." The saint saw more and more the vanity of worldly things. She wished to remain in her state of abject poverty. "And, therefore," continues the legend "in order that she might be quite free from worldly cares, she prayed to her Lord Jesus that He should enable her to despise all earthly interests and pleasures, and even to forget her children and cease to love them thenceforth." And from that day she beheld wondrous visions, heavenly voices spoke to her, and much comfort and bliss were vouchsafed to her from the heavens above.

We have seen that to the thought of the day, heaven and earth, the natural and the miraculous, were all blended into one, and in the people's idea of time there was the same lack of discrimination. They knew of no difference between the people of one period and those of another. As the world was then, so it had ever been, and would for ever continue to be. Even the most learned men had not the faintest conception of the enormous changes which had taken place in men's thoughts, their laws and habits, and in human life altogether. That their age was itself the result of a long historical development, and the starting-point for a further course of change in the whole mental and material condition of mankind, never occurred to the human mind during the thousand years of the Middle Ages. Men knew nothing with certainty of the past, and to the future they gave no thought. To improve the conditions of their own life, or to lessen the burdens of humanity, was no concern of theirs. The very idea of progress was foreign to their minds. Hence the great *naïveté* with which the painter of that time treats his almost solitary subject, the Bible. The characters of the Old and New Testament are to him exactly like the people he meets every day, so that all his representations of the past are full of internal and external anachronisms.

This want of knowledge gave the artist a kind of assurance, the boldness of *naïveté*, but his work is far inferior to reality. The frescoes in the cathedral at Kassa, representing Jerusalem at the time of Christ, make it look exactly like the town of Kassa in the fifteenth century.

It is this lack of the chronological sense which has falsified the chronicles. In them the times of Attila the Hun, and the Hungarian Árpád, are mixed up together, although they were really separated by an interval of five hundred years. They tell us that the Hungarians occupied the country some ten or twenty years after the death of Attila, whose two grandsons fought under the banner of Árpád. One of the earliest chroniclers, the "anonymous scribe of King Béla" (*Anonymus Belae Regis notarius*) actually took the names of the Hungarian leaders from Dares Phrygius's *Destruction of Troy*, where the author describes Castor and Pollux, Hector and Paris. To the chronicler, the Trojan War and the doings of Attila and of Árpád, were very much the same.

Any one who fails to realise the vast difference between the mental life of that day and of our own, as the rationalists of the eighteenth century failed, and as also did George Bessenyei, a follower of Voltaire, in Hungary, will never understand the real spirit of the Middle Ages, and neither will he who is content with merely following the political controversies of the period. It was to the absence of any control over the impulses of the natural man that many an outburst of violence was due. How many cruel and thoughtless deeds may be found even in the life of St. Stephen himself. He blinded his relative, the innocent Basil, in order that he might not claim the throne. Yet Stephen was one of the most pious and thoughtful monarchs of the Middle Ages. Foreign chroniclers, when describing King Kálmán the Wise, agree that he surpassed all contemporary monarchs in knowledge and wisdom, yet he, also, punished his rebellious brother Álmos and his young son by depriving them of sight. Even Louis the Great and John Hunyadi displayed some of the wild ferocity of the times in their wars.

In Hungary, the Middle Ages were less marked by religious zeal and exaltation, and also by intolerance, than in the Western countries. The character of its people has always been distinguished for sobriety and reserve. This, undoubtedly, was advantageous in so far as it aided political development, but, on the other hand, it deprived the nation of the literature of religious fervour. Nevertheless, Christianity was blended with the strong national feeling of the Hungarians, and each profoundly modified the other instead of developing along separate lines. Proof of this is furnished by many historical tales and monuments.

The Blessed Virgin is not only a religious idea, but also the patron saint of Hungary. One of the Hungarian kings, St. Ladislas (1094), was canonised, and renowned as a most pious Crusader, yet he was at the same time the most popular and chivalrous soldier of the battlefield. He is the only king whose memory has been enshrined equally in the folk-lore, in sacred legends, and in the frescoes on the walls of churches. He forms the favourite subject alike of the sculptor and of the writers of the clumsy but well-meaning lyrics sung by the priests. Miniature painters, chroniclers, poets, metal workers, and coiners all glorify him. He was the first national ideal of the people to be immortalised in art, and his equestrian statue is the finest relic of the sculpture of the Middle Ages. The church, the folk-lore, and the Latin verses in the *Peer Codex* have all helped to preserve some remembrance of this ideal knight. The idealistic and chivalric qualities of the Middle Ages in Hungary reached their zenith in his personality.

The spirit of an epoch is expressed not only by the written word, or by statues and pictures, but also by its architecture. In Hungary, as in most other countries, all the great edifices of the Middle Ages were ecclesiastical. Men were content to live in small, dark houses and narrow streets, but their cathedrals were lofty and magnificent buildings, embodiments in stone of their religious zeal. The four most famous ancient monuments in Hungary are all creations of the religious spirit ; the Norman cathedral at Ják, the Gothic dome at Kassa, the basilica at Pécs, and the high altar at Lőcse. Every branch of art received its inspiration from religion, and statues and pictures reveal exactly the same *naïveté* and the same religious fervour as the parchment books of that little library which has been bequeathed to the present generation as the Hungarian literature of the Middle Ages.

The type of ancient Hungarian ecclesiastical architecture is a cathedral, with strongly-built, fortress-like towers at each of the four corners, showing the two prevailing sentiments of the times—the religious and the warlike— cathedral and fortress in one.

Individual characteristics had not much chance of development, and there is accordingly a great scarcity of subjective lyric poetry. Every man, whether knight, priest, or artisan, was a member of a community. It is the normal which thrives best in such associations, and distinctively individual features are little cultivated. Whenever we find feelings other than those of religion, in the poetry or art of the Middle Ages, we are struck by their nebulous, indistinct character. The human soul seems to have been hidden from men by a veil, as Nature was, and consequently psychological observation did not exist; people examined neither their own souls nor the souls of others. In the poetry of that period action was everything, and the inner, psychological process which precedes action and leads to it was nothing.

If we may be permitted to use the language of geology, the soul of the Hungarian people during the Middle Ages might be said to show in section three different strata. At the bottom is the primitive pagan nature, brought from their Asiatic home. The next shows a more cultured mental condition, the result largely of intercourse with Turkish, Slavish, German, and Italian neighbours. Last comes Christianity, introducing a multitude of new features into the life of the people. In the absence of sufficient literary remains we can only gather as best we may, by the aid of analogy, what are the thoughts and feelings which belong to each stratum.

IV

THE RENAISSANCE

HUNGARY was one of the first countries to be stirred by the Renaissance. For this she was indebted to one of the greatest men of that great age, King MATTHIAS CORVINUS, who was born in 1443, and who reigned from 1458 until his death in 1490.

Matthias, who had been brought up by eminent humanists, was a thorough Renaissance monarch, like his Italian contemporaries, Lorenzo the Magnificent, and the rulers of Urbino and Milan, Federigo Montefeltre and Lodovico Moro. They were all passionately fond of the new artistic luxury, and highly prized every relic of classical times, fragments of the glorified Greek age, as well as the elaborately illustrated vellum books, some of which cost more than a picture by Raphael. Italy was then the centre of culture, so King Matthias endeavoured to create a channel through which that culture might make its way to Hungary. In view of that effort we may call King Matthias the first modern Hungarian. All that was most eminent and characteristic in his father, John Hunyadi, is suggestive of the Middle Ages, while Matthias is a new type—the Renaissance ruler ; between him and his father there is the gulf which separates one historical epoch from another. Naturally, even in Renaissance times, there still persisted elements belonging to the Middle Ages, just as with the rosy light of dawn there is mingled something of the darkness of night; so in the character of Matthias we may discern features which link him to a bygone age. It was the same with the men who were his spiritual kindred, Lorenzo the Magnificent or Alfonso of Arragon; but like them Matthias was essentially a man of the Renaissance. Italy herself could not show us a more striking type of the new genus. It is not only that he surrounded himself with the very best works of art of that period, but his whole personality showed that he had drunk deeply of the waters of that enchanting stream which reached Hungary earlier than other countries. His character and education, his tastes and prejudices, his imagination and temperament, were all rooted in the soil of the Renaissance.

Great vitality and uncurbed emotions are frequently to be found linked with a sense of beauty in the typical man of that age; but his lively imagination and his manifold abilities were often mingled with craftiness and rhetorical volubility; he admired the classical world in an intellectual way, and yet was not entirely free from superstitions; finely turned wit and indomitable energy existed side by side in his nature. All those features appeared in Matthias. His imagination was powerful and undisciplined. Gigantic plans seethed in his mind like precious metals in a furnace, rich, yet mingled with dross. At one time it was the crown of Bohemia which he attempted to seize, at another it was the German imperial title. He dreamed of reconquering the territories near the Danube, chasing the Turks back to Asia, or converting them to Christianity. Later on, he found a wild pretext for laying claim to the throne of the Sultan, on the ground that an aunt of his had been carried off to that monarch's harem.

The Renaissance developed, to a very great degree, the consciousness of individuality in Matthias's contemporaries ; no longer were they merely subordinate parts of some vast machine, they felt themselves free as air. At such a time there were many who, in the intoxication of their newly found freedom, would brook no restraint of their passions or ambitions, and so we meet some very strong personalities and some very violent ones. The effect of this new development upon political life was to create autocrats and tyrants. Italy was full of despotic rulers in the fifteenth and sixteenth centuries.

The same unbridled strength appeared in Matthias, and often led him to extremes. For instance, in defiance of popular opinion, he bestowed the title of Primate of Hungary on a handsome, seven-year-old Italian boy, so that from Ferrara people sent the Primate toys ; he imprisoned his own uncle ; he suddenly raised his friends to the highest posts and, if it pleased him, as suddenly hurled them down.

Notwithstanding, he possessed features which distinguish him from all the other tyrants, and raise him to the level of the "great Italians" of the age. He never failed to select the necessary means to achieve his end. In politics, as in all else, his plans were on a grand scale, and covered the whole political stage of his time, the Holy Land as well as Bosnia, Bohemia and Turkey, Brandenburg and Venice. They were all as pieces on his chess-board, as also were France, Spain, and the Pope.

The subtle threads of his diplomacy stretched from the Court of Burgundy to Teheran. He was in touch alike with Turkish dignitaries and with the Czar. He threatened the Turks with the Pope ; the Pope, again, with the Turks.

"If the Holy Father does not comply with my wishes, I swear by the sacred Cross that I will help the Turks to enter Italy," he declared to the Nuncio. He might have said, with the Latin poet, "*Si flectere nequeo superos, Acheronta movebo.*"

His fertile and vehement imagination, and his far-seeing, calculating intellect, combined in effecting his purposes. He flattered and threatened, he implored and commanded, he convinced or conquered or bribed his enemies. If he did not attain his ends by his logic and persuasive eloquence, or by his princely gifts, with swift dexterity he resorted to force. But if violent methods did not promise success, he forgot his former plan and once again became tranquil.

As a statesman, then, as in other respects, he was typical of the Renaissance. His cunning in design, his vigour in execution, the grand scale of his plans, and his indifference to the means, so long as the ends were achieved, made him seem like a pupil of the great Machiavelli, though long before Machiavelli's time. It is characteristic of the Renaissance politicians that they enlarged the stage for their combinations by involving one European country after another, and this feature may be seen in Matthias. His mind, his fertile imagination, and his feverish energy were typical of the fifteenth century. In respect of certain wild but majestic features in him, he had something in common with the famous lions which he used to keep in an enclosure of his palace, and which are mentioned by the poet Janus Pannonius.

Matthias was a consummate artist, with all the artistic intuitions of his age, but his art was politics, as that of Giovanni Dalmata was architecture, and that of Benedetto de Majano sculpture. In his great plans he generally counted upon two weaknesses in human nature, vanity and love of money. He lavished appreciative words as well as gold upon those whom he wished to impress. The age of the Renaissance was the age of rhetoric, and Matthias was a true representative of it in that respect. If his plans required it he used refined rhetoric and artistic periphrases, to which his perfect courtesy lent effect. Polished manners were a new thing in his day, though they had been generally adopted by the Italian nobility. But in spite of his suave methods Matthias sometimes found his politeness thrown away and his plans threatened with failure, and then his vehement nature would burst out with uncontrollable fury. " He got into a passion," says an Italian ambassador, "like a raging lion." When the king was angry it seemed as though "flames burst from his eyes and mouth and nostrils."

But above all, it was his great love for art that made Matthias so thorough a representative of the Renaissance. He endeavoured to transplant the new culture into Hungary. He invited the most prominent humanists and the best artists from Italy, and when they could not come themselves he brought their works, at least, to his country.

He collected antique treasures and founded a fine library, the so-called Corvina library. He adorned his palace in Buda with choice Italian works of art; he commissioned statues, pictures, books, and furniture from Italy, and especially from Florence, the home of the new art. Outside Italy no man in Europe was a better judge of works of art and of literature. His liking for the new ideas may be explained by three circumstances : in the first place, he had been educated by eminent humanists, who taught the impressionable youth to admire the classical world ; when he became king, the most influential men of his Court and amongst the clergy had nearly all studied in Italy and brought home the ideas of the new cult ; and, furthermore, the direction taken by his tastes was largely influenced by his marriage, his Queen Beatrice having been brought up at the Court of Naples, where knowledge and art were enthusiastically beloved. Her grandfather, the noble Alfonso, was the best connoisseur of art of his time. Her father, though harsh and crafty by nature, was endowed with much artistic taste ; he founded a scientific academy, and zealously collected books. It must be remembered, too, that in the middle of the fifteenth century, there was a constant intercourse between Hungary and Italy, for not only did merchants and pilgrims pass to and fro frequently, and in large numbers, but also scholars, students, and painters. Filippino Lippi, Verrocchio, and Caradosso could not accept the King's invitation to his Court, but their works were well represented there. The artist who worked for Matthias the most, and who spent the longest time at his Court, was Giovanni Dalmata. All his works in Hungary were destroyed by the Turks, but it is well-known that he executed a great number for the King, who conferred upon him a title equivalent to knighthood. On the death of the King he left Hungary. He was one of the most refined sculptors of the Renaissance, and possessed something of the graceful Attic spirit, which is only to be observed elsewhere in works of the early Florentine Renaissance. His works represented historical Hungarian person-ages, such as John Hunyadi and his son Ladislas (then recently beheaded) as well as mythological characters. The statues had a curious fate. Half a century later they were in Constantinople, among the ruins of the Byzantine Emperor's hippodrome, carried thither by the victorious Turks. And the statues, relics of Hungarian Renaissance times, stood there side by side with other interesting objects. Next to them was the famous brass serpent and the golden tripod, which the victorious Greeks erected at Delphi to commemorate the siege of Thebes. There too were the Egyptian obelisk of Theodosius the Great and the triumphal column of Constantine. All the nations whose victories had been celebrated by these monuments were then beneath the Turkish yoke.

A great hurricane of historical events had swept the wrecks of the golden age of Egypt, Greece, Byzantium and Hungary into one heap. Such is the irony of fate— relics reminding us of Thothmes III., of the conquerors of Salamis, of Theodosius the Great, and of Matthias Corvinus, stood on the site of the circus which the Turks used as a stable. The statues taken from the palace of the Hungarian King were destroyed in the sixteenth century ; some of the other relics are still to be seen among the ruins of the Hippodrome.

Among the artists of the early Renaissance who worked for Matthias was Andrea del Verrocchio, the creator of the finest equestrian statue in the world—the Colleone statue in Venice. Later, the Prince of Milan, Lodovico il Moro, commissioned Verrocchio's great pupil, Leonardo da Vinci, to paint a Madonna for King Matthias, adding that " he is able to value a great picture as few can."

Filippino Lippi could not accept the King's invitation, but painted two pictures for him in Florence (*due tavole molto belle,* says Vasari). One was a portrait of Matthias, and the other the Lord's Supper.

It was probably the famous Caradosso who made the masterpiece of Renaissance goldsmith's work, the Calvary at Esztergom, for the king, which was afterwards given to the Primate Bakócz by the king's son, John Corvinus.

The most talented Italian artist at the Court of Matthias was the young Benedetto da Majano, afterwards the architect of the splendid palace belonging to the Strozzi family.

Matthias would not have been a typical Renaissance ruler had he not been passionately fond of fine vellum manuscripts, adorned with miniatures. He and the Italian princes were rivals in book-collecting, and as he could easily afford it, he used to spend as much as 30,000 golden florins annually on his library, which must have cost, in our money, some hundreds of thousands of pounds. His agents wandered as far as the Levant in order to procure interesting Greek manuscripts. The most eminent Florentine masters worked for his library, and he paid Attavantes for a single manuscript the price usually given for a masterpiece of painting. The miniatures on the parchments of Attavantes combine the fresh beauty of the early Renaissance with the most refined Greek taste.

In that age, love of art went hand in hand with admiration of antiquity. Italian potentates were all eager collectors of antique treasures. People did not always understand the Greeks and Romans, but they always venerated them. Matthias began collecting ancient relics, sarcophagi, tablets, bronze casts of coins, and both he and his favourite writers and artists speak of the Romans with the greatest reverence. "The King," writes a well-known Italian humanist, "reads even late at night in bed. Quintus Curtius' *History of Alexander the Great* or the works of Livy may be found under his pillow." His conversation and his frequent quotations showed how well read he was in the Roman authors, especially in Virgil, while Queen Beatrice was equally well versed in them.

It is only natural that the men who were engaged in bringing to light and spreading this classical culture should be highly esteemed. Nearly all the monarchs had famous scholars living at their Courts ; one prince invited them because of his real interest; another, perhaps, merely because it was the fashion. These scholars used to wander from country to country, as famous actors do nowadays, their contracts with their hosts, the Kings, being for a year or two only, and they were handsomely paid for their visit. When the term expired they left for some other Court. Matthias had a large number of philosophers, cardinals, physicians, orators, philologists, brilliant conversationalists, famous astronomers, astrologers banished from their own country, and chiromancers at the court ; in a word, the most as well as the least valuable classes of that singular, yet great age. In 1471, King Matthias wrote to a famous Roman humanist : " Scholars, how happy are you ! You strive not after blood-stained glory nor monarchs' crowns, but for the laurels of poetry and virtue. You are even able to compel us to forget the tumult of war."

Let us cast a glance at the polite society of the period, and enter one of the halls in the palace of Buda. It is furnished with all the luxury and artistic taste of the Renaissance. On the walls are wondrous tapestries interwoven with gold, alternating with frescoes representing scenes from Hungarian history. Nature lends her beauty to that of art, for if the guest lift the heavy silk curtains and look through the porphyry-framed windows, he sees the striking panorama of Buda and Pest; below him the Danube, like a silver ribbon dotted with green islets; to the right the hills, and to the left the wide-stretching plain. Then, if he look around him in the hall, he sees beautifully carved tables, glass cases filled with treasures dear to the heart of the connoisseur, Venetian mirrors, golden statues, old bronzes, medals; in one corner a Roman couch covered with brocade; farther on, antique tripod chairs "like those at Delphi." Along the walls are carved bookcases with crimson silk draperies. On the shelves, the literary works of classical antiquity stand side by side with those of the new revival, all of them bound in silk, while the workmanship of their silver clasps and corners is as worthy of admiration as the miniatures to be found inside, which display the rich imagination of the Renaissance blended with that of antiquity—graceful garlands of flowers and fruit, Cupids riding on fawns or playing with rainbow-coloured butterflies, Tritons and nymphs sporting, and, as a border, antique gems, and delicate climbing plants with golden flowers.

Seated in one of the Grecian chairs we see the royal host, King Matthias, the centre and soul of the gathering. His long fair hair falls over his shoulders, his cheeks are ruddy, his forehead high, and his large shining eyes betoken a great mind and a passionate temperament. Near him stands a tall and remarkably handsome ecclesiastic, the King's favourite, and the best Latin poet of the century, JANUS PANNONIUS (John Csezmiczey) (1434–1472). The sadness of this young man's future has not yet cast its shadow upon him; he is

still the favourite of the King, who distinguishes him
in every possible way, but he was soon to fall into
disfavour ; his former benefactor became his persecutor,
and he was forced to fly in disguise to a remote fortress,
there to die young and forgotten.* Janus Pannonius
belonged to the best class of Renaissance scholars. It is
only in that age that we find such ardent admiration of
and genuine enthusiasm for everything connected with
classical culture. Pedantry and dry scholastic study had
not yet made the world tired of the past, and for the
Renaissance scholar the classical authors had the dignity
of antiquity, together with the zest of novelty.

The Florentine Vespasiano, the wealthiest of the
dealers in books and manuscripts, speaks in a pathetic
manner of Pannonius, years after he had met him.
Pannonius had been educated at Ferrara, where he far
excelled all his fellow students in his knowledge of
Greek and Latin. When his uncle, John Vitéz, the
Archbishop of Esztergom, urged him to return to
Hungary, he went, on his way back, to Florence, to
see the great men of the day—Cosimo de' Medici,
Poggio, the great humanist, and the Greek Argiropolis,
the commentator of Aristotle. " Once," says Vespasiano,
" there came to me a remarkably handsome youth, of
dignified appearance, clad in a crimson robe. I cried
out joyfully, 'Welcome here ! You are a Hungarian,
are you not ? ' On which he greeted me with great
warmth, and told me in his own charming manner 'that

* In 1464 Matthias writes of Janus Pannonius that he is the
pride of his Court, and that he is always striving to anticipate the
King's wishes, but eight years later he writes to the Prince of Saxony
requesting him to imprison Janus, should he enter Saxony, and
declares himself ready to return this " friendly service " in a similar
way, if necessary.

I had judged correctly, and that he had come to see the great humanists.' " Vespasiano then took him to the Villa Careggi, the home of the first Renaissance Platonic academy; also to Cosimo de' Medici, who was completely fascinated by the brilliant and learned youth ; then to Argiropolis, whom Pannonius heard lecturing ; and to Poggio, at whose house he recited some of his poems with remarkable success. Vespasiano writes of him : " Every one felt the charm of his personality, even those who knew him only by sight. Every day added to his reputation. We looked upon him as the delight of the world (*le delizie del mondo*)." The chief work of Pannonius is a long Latin epic poem, wholly classical in its conception, praising the achievements of his friend Marcello, the Venetian leader.

Another remarkable figure at the Court of Matthias was Regiomontanus (1436–1476), the greatest astronomer of his century, and the inventor of modern trigonometry. He was the friend and pupil of the great Greek cardinal Bessarion. Matthias placed him in charge of his library and astronomical observatory, at a salary of two hundred golden florins. The observations of Regiomontanus constitute the beginning of real scientific astronomy. His work, the *Ephemerides*, was dedicated to King Matthias, who rewarded him with twelve hundred golden florins. The book is a kind of nautical almanack, enabling an observer to find his geographical situation by means of the stars. Columbus used the book during his first voyage, so that it played an important part in geographical discovery.

Near the King we cannot fail to see his literary familiar, the ingenious Galeotto, who has a hand in everything going on in the new classical society.

Galeotto had been the friend and tutor of Janus Pannonius at Ferrara. Later on, he went to Hungary as the guest, and partly as the jester, of the King, and of the humanists among the bishops. He had travelled in France, staying at the Court of Charles VIII., and in Spain and England. He composed bombastic praises of Lorenzo the Magnificent. He knew a little about everything and yet not much altogether, but he seems to have had a consummate knowledge of the art of being a parasite. He was witty, well-read, and clever, and easily became a favourite with everybody as an amusing though superficial conversationalist.*

The other historian of the King is Anthony Bonfini (1427–1502), a man of a less vivacious temperament than Galeotto, but more dignified, more learned, and more distinguished. Matthias preferred him to all the other foreign scholars, and kept him at his side even during his last years. What we learn about the King from the superficial, talkative Galeotto, is chiefly in the form of anecdotes, while Bonfini, on the other hand, wrote a careful treatise concerning the King's reign, in a style modelled on that of Livy.

It would be impossible to describe all the bright planets which revolved about that gorgeous sun, Matthias Corvinus. Such a society had never before been seen in Buda. Even at that epoch, it was perhaps only the Villa Careggi, the palace of the great Lorenzo, that witnessed gatherings rivalling those at Buda. The guests have just finished the feast. They are in the banqueting hall, where the King has been listening to

---

* Galeotto appears in Sir Walter Scott's *Quentin Durward* as a fascinating and eloquent astrologer, princely in appearance, but cunning and treacherous.

the Hungarian bards as they sang the deeds of the King, and of his great father, John Hunyadi.* Inspired by their song Janus Pannonius expresses his resolve to write an heroic epic about John Hunyadi. Now they are in the library, talking about the great philosopher Plato, who has been recalled to life, as it were, by the Renaissance. The heads of the State of Florence, Cosimo de' Medici and Lorenzo the Magnificent, are most enthusiastic disciples of the philosopher : a society was soon formed for the study of Plato, and men recognised in him the greatest prose-writer of classical times.

Janus Pannonius was a keen student of Plato,† and he translated the works of his follower, Plotinus, into Latin. Matthias was especially fond of the Platonic philosopher Apuleius.

Thirteen centuries before, there dwelt in Hungary a man familiar with Plato, the Roman Emperor Marcus Aurelius, who wrote his philosophical works near the banks of the river Granua (Garam). And at the end of thirteen centuries there were again lovers of Plato in "the land of the four rivers." The great fascination exercised by Plato upon the minds of men in the fifteenth century is clearly shown in the letters written to King Matthias by the great Florentine Platonist Marsilius Ficinus, all of them full of allusions to the philosopher and enthusiastic in his praise.

The centre of the gathering in Buda was always Matthias, not the most learned there, but the most

* One of these songs, describing the siege of the fortress of Sabácz by Matthias, was found in 1871.

† " When he spoke in Greek," Bonfini says of Pannonius, " you would think he must have been born in Athens." And Vespasiano says, " It seemed as if Janus Pannonius had been brought up by Socrates himself."

gifted, his vast mind open to every new impression, his attention always keen, and his curiosity insatiable. He was continually learning, not alone from books, but from the conversation of those around him. But something of the spirit of the Middle Ages still remained in the man. His studies were wide and many-sided, rather than profound ; his mind delighted in logical subtleties ; he often confounded science with superstition, luxury with artistic beauty. The society around him showed that although the new ideas had triumphed in men's minds the victory was scarcely won. But we become conscious of the triumph of the new spirit as we listen to the guests while they discuss the great questions of the day : the scientists weighing their facts, the philologists quoting the poets, while every now and then there breaks in upon the learned talk the sound of merriment, the cheerful spirit of the Renaissance having restored wit to its proper place, wit, too, divested of its former coarseness.

It was under Matthias that printers first came to Hungary. Andrew Hess, coming from Rome, printed, in 1473, and in Roman characters, the book called *Budai Krónika*, which contained the history of Hungary up to the time of Matthias. And so Hungary forestalled England in the art of printing.

Matthias, like all the rulers of his day, was exceedingly fond of gorgeous festivals and brilliant pageants. He was *maître de plaisir* as well as statesman. In the fifteenth century Venice was famed throughout the world for its luxury, yet the Venetian ambassador himself was amazed at the pomp of the Hungarian monarch's court. The papal nuncio also, who had seen much grandeur in his own circle, spoke rapturously of the castle at Visegrád, calling it a paradise on earth. Another ambassador declared that the castle had no equal in Europe, that only the *Palais de Justice* in Paris could be compared with it.

But the Renaissance also brought great changes into the habits of every-day life. People began to pay more attention to cleanliness, houses were better ventilated, and in Italy clean linen and good manners at table became the hall-mark of the gentleman. All his foreign guests spoke of Matthias as exemplary in such matters.

There is one more point of similarity between Matthias and his great Italian contemporaries, in that he established a new kind of title to the occupancy of a throne. At the beginning of the Renaissance period, the Italian thrones were in the possession of men who were not of royal descent, but were either successful generals, or their sons. Such monarchs had no family traditions to lean upon, no inherited claim upon the people's loyalty; that had to be won. They therefore occupied themselves with affairs of State more than members of the old dynasties had been accustomed to do; and in their anxiety to acquire dignity they also displayed greater luxury. In default of an ancient name they had recourse to their wealth, and they loved to surround themselves with eminent men in order to add splendour to their court. Such a monarch was Matthias, himself sprung from no royal race, but a son of the great general John Hunyadi.

It is consonant with the opinion of their time that the monarchs of the fourteenth and fifteenth centuries, autocrats, men of strong personality and of sensual tendencies, should try to secure their thrones to their illegitimate sons, and Matthias endeavoured to do so on behalf of his son John Corvinus.

Matthias was of his age even in its smallest feature. With the literature and philosophy of the classical period, much of its superstition also had been revived. Astrology and chiromancy were practised in every court in Europe. Matthias, too, liked to hear and to talk about the "ars magica," and before taking any important step invariably sought the advice of his astrologer.

To sum up, Matthias expressed the spirit of the Renaissance to perfection in his character and talents, as in his faults. He represents that age as faithfully as a statue by Verocchio, or a picture of Mantegna, or a cathedral or campanile by Brunelleschi, or the miniature-adorned manuscripts of Attavantes. If his learning was less wide than that of Lorenzo de' Medici or Federigo da Urbino, his natural talents and inventiveness were greater. He thoroughly realised the importance of the Renaissance, and wrote on one occasion to Galeotto Marcio: "We may pride ourselves on having raised the glorious past, eternal in its influence, from the dead."

The poetry of the Middle Ages was chiefly religious, but the era of Matthias produced some secular poetry, and its light falls upon the figure of the King. The most important works were written in Latin, for the admiration of the classics was too enthusiastic and exclusive to allow of much favour being shown to poetry written in the vernacular. Janus Pannonius, in Hungary, used Latin for his epics, just as Petrarch did in Italy.

The same era also saw a late flowering of legend. The first long epic poem written in Hungarian is the story of St. Catherine of Alexandria. Her history inspired many of the great Renaissance painters : the most famous picture representing her is that by Raphael,* who painted the virgin saint with visionary eyes and her well-known symbol, the wheel. The legend of St. Catherine must have been the work of some one living outside court circles, where Italian taste was prevalent, and yet of some one in touch with the Renaissance, for the plan and treatment of the work show the influence of the new spirit. Literary works of the Middle Ages, with the exception of a few real masterpieces, lack plan, and are frequently obscure in parts because they are wanting in logical order and in proportion. It was one result of the revived interest in the Latin writers that logical method and clearness came to be essential in literature. The Romans were preeminently gifted with the capacity for organisation, and they brought that power into play in their literary activity ; their works became a standard of literary excellence and their methods became rules for their Renaissance admirers.

In the legend of St. Catherine we notice subjective features; behind the facts, we detect the springs from which they flow. In that respect also the author of the poem is typical of the age in which he lived, an age which had learnt to place a new value upon the individual.

* The picture is in the National Gallery in London.

V

THE REFORMATION

HUNGARIAN culture in the sixteenth century was influenced by two great events : the Reformation and the disastrous battle of Mohács (1526), in which the Hungarian army was annihilated by the Turks, and in consequence of which nearly the whole of Hungary fell beneath the Turkish yoke, losing at one blow her king and her liberty.

At the time of the Reformation the country was torn into three parts : the central portion, with the capital, Buda, was in the possession of the Turks ; the north-west belonged to Austria, while, in the east, Transylvania formed an independent dukedom.

Both the Reformation and the battle of Mohács left deep traces on the mental life of the nation. Some superficiality and frivolity, some arrogance, too, and rashness of thought were often mingled with the spirit of the Renaissance. But those two events stirred the soul of the Hungarian people to its depths.

The Reformation was a great international movement which spread over the whole of Europe, bringing everywhere the same intellectual changes. The battle of Mohács was a national sorrow, which stamped a peculiar character upon the mind and the literature of the nation. The two events were very near together in time. In

1524, eight years after Luther's action at Wittenberg, the royal court in Buda was torn by a violent religious controversy, and a Bill was passed in Parliament ordering all Lutherans to be put to death. Two years later came the battle. National and international, religious and political events struck a blow at the new culture.

The chief effect of the Reformation was to heighten religious feeling and to deepen the reverence for conscience. It also influenced literature, developing the technique of both prose and poetry in a surprising way. The religious revival affected Catholics and Protestants alike. Never had religious convictions obtained a firmer hold upon the minds of men. But the fervour of religious feeling was different from the fanaticism of the Middle Ages. The imagination was more restrained, the element of superstition was suppressed, and religion became more and more an uplifting of the heart, and a submission to the guidance of conscience. It was the most cultivated class of men, the humanists, heirs of the Greek and Roman culture, who stood at the head of the new religious movement. That circumstance made itself felt in all directions, and especially in the development of every branch of literature.

The Reformation gave an impetus to Hungarian prose in two ways : by stimulating biblical translation and by fostering religious controversy.

Luther advocated the principle that the Bible should be made accessible to all, and the invention of printing made it possible. Deeper and deeper did the Hungarian nation drink from those eternal wells of poetry, the Old and New Testaments. It is true, there had been translations of the Bible before the Renaissance, but they were mere fragmentary transcripts.

The most valuable was made at the beginning of the fifteenth century, under the influence of Luther's great predecessor, John Huss. The doctrines of Huss began to spread throughout Hungary to such an extent that the Pope found it necessary to send an inquisitor. Two Franciscan monks, Thomas and Valentine, were banished for their heresy, and went to Moldavia, where a great number of Hussites were then living, and there, inspired by their master, they translated the Bible into Hungarian. It is the oldest translation in that language. One fragment of it found its way by chance into the Imperial library of Vienna, another to the library in Munich, and a third is preserved in Hungary.

The first complete translation of the Bible dates from the time of the Reformation. It was made by a Protestant, JASPER KÁROLI (in 1589-90), and is widely used by the Protestants even now. It has recently been revised with the aid of the British and Foreign Bible Society, and that edition has the largest circulation.

The Catholics were not far behind the Protestants in making a translation. That which they had used for two centuries was the work of a Jesuit, George Káldi, but the new one dates from the seventeenth century. This Catholic translation was even patronised by Gabriel Bethlen, the Protestant ruler of Transylvania, who fought so heroically for the Protestant cause during the Thirty Years War.

The spread of the new faith was furthered as well as followed by controversy. The Protestants began a general attack, against which the Catholics at first offered scarcely any defence. The success of the Protestants was largely due to the fact that they used the new weapon which the printing-press had placed in their hands.

The greater part of the polemical religious literature was written in Latin, but some of the Protestant publications were written in the vernacular. This controversial literature had a salutary influence on Hungarian prose.

But the Reformation did not only develop prose, it also created a new epoch in the history of hymns. There had been hymns written in the native tongue long before the Reformation, but Luther placed new emphasis on the principle that everything relating to religion should be made as simple as possible for all believers. Protestants began the work, and the Catholics soon found how right they were.

At the end of the sixteenth century, the Catholics also began to use the new all-powerful weapon which had given such tremendous assistance to the Protestants— the art of printing. We have seen that printing was introduced into Hungary in the reign of Matthias, earlier than it was adopted by most European countries, but after the death of Matthias that progressive movement, together with many others, was checked. Printing almost ceased, and it was not until the time of the Reformation that the printing-press commenced to play an important part.

Controversy introduced a dogmatic style and a harsh tone into literature. Writers were carried away by their heat in affirmation or denial, and we find ourselves, at that period, far removed from the oratorical elegance of the previous century. The most cultured of the scholars had not been educated in smiling Ferrara or Padua, but in gloomy Wittenberg, the town where the melancholy Prince Hamlet studied.

The century which saw the Reformation was, above all things, sober and practical. These qualities have always characterised Hungarians, whence the great effect of the movement upon the people. Only once has the soul of the nation been stirred more profoundly, and that was during the first half of the nineteenth century, when the new democratic ideas took hold of the popular mind. The catastrophe of Mohács had an equally great effect on people's minds. It strengthened the feeling of patriotism just as the Reformation increased religious fervour. The Hungarians became zealous both for their fatherland and for religious liberty. Great national misfortunes always light the flame of patriotism, which in times of security often becomes extinguished. Hungarian poetry of this period echoes the patriot's grief ; the note is now soft, now harsh, but always the expression of real affliction ; and in some of the poems we find the sadness of the patriot blended with fervent religious feeling. Melancholy became a dominant note of the lyric up to comparatively recent times.

Fervent love for the fatherland, and bitter grief at its distresses, are revealed in the poetry of the chief Hungarian lyric poet of the sixteenth century, Valentine Balassa. The same feelings inspired the greatest epic poet of the seventeenth century, Count Nicholas Zrinyi ; and the same note is heard from the lyres of the eighteenth century poets, especially those of the classical school. Even in the nineteenth century we still see men turning in thought towards Mohács—Charles Kisfaludy, for instance, "greeting with sighs the tomb of our greatness" ; Berzsenyi, however, speaks of the event with frigid stoicism, while Kölcsey's tone is one of profound melancholy, and Vörösmarty's peerless hexameters possess a gloomy grandeur.

But suddenly, during Vörösmarty's lifetime, came the

period of Count Stephen Széchenyi's reforms, and a vision of the "future Hungary" rose beside the spectre of the past, and, in the imagination of the poet, the two forms strove with one another.

It is this ever-present patriotic feeling which distinguishes Hungarian poetry from that of other nations. In no other poetry of the time is the note of love for the Fatherland so powerful and so fundamental. With other peoples the feeling of national unity was still lying dormant, while in Hungary it moved the heart of the nation with the unconscious but mighty force of an universal instinct. The fire of the Turkish wars only served to make this element in the Hungarian character as strong as iron ; and the development, in the sixteenth century, of the feeling of nationality, was one of the most important phases of the evolution through which the nation's mind has passed.

Their religion and their country were the two ideals which inspired the poets of the sixteenth century to sing their songs of joy or sorrow, and it was for his religion and his country, both of which were constantly threatened by neighbours to north and south, that the Hungarian statesman trembled. The Hungarian still fought for "God and the Fatherland" as he did in the Middle Ages—only the foe had changed. And the two-fold cry echoed by the nation's poetry is "God and Fatherland."

The sixteenth century was controversial, and consequently an age of prose. There were, however, a few poets, both in the first, and in the latter half of the century, who deserve attention. One was a wandering minstrel, Sebastian Tinódi ; and another, a passionate warrior, a troubadour-knight, Valentine Balassa.

SEBASTIAN TINÓDI, who died about 1559, was by no means a poetical genius; he was a brave patriot, and a thoughtful, conscientious man, but he had little imagination. He is interesting as the best-known and most typical representative of the class of poets called minstrels. To some extent the minstrels discharged the functions now performed by the newspaper; they wandered from town to town, and half sang, half recited, their tale of the latest political events, or of battles, accompanying their song with an instrument not unlike the guitar. Sebastian Tinódi was one of these wandering poets or singers. And there was matter enough for his song! The Turks penetrated further and further into the very heart of the country; the great leader, Valentine Török, in whose castle Tinódi had worked as a scribe, was treacherously lured into the palace of the Sultan, and died in a Turkish prison.

Next came the wonderful deed of valour performed by George Szondy, captain of the fortress of Drégel. With a handful of soldiers he withstood for a long time the united forces of the Turks, and when called upon to surrender, he preferred death, and died fighting for his Christian faith and his Fatherland. Only for his two faithful pages did he ask from the Turk the mercy which he scorned for himself.

Another fortress, that of Temesvár, was just as stubbornly defended by Stephen Losonczy. When the defences were completely destroyed, the Turks assured Losonczy that they would allow him and his soldiers to depart from the ruins in safety, but the faithless foe broke his word, and fell upon the little band and their leader, killing them to a man, after a desperate fight.

Those sad events were witnessed and narrated by

Sebastian Tinódi. He was not only a patriotic minstrel, but also a reliable eye-witness, who related historical events in all their details ; contemporaries, it is well-known, are much more interested in details than are historians when writing of past ages. He visited the battlefields of which he sang, in order that he might give a faithful account of the conflicts they had witnessed. He was much more accurate, but much more prosy too, than most of the historians who were his contemporaries. The technique of his versification is primitive and his language is as monotonous as his rhymes. His poems may be divided into three groups. The first treats of the political events of the day, the constantly renewed attacks by the Turks, and the defence of the fortresses by the Hungarian leaders. The subjects of the second are taken from the Old Testament, and in that part of his work he clearly showed the influence of the Reformation, which made the Bible known to a far wider circle than it had been before. Typical of this class is his *Judith*. In the remainder of his work the influence of the Renaissance may be clearly traced, for he turns for his subjects to the classical world, choosing from its mythology such topics as those contained in his *Chronicle of Jason and Medea*.

The most prominent poet in the second half of the sixteenth century was VALENTINE BALASSA (1551–1594). He himself was a picture in miniature of the times in which he lived—warlike, unhappy, and wild. Like the youthful Sophocles at the rejoicings after Salamis, he first attracted attention by his stately dancing. At the coronation of the Emperor and King, Rudolph II., he was chosen to lead the Hungarian national dance. The fact is mentioned in the Latin chronicles of Istvánffy a Hungarian historian, and we may judge how deep an impression the remarkably handsome youth and his elegant dancing must have made on all who beheld him, when we read the enthusiastic description of the event written many years later. The youth was sent to Eger to "learn chivalry," or knightly ways. The fortress of Eger was an important military centre; the heroic and successful defence of the town by Stephen Dobó was known and applauded in all the neighbouring countries, and so, too, was the magnificent part which the women of Eger had played in that piece of heroism. Balassa's first love-songs were addressed to the daughter of the same Stephen Losonczy who is mentioned above as the valiant defender of Temesvár. Balassa's father was himself the captain of a border-fortress, and by his intrepidity drew upon himself the wrath of the Sultan. It was in this warlike atmosphere that the young poet grew up, and his private life was as perturbed as the age in which he lived. It was a restless life indeed, full of litigation, full of discord. His marriage is characteristic of his whole life, and reveals his disposition. He wished to marry a cousin, a member of the Dobó family. The lady was entitled to one part of the large fortress and town of Sárospatak (the fortress having several owners). The family, however, strongly objected to the match, because the pair were cousins, so Balassa determined to acquire both bride and fortress by one bold stroke..

On Sunday he went to church at Sárospatak with several of his armed men; he waited until the service was over, and then stepped forward boldly, grasped the hand of Christine Dobó, and compelled the priest to marry them. After the wedding, he led his wife to the courtyard of the fortress, and addressed the garrison in a fiery speech, telling them that the fortress was his, and that he claimed their obedience, and threatening them with his own troops. Finally, he took possession of the keys, and compelled the soldiers to take the oath of allegiance. Not for long, however, was he suffered to remain in undisturbed possession of either bride or castle. The latter was taken from him by force, and the family caused him, after lengthy litigation, to be divorced from his wife on the ground that the consanguinity of the contracting parties made the marriage invalid.

The violent proceedings of Balassa in contriving his marriage were equalled by the merciless hatred of his relatives, who even accused him of having become a Mussulman, and of bringing up his son in that faith.

After estranging the affections of his relatives, Balassa left his Fatherland. For a long time he wandered about aimlessly in Poland, and at length went to Dantzig. Some years later he returned to Hungary, and, like his great successor, Alexander Petőfi, died on the battlefield. A few days before the fortress of Esztergom was retaken from the Turks by the Hungarians, Balassa fell, mortally wounded. How can the life of this violent, quarrelsome man possess any interest for us ? Because Valentine Balassa was the only real poet to be found in Hungary during the sixteenth century, and remained her best lyric poet until Alexander Petőfi appeared in the middle of the nineteenth century.

The range of Balassa's poems is not wide, but they are instinct with feeling. In some of his verse he reveals his restless and stormy soul, distraught with the pangs of love. In others, he praises the life of a soldier, which in those days was a very different thing from modern garrison life, and chiefly meant camping in the open air, with a constant succession of adventures demanding resource and courage. We seem to breathe the bracing air and the fresh scent of the meadows in those poems. In one song, he, like Othello, bids adieu to life in the tented field; he also bids farewell to Hungary, the bulwark of Christianity, and the home of heroes; to his comrades, whose fame is sung even in far distant lands; to his swift "eagle-winged" charger; to the groves and banks, to his friends, and to his many enemies.

The poems written during his wanderings form a class quite distinct from the rest of his work; they are full of yearning for the distant Fatherland and his dear ones there. "A pilgrim in far-off lands, soberly apparelled and gloomy in heart, longing for the wings of a bird, that he may fly to those he loves."

In all his troubles religion was his one consolation. He was chiefly a religious poet, and in that respect was a characteristic product of his times. The unrestrained vehemence of his feelings, the feature of his character, which in his private life proved a blight, was an advantage in his poetry. He was one of the first who prepared the way for the expression of genuine feeling in poetry. But his verses are not only remarkable for their sincerity and depth of feeling, but also for their technique. What a difference between the prosy language of Tinódi and the graceful stanzas and sonorous rhymes of Balassa !

There is one other new feature in his poems—a sense of the beauty of nature. Appreciation of the beauty of nature seems to have awakened at the dawn of the New Age, and Balassa was the first among Hungarian poets to give expression to it; it attained its greatest perfection in the nineteenth century in Petőfi, who is unrivalled in his

D

appreciation of external nature. Until the advent of
Balassa, the man of extremes, the dreamy yet passionate
troubadour, external nature had found no voice in Hungarian poetry ; she was a world waiting to be discovered
by poets. It was he who first, of Hungarian poets, felt
the beauty of the landscape and saw symbols of his own
inner experiences in the phenomena of nature.

During the time of the Turkish wars a large number
of stories were written in verse, telling some tale of love
and war. Many of these were inspired by the works of
Boccaccio, though some of them only to a slight extent.
Such a story is that of *The Faithful Griseldis*, written by
PAUL ISTVÁNFFY, who was educated at Padua. It tells
us of the mental anguish of a wife whose fidelity and love
were put to a severe test by her husband on account of
some wager. Another group of these stories was based
upon the *Gesta Romanorum*. There were also translations
from the Italian, such as that fine fairy tale which was
adapted by ALBERT GYERGYAI under the title of *Prince
Argirus*, and which served as a basis for Vörösmarty's
delightful fairy play *Csongor and Tünde*. But more
important than any of these, by virtue of its being purely
Hungarian, is the story of *Szilágyi and Hajmási*. Two
Hungarian warriors are taken prisoners and carried to
Constantinople. On a certain Whitsunday, one of them,
Szilágyi, more moved than usual by the memory of his
beloved country, takes up his lyre and sings mournful
songs. The Sultan's daughter hears, and feels pity for
the captive, and her pity is soon changed into love. " If
thou wilt promise to be faithful to me in thine own land,
then will I set thee at liberty and follow thee." The
young hero promises to be faithful, and he and his companion are set free by the princess, and they all three fly

on horseback. The Sultan sends a troop in pursuit, but the fugitives reach the Hungarian frontier in safety. Here a new danger arises, for the other Hungarian, Hajmási, has also fallen in love with the princess and challenges Szilágyi to fight. He is, however, defeated, and retires from the scene in a repentant mood.

The early part of the seventeenth century was in Hungary, as everywhere else in Europe, the age of the anti-Reformation. It has already been said, when speaking of the influence of the Renaissance and the Reformation, that all great intellectual movements having their origin in other countries, profoundly affected Hungary too. The "fair" Danube rises in distant lands and flows into Hungary, where she receives the tributary streams of that land. So is it with the current of the nation's thought; foreign and native elements combine in it, and any great change without must sooner or later profoundly modify it. Those changes are reflected in the nation's literature.

The dominant idea in the seventeenth century was that of undoing the work of the Reformation, and the centre of the movement was Spain. In Hungary, Cardinal Peter Pázmány, the Bossuet of Hungary, was the intellectual leader of the Catholic revival, and the most remarkable author of his time. During the sixteenth century Protestantism had attained the greatest importance and influence in Hungary. The greatest thinkers, and leading men, were all Protestants. Balassa was perhaps the only Catholic among them.

The majority of the nobles were Protestant, and it happened twice that the Palatine, the representative of the king, was of the same faith. At the end of the century, the Papal Nuncio returned to Rome with the alarming news that there were only three hundred Catholic divines in the whole of Hungary, whereas in Italy that number was the average for a single town. It seemed as though Hungary would rapidly become exclusively Protestant.

It was at this moment, which threatened imminent danger to the Catholic Church, that PETER PÁZMÁNY appeared (1570-1637). Under his guidance, Catholicism regained nearly all it had so suddenly lost. We might almost say that Pázmány was born in a Protestant country and died in a Catholic one. His parents were Protestants, but Nagyvárad, where they dwelt, to a great degree predestined him to his future vocation, for it was the headquarters of the Jesuits. The first Hungarian Jesuit, Szántó, lived and preached in that town, and it was he who converted the parents of Pázmány. Their son entered the Order, and when twenty-one years of age went to Rome. Here he was most powerfully impressed by the great Jesuit writer and orator, Bellarmin. He resolved to become the Bellarmin of Hungary, and to restore its former greatness to the Catholic religion. He devoted his indomitable energy, his wonderful gift of eloquence, and his brilliant literary style to that end. He rose rapidly in fame and influence. At the age of forty-six he was the highest ecclesiastical dignitary of the land, the Archbishop of Esztergom. He also acquired great influence at the court of Vienna.

The Emperor Ferdinand II. sent him on an important secret mission to Rome. This was at the time of the Thirty Years War, when the whole of Europe was divided into two vast camps of embittered enemies. Cardinal Richelieu, the great adversary of the Habsburg dynasty, supported the Swedes against the Austrians. That a cardinal, with the knowledge of the Pope, should support the Protestant Gustavus Adolphus against his most Catholic Majesty the Austrian Emperor, seemed to Pázmány infamous. Such a state of things had to be put an end to, for the Catholic supremacy was at stake. Pázmány was therefore sent to Rome, to ask the Pope to interfere in the interest of the Habsburgs. The Rome which he had left as a poor, unknown Jesuit monk, he now entered with princely splendour and an immense retinue, through the Porto del Popolo. He was received everywhere with great politeness, but gained nothing but fine speeches and effusive promises, so that at last, Pázmány, who had worked harder than any one else for the Catholic Church, left Rome with bitter disappointment in his heart. His desire remained unfulfilled, for he was unable to defeat the French policy. Neither did he succeed in creating a Catholic alliance strorg enough to arrest the triumphant progress of Gustavus Adolphus. "It is with more joy than I received from all the signs of favour shown me at the Papal court" said Pázmány, just before leaving Rome, "that I now take my leave." But he nursed his anger, and at Ancona, before embarking, his bitter indignation found vent, and the Hungarian cardinal gave utterance to the following sentiments concerning the Pope, in the presence of the Roman divines. " Alas, I see that the Pope pays no heed to the dangers which threaten Christianity, and gives no aid to the Emperor. On the contrary, his Holiness supports the Emperor's foes and seeks an alliance with the French and Swedish against the most Catholic monarch." It was said that his failure grieved him the more because he had hoped that in undertaking the mission, he was at the same time paving his way to the papal throne.

Pázmány was not only the leader of the Anti-Reformation movement, but he was also the first great master of Hungarian prose. Before his time authors wrote in a flat, colourless, verbose style, as beginners often do. Suddenly Pázmány stepped forth without any predecessor, and expressed his ideas forcibly, with striking brevity, and with many an unexpected turn in his concise sentences. His best works are his *Sermons*. He possessed the gift, peculiar to great preachers, of illuminating the obscure and mystical dogmas of the Catholic religion by means of the simplest similes. Abstract ideas became intelligible under his treatment of them. His chief work on theology is *A Guide to Divine Truth*. The first half of the book treats of Christian dogma in general, and the second contains an attack on the arguments of the Protestants. He was very successful in religious controversy. His style is terse, forcible, caustic, and, in accordance with the habit of the theologians of that day, often harsh. One of his most bitter controversial pamphlets, in which he attacks the Protestant doctrines with withering sarcasm, was translated by the Protestants themselves, in order that it might be answered by a famous German scholar. When the answer was ready, the book containing it had to be translated into Hungarian. Controversy was thus a slow affair, and it was sometimes years before a reply was forthcoming. Time did not move at the same pace then as it does now, and men were more inclined to take things leisurely.

Pázmány was also famous for the schools which he founded. The number of priests being insufficient, he established a seminary which is called after him the Pázmáneum to this day. The Jesuits firmly believed that the future of a party depended upon its schools, so Pázmány built a large number of grammar schools, all of them at his own expense, and he founded a University at Nagyszombat. Out of that foundation grew the University of Budapest, which is now one of the largest in Europe.

The Protestants founded several schools. The two most important high schools were those at Gyulafehérvár, in Transylvania, and at Sárospatak. The school at Gyulafehérvár owed its origin to an eminent ruler of Transylvania, a man not unlike the great Matthias ; he was self-willed and violent, but he possessed an original mind, and was an ardent lover of knowledge and the arts.

This Prince was Gabriel Bethlen, the brother-in-law of Gustavus Adolphus, and the ally of England. In the latter capacity he took part in the Thirty Years War, and had he lived longer, probably the war, and consequently the fate of Europe, would have taken a different turn. In the high school which he founded there lectured the first Hungarian philosopher, the attractive but unfortunate JOHN APÁCAI CSERI (1625–1660), son of a poor serf. He had studied in Holland, where he became acquainted with the works of Descartes. The founder of modern philosophy fired the soul of the poor Transylvanian student. Cseri began to write his chief work, the *Hungarian Encyclopædia*, at Utrecht, at first in Latin, and afterwards in his native tongue. In this book he treats of all the branches of knowledge, dealing with philosophy in accordance with the system of Descartes, within five years of that philosopher's

5

death. He was one of the very first to make Descartes known in Europe. On his return to his native land, he determined to plant the young tree of philosophy in Hungarian soil, to spread knowledge and culture, and to found a scientific academy. Unfortunately he was not a man of commanding and original genius, and he had to contend with the difficulties that invariably beset the pioneer. People did not understand his ideas, and his efforts failed. Cseri was first, among Hungarian authors, to raise his voice against serfdom.

The catastrophe of his life was connected with the visit of the English scholar, Isaac Basire, to Transylvania. Isaac Basire's life was a chequered one. He was born at Rouen in 1607, and became chaplain to Charles I. After the king was beheaded, Basire went to Constantinople as a doctor, and from Turkey to Transylvania, where one of the successors of Gabriel Bethlen, George Rákóczy II., made him a professor at Gyulafehérvár. Here he at once came face to face with Apácai Cseri. The latter, after studying in Holland and England, had carried Presbyterian principles home with him, while Basire, the Court chaplain, was naturally Episcopalian. The controversies of the English Church were thus transplanted into Transylvania, and the prince commanded the two scholars to discuss their differences in public debate. The debate took place, and the Episcopal doctrines of Basire found favour with the audience, and he carried the day. On his defeat, Apácai was deprived of his chair at the high school, and given employment at a much less important school at Kolozsvár, where the great idealist died at the age of thirty-five. The victorious Basire then returned to England and entered the service of Charles II.

The other Protestant high school was that of Sárospatak.

The wife of Prince George Rákóczy, the highly cultured and studious Susan Lorántfi, invited thither the famous professor, Amos Commenius, one of the founders of modern pedagogy. Gabriel Bethlen wished to secure for this school the services of ALBERT SZENCI MOLNÁR (1574–1634), the enthusiastic champion of Protestantism. Molnár did not accept the invitation, however, preferring to wander restlessly through Europe.

Molnár was a truly representative figure of the times. He was all enthusiasm, all fervent and untiring study, all restlessness, and his career was all adversity. He was born in Hungary, and died there, but the greater part of his life was spent abroad. Of this Hungarian philologist, writer, theologian and poet, Bisterfeld, a contemporary, said : " He was a favourite of the Muses but not of Fortune. Germany became his home and shelter, and to his native land he was as a stranger." He passed some years in Switzerland and in Italy, but lived chiefly in Germany, where he worked assiduously in the field of Hungarian literature. In Germany he endured much misfortune. A sketch representing an atrocious incident in his life forms the frontispiece of one of his books, a translation of Calvin's *Institutes*. At Heidelberg, when the inhuman army of Tilly destroyed the town, Molnár was reduced to beggary, and then tortured. The sketch shows him raised aloft on a high post, while a Spanish soldier scorches him with a torch.

Molnár was one of the most important Protestant writers. His best work is a *Translation of the Psalms*, from the versions of Clément Marot and Théodore Béza. The Hungarian Calvinists still use that translation, which is remarkable for its perfection of technique. The verses are very melodious, rich in euphonious rhymes, and perfect in metre. Molnár was remarkably industrious and wrote, amongst other things, a Hungarian grammar.

We have seen that the Reformation gave an impetus to serious study, and also led to the creation of different sects. The most interesting was the Unitarian community. There was a time when the greater part of the population of Transylvania belonged to that body. Just as the champion of the Episcopal church in Transylvania was a foreigner, Basire, so too the Unitarian doctrine was first propagated in Transylvania by the foreigner John George Blandrata, a physician, who had been banished from several countries. In Transylvania Blandrata became Court physician to the ruler, John II. That prince was converted to Unitarianism, and his chaplain, Bishop Francis David, became the most ardent apostle of the new faith. This was the most prosperous period of Transylvanian Unitarianism, but soon after the death of John II., Francis David was cast into prison, where he died. Though he perished, his cause lived on, and still has a large number of adherents in Hungary. Some of them split off from the main body and formed the Szombatos sect, whose members keep Saturday instead of Sunday as the Sabbath day. The founder of this long persecuted sect was Simon Pécsi, the Chancellor of Gabriel Bethlen.

VI

COUNT NICHOLAS ZRINYI

In the year 1626, a young nobleman, at the point of death, was carried into the castle of Archbishop Pázmány, in Pozsony. The dying man was Count George Zrinyi, Commander of the Hungarian army, the King's favourite, the finest soldier of his time, and also the best hunter. It was commonly said of him that he could bring down the game with his lance while riding. He was now brought to his friend Pázmány, who had some years before reconverted him and his family to the Catholic faith. Some said it was the plague that killed him, but certain vague rumours were whispered abroad, that he had been poisoned. Wallenstein, the commander-in-chief of the Imperial army during the Thirty Years War, wished, it was said, to get rid of so formidable a rival, and had the radishes poisoned which he offered to his guest at dinner.

Count George Zrinyi was the head of the most distinguished family among the aristocracy. His grandfather, the famous Count Nicholas Zrinyi, died a glorious, self-sacrificing death, during the defence of Szigetvár, which he had held with a handful of men against the army of Soliman, innumerable as the sand on the sea-shore. Count George Zrinyi had two little sons, Nicholas and Peter, and the dying

father entrusted the children to the care of Archbishop
Pázmány.

If the veil which hides the future could have been
lifted for one moment, and he could have seen the fate
which awaited his two sons, and his grandchildren, a
series of the saddest pictures would have been presented
to the closing eyes of the dying father. He would have
seen one of his sons, Peter, in a vast hall, kneeling on a
platform draped in black, with an awe-stricken crowd
around him, while the German headsman severed the neck
of the condemned hero with his heavy sword. He would
have seen his other son, Nicholas, to whom the laurel
wreath both of poet and hero had been awarded, lying
dead on the bloodstained grass, in the depths of the
forest of Kruzsedol. Another picture would have shown
George Zrinyi his great granddaughter, Ilona Zrinyi,
defending for years the fortress of Munkács, the last
bulwark of Hungarian independence, against the
Austrian army, and at last dying in exile, far from the
fatherland, in a town of Asia Minor. And the last
member of the family would have appeared to his dying
ancestor, with his heart pierced by Turkish lances.

The sons of Count George were brought up by the Archbishop. NICHOLAS ZRINYI (1618–1664), the elder, soon
proved to be the more talented of the two. He became
the greatest epic poet of the century, and at the same time
an eminent statesman, and one of the best strategists in
Europe. His whole life was remarkable. At an age
when other children merely play at warfare with toy
swords and tin soldiers, little Zrinyi was introduced to
real war by his father, who was fighting the Turks. The
warlike spirit was soon awakened in the child, the more
so as he lived in a border fortress where they had to be

ready at any moment to repel the raids of the Turks ; and where his eyes became familiar with fierce foes and deadly weapons.

Such was the childhood of the future hero and bard of battles. At the age of sixteen he went to Italy and visited the papal court. In Rome he became acquainted with the works of the poet, who, next to Virgil, made the deepest impression upon him—Tasso. The whole career of Zrinyi was one of rapid progress. At eight years of age he was one of the bannerets of Hungary, and accordingly had certain official duties to perform. At twenty-one he was the ban of Croatia. He was twenty-six when his grand epic, the *Zrinyiász*, was published. As a soldier he first greatly distinguished himself in 1663. But when, after a long battle, and in spite of the victory of Zrinyi, the Austrian Court agreed to the shameful peace of Vasvár, the terms of which made it seem as though the Turks had won the battle, Zrinyi retired, deeply grieved and indignant, to his fortified castle at Csáktornya. He had consecrated his whole life, his talent as a military writer, as commander and as poet, to one aim, the deliverance of his fatherland from the Turkish yoke. And after all his efforts, he was forced to see Austria withhold justice from Hungary, and to realise that she probably would never do her best to deliver a Christian sister-country from the dominion of the Turk. We must not forget that from the sixteenth century Hungary was divided into three parts. The largest portion was under Turkish rule, the northern belonged to Austria, while the eastern part formed the independent dukedom of Transylvania. Zrinyi saw that he could not trust Austria, and knowing that the continued rule of the Turks meant utter ruin to Hungary, he resolved to deliver his country by means of foreign aid. He began to weave the threads which, after his death, led to the conspiracy of Wesselényi and his party, the same conspiracy of which his brother Peter Zrinyi was the victim. While occupied with these plans, his life was suddenly brought to an end by an accident. During a hunt, he was found dying in the forest, his throat ripped open by the tusks of a wild boar. The people, however, were convinced that their hero had been treacherously slain by his rival, Montecuccoli, the commander-in-chief of the Austrian army, who felt as if under a cloud.

Zrinyi's chief work is a long epic poem which was published with a Latin title : *Obsidio Szigetiana—The Siege of Szigetvár*, popularly known as the *Zrinyiász*.   In it, he glorifies his great-grandfather, the first Nicholas Zrinyi, Szigetvár's valiant defender.   In the choice of his subject the poet was influenced partly by family traditions, and partly by the similarity of his own life to that of his hero.

The poem opens with a scene in Heaven. The Hungarians, through their civil dissensions, have roused the wrath of God, who resolves to chastise them by sending the Turks upon them.   In the end, Zrinyi sacrifices himself for the Hungarians, and when he sees that the fortress cannot hold out any longer, sallies forth for one last fierce conflict, slays the Sultan, and dies with all his heroic comrades.

The poem is of the purely national epic order, in the style of Virgil and Tasso.   Its language, although at times rough and unpolished, is wonderfully powerful. The chief value of the poem lies in its structure and its character drawing.   The men are all real and drawn from actual life. Tasso also depicts soldiers and Turks, but his writings reveal his ignorance of military life, and his Turkish heroes are mere opera-Turks. In the world of European literature Zrinyi stands high amongst those who can characterise whole races. We are struck by the truth and reality of his sketches of both Turks and Hungarians. He depicts battles, camp-life and councils of war, as one who knows them by personal experience, and who is as well acquainted with the enemy as he is with his own army. It may be that in many details Zrinyi unconsciously imitated Tasso, but for all that, he is thoroughly national and original. His work reveals the energetic, emotional yet laconic, and proud but generous Hungarian aristocrat and general, just as in the works of Tasso we detect the religious, highly refined, sensual Italian.

The martyr's death of the hero of Szigetvár was not really a decisive event, and did not mark a turning point in the history of Hungary, brilliant as it was as an episode of the Turkish wars. But the poet so groups the events as to give the incident greater importance. Zrinyi is made to appear as one who voluntarily sacrifices his life for the salvation of his country, and he is rewarded for this deed by a vision announcing that God accepts his sacrifice, and that after four generations have arisen, Hungary will be delivered from the Turk. The fourth generation was that to which the poet himself belonged, and it was as if by a prophetic inspiration that he foretold the coming deliverance of Hungary, for only his sudden death prevented him from seeing the realisation of his visions. Twenty-two years after his death, the fortress of Buda, which the nations of Europe had always regarded as the key of the Turkish dominion, and also of Jerusalem, was reconquered by the Christians.

In 1664, the year of Zrinyi's death, an epic poem appeared which became vastly more popular. The subject of the poem was the romantic marriage of Count Francis Wesselényi (afterwards Palatine of Hungary) and the beautiful Countess Maria Széchy. Its chief interest for us lies in the fact that it marks the beginning of an entirely new literary style, which quickly became popular throughout Europe.

The title, *The Venus of Murány allied to Mars*, is in itself enough to show the nature of the new style, which was characterised by florid metaphor and mythological allusions. It is the Baroque style, which influenced every department of life during the second half of the seventeenth century. The palaces display it as much as the pictures ; the laying out of gardens, as the binding of books ; literature not less than hairdressing. In all things there was something grotesque and over-ornamental, originating in the exaggeration of the Renaissance.

The change of taste introduced the Rococo period. The restful straight lines of the Renaissance buildings suddenly became twisted, curved, or broken. There was more wealth of detail but less dignity. Everywhere were rounded corners, shell - shaped hollowed surfaces, or intersecting lines. Sculpture, too, assumed an entirely different character. The statues as it were became restless. The ample and twisted folds of their garments seemed agitated by the wind, and their very gestures became nervous or excited, although the spectator could not possibly tell why. It was as though some emotion stirred them, the source of which could not be divined. The unexplained or gratuitous vehemence of their gestures was the ruling feature of the Baroque, and above all of the Rococo statues.

The same departure from naturalness was manifested in the realm of fashion. Elaborateness was the order of the day. People were even dissatisfied with their own hair, and wigs made their appearance in order to add to the wearer's dignity. Artificiality invaded the garden. Trees and shrubs were shaped into geometrical figures, triangular or square, until the garden showed nothing but a continuation of the stiff lines of the buildings.

Poetry shared in the infection, and poets revelled in allegory, myth and metaphor. What they learned from their antique models they spoiled by exaggeration. The structure of the epic poem lost its noble harmony, because the poets drew its component parts in too sharp outlines. The mythological element became aggressively pompous, and yet the deities lacked dignity.

The new tendency may be discerned in Hungarian poetry, and a good illustration is provided by the *Venus of Murány*, written by the favourite poet of the period, STEPHEN GYÖNGYÖSSI (1625-1704). His subject is an incident of European fame. Although the story seems pure romance, it was based on an historical event which occurred in the year 1644. Francis Wesselényi, a general belonging to the imperial party, and afterwards the leader of the Wesselényi conspiracy, was attacking the strong fortress of Murány. The defender and captain of the fortress, which belonged to the national party, was Countess Maria Széchy, famous for her great beauty. In the course of the siege the two hostile leaders, captivated by each other's fame and valour, fell in love, and Maria Széchy enabled the leader of the besiegers to gain an entrance to the fortress, together with a number of his men. That event gave Wesselényi possession of the strongest fortress and the loveliest woman in the land. With Richard III. Wesselényi might have asked

> " *Was ever woman in this humour woo'd ?*
> *Was ever woman in this humour won ?* "

Stephen Gyöngyössi was in the service of Wesselényi, and it was in accordance with Wesselényi's suggestion that Gyöngyössi made the history of the lover-combatants the subject of his poem. The poet, like the other writers of his day, used the somewhat conventional and mythological *deus ex machina*, and commenced by saying that Cupid, the son of Venus, wounded Wesselényi and Maria Széchy with his arrows. It is not only in its mythological element that Gyöngyössi's poetry reveals the influence of the Baroque taste, but also in an exaggerated use of ornamental metaphors, such as " The arrows of the sunrays wound the clouds," or "The lustre of the diamond challenging the sun."

The calm and critical eye of history does not see as much romance in the marriage of the *Hungarian Mars* and the *Venus of Murány* as the poet did. History tells us that Maria had not lived very peacefully with her relatives, and wished to make herself independent of them. Wesselényi, on the other hand, certainly had an eye to the advantages which such a marriage would bring him. It was regarded as a *mariage de raison* on both sides, and there is one delicate point in it which no poet or historian can quite ignore, and that is the undoubted treason of which Maria was guilty.

The personality of Gyöngyössi was very different from that of Zrinyi. Zrinyi died young, and Gyöngyössi, who was born almost in the same year, outlived him by forty years. Zrinyi possessed a certain austere dignity. He did not regard fine, grandiloquent language of great importance in poetry, and his strength lay chiefly in composition and character drawing. He was a great general who employed his master-hand in carrying out great plans and in the wise government of his men.

Gyöngyössi, on the other hand, was a poet of the Ovidian order, full of softness and melody. His technique is highly developed, and in descriptive and lyric poetry his style is remarkably pleasing.

Another elaborate allegorical work by him is entitled *The Phœnix that Sprang to New Life from his Ashes, or the Memory of John Kemény*. It also treats of a stirring historical episode, and is no mere adventure of love. Charles X. of Sweden invaded Poland and asked the help of the Prince of Transylvania. The Prince consented and one of the heroes in his army was John Kemény, a Transylvanian magnate. But the war was brought to a sudden end by a great catastrophe. The Poles were helped by the Tartars, who decoyed the Hungarian army further and further, until at length, having received reinforcements, they were able to take most of the Hungarians prisoners. Among them was John Kemény. A Tartar prison meant slavery, and that became the fate of the unfortunate captives.

In the first part of the poem, Gyöngyössi's theme is the suffering of his hero, while in the second he relates how Kemény was delivered, became Prince of Transylvania, and married Anne Lónyay, to whom he wrote touching letters from his prison.

VII

THE AGE OF DECADENCE

At length, in the year 1686, the day came when an epoch-making event was to take place, an event on which the very existence of the country depended, one for which the way had been prepared by Zrinyi and which was expected by everyone with mingled hope and fear. Hungary, with the co-operation of Austria, cast off the Turkish yoke, and Buda was regained for Christianity. The deliverance was effected by the troops of Prince Charles of Lorraine; every country in Europe was represented in them, including the remote highlands of Scotland.

Hungary was free. But strange to say, the period which followed that glorious historical event was from the literary point of view not one of advance but of decadence. Literature seemed extinct. Mikes, the one really original writer of the period, lived in exile far from his country, on the shores of the Sea of Marmora. There he wrote the works, which only became known several decades later. In Hungary itself, literary production seemed to have come to a standstill. There were few writers and few readers. The explanation of this curious fact lies in the circumstances which benumbed every organ of the body politic. The desolate state of the realm of literature was largely due to the desolation which reigned everywhere in the country, a result of the frightful depopulation to which it had been subjected. The Turkish Supremacy, which had lasted for more than one hundred and fifty years, had terrible consequences. When the enemy was finally expelled, there scarcely remained more than a million Hungarians. Not only had the Turks slain enormous numbers of them, but they had carried off almost as many, to serve as soldiers or as slaves. The Lowlands, the most purely Hungarian parts of the country, were the chief sufferers from the devastation.

Another cause of decadence was the universal poverty. The Turkish rule had a depressing effect on the financial condition of the country, and when that evil was removed the Austrian Customs' system followed.

It was this period which gave birth to the sarcastic proverb, *Hungary will be choked in its own fat.* The export of farm products was deliberately made more difficult, and the import system was so arranged that all industrial products had to be purchased from Austria. Hence, of course, the price of Hungarian products was sadly depressed, and the nation was compelled to buy manufactured goods dear in Vienna, and to sell its raw material cheap. The Austrian troops quartered upon the inhabitants consumed and wasted as much as the Turks before them. The large estates became the property of Austrian officers. The value of money decreased while the taxes remained high.

A third reason for the decline of literature was the disfavour in which the native tongue was held. Scholars wrote in Latin, and Latin was spoken by the deputies in Parliament. The wealthy aristocracy felt more and more drawn towards Vienna. There were no large towns in

Hungary, and even in such towns as there were, most of the wealthy burgesses spoke German.

The most important event of the eighteenth century in Hungary was the war for freedom waged by Prince Francis Rákóczy II. against the Habsburg dynasty. Rákóczy's mother was Ilona Zrinyi, already mentioned as the heroic defender of the fortress of Munkács against the Austrians. Afterwards, she married Imre Thököly, who became a prominent leader in the wars of Rákóczy II., and died in exile in Asia Minor. When Austria treated Hungary as a conquered province, Vienna looked upon Rákóczy as the centre and soul of the national efforts to secure independence. The war lasted from 1703 to 1711, and ended in Rákóczy's exile.

But in spite of these depressing circumstances, there were two brilliant literary phenomena, both of them connected with the magic name of Rákóczy. One was the masterly prose of Rákóczy's faithful follower, Count Kelemen Mikes, and the other, the poetry born in the camp of Rákóczy's soldiers, called the Kurucz army.

There sprang up among Rákóczy's soldiers an interesting, folk-like poetry—the Kurucz poetry,* sometimes uncouth, but full of strength and genuine feeling.

The poems do not all belong to the time of Rákóczy's war (1703–1711), for some were written during the earlier Kurucz wars, in which Imre Thököly, Ilona Zrinyi's husband, was the leader. But the most characteristic

* The word *Kurucz* is derived from the Latin *crux*, a cross. In the sixteenth century the powers wished to form an army of crusaders to march against the Turks. In the course of the proceedings, however, some regiments revolted against the nobility or their generals. Rebels were first called *Kurucz* on account of their symbol the *crux*. Later on, when the armies of Thököly and Rákóczy were rebel troops, the name *Kurucz* was also attached to them.

were written during the stirring and enthusiastic years of Rákóczy's campaign. It is chiefly the poetry of the camp, sung by soldiers to soldiers. The poems were recited, sung, and occasionally copied, but never printed and published. It was not until one hundred and fifty years later that they were collected. The songs are among the finest treasures of Hungarian popular poetry, the richness of which inclines us to say that the greatest Hungarian poet is the Hungarian people.

As they were songs for the camp, they naturally contain at times an element of aggressive and crude strength. But the good fortune of the Kurucz army waned, and the foreign and imperial party gained the upper hand, a fact that accounts for the note of melancholy so common in the songs. Moreover, as the Kurucz party were often prosecuted for their Protestant faith, it is only natural that a fervent religious element should reveal itself in their poetry.

Its dominant feature is the exaltation of racial and national feeling. No other popular poetry can be compared with it. Even its bursts of anger, indignation, sorrow, or bitter sarcasm contain a certain noble dignity. Some of the poems are purely lyrical, breathing the prevailing sentiments of the times— fervent patriotism, or embittered hatred of the enemy ; others, however, are of the nature of epics, relating the events of the campaign in the form of a dialogue, and so resembling the Scottish ballads. One of the best is the song about *Ocskay's Treason*. Another is a plaintive song of the homeless soldiers, who, with no secure shelter, wander about the plains and forests. Very touching is the *Farewell of Rákóczy*. There are several songs written by Protestant pastors, who had been carried away to

6

become galley-slaves.   When we read them, we seem to hear the unhappy captives singing plaintively of their sufferings, to the tune of some hymn they had loved in happier days.   The world-famed *Rákóczy March* did not receive its present form until the year 1806, yet even in its original shape it is a powerful creation, and expresses strikingly the two contending feelings of the time, a fierce love of fighting and a profound melancholy.

When Francis Rákóczy went into exile, never to return, he left his family, his dreams of freedom and glory, his crown, and his immense wealth behind him, and became a homeless wanderer.   There were still some, however, who clung faithfully to him in the days of his exile ; among them was a young nobleman, twenty-one years of age, Count KELEMEN MIKES (1690–1762).

He accompanied Rákóczy in all his wanderings.   First they went to Poland, then to England, and at length to France, where another exiled prince, James II. of England, had been hospitably received in the hope that some diplomatic advantages might follow.   At the French Court Mikes became acquainted with French literature, and translated several books, chiefly religious works.

The   Hungarian   exiles   did   not   stay   long   at Versailles.   They went to Turkey, and finally took up their abode at Rodosto, on the coast of the Sea of Marmora.   Here Mikes dwelt until his dying day, spending thirty years in exile.   On peaceful evenings the exiles watched the sun as it sank into the blue waves of the Marble Sea.   In the morning they saw it rise above the minarets, never, alas, to herald the day of their freedom.

Years rolled by, and Rákóczy died.   He was soon followed by his faithful general, Bercsényi, and one by one the little band were laid to rest in the land of their exile. Mikes outlived the others, and remained a solitary stranger in a strange land. It was on October 2, 1762, that the closing eyes of the last Kurucz watched the sun sink into the sea for the last time.

It cannot be said that as a writer Mikes was a powerful or remarkable personality, but his style is wonderfully attractive. His chief work, the *Letters from Turkey*, was not published until the end of the eighteenth century.

The letters are mostly dated from Rodosto, and are addressed to a lady cousin living in Constantinople. They were copied into a book, and after the death of Mikes, were found collected in one volume. It is not known whether the letters were ever actually despatched. At first sight we are inclined to believe they must have been. They are all properly dated, their beginning and end are exactly like those of ordinary every-day missives, and their contents are just the news of the day. On the other hand, the fact that they were carefully copied into one volume and that no relative of Mikes has ever been heard of as living in Constantinople is against that supposition. In addition, the letters may be divided into well-defined groups, as if the author had arranged them according to their contents. Accordingly, many scholars feel sure that this collection of letters is really his diary, or autobiography, a work almost unique as to its form.

The letters are full of the most charming humour. They supply us with the merriest accounts of his every-day life, and contain many interesting ethnographical notes, while here and there is a touch of real pathos. There is much real, earnest religious feeling in them too, but—and this is characteristically Hungarian—absolutely no sentimentalism. There is nothing in contemporary

Hungarian literature to equal their pleasant, fluent, conversational style. There is no pompousness, no affectation ; all is life and grace and transparent sincerity. Three groups of the letters are especially interesting : those dealing with the life of the Hungarian emigrants, with Turkish life and customs, and those relating historical anecdotes.

Those which tell of the personal history of the unfortunate Prince Rákóczy make the strongest appeal to us. Mikes describes the sad, lonely life which the Prince led. Deeply religious, he never missed the Church services. His leisure, and, alas ! he had plenty, was usually spent in carpentering or at his joiner's bench. Mikes adds "how very well he did even that work." Some years after the Prince's death, his son Joseph made an unlucky attempt to enter Hungary, but the enterprise failed, the small Hungarian army had to retire, and young Rákóczy died, as his father had done, in the arms of the faithful Mikes. " A curious world," writes Mikes in his last letter. " How many changes have I witnessed ? When I wrote my first letter to you, dear cousin, I was but twenty-seven, and now sixty-nine years weigh upon me."

The letters give us a perfect picture of the inner and outer life of a man whose strength was sustained by the priceless blessings of a calm confidence in God and a happy optimistic view of the world around him.

The literary life of Hungary in the eighteenth century presents a desolate picture.

Even the two men who may justly be regarded as the most notable figures of that day lived far from their fatherland —Mikes on the shores of the Sea of Marmora, and Francis Faludi in the heart of the Eternal City, at St. Peter's in Rome. For several years Faludi was a confessor there.

FRANCIS FALUDI (1704–1779) was a Jesuit. Toldi, the first writer of literary history in Hungary, said of Hungarian monks, that they had all the merits of monks, without their faults. It was certainly true of Faludi, who was a quiet, humble-minded man, of untiring activity, of a placid and kindly disposition, filled with a great love for his fellow men, and for beauty of every kind. Occasionally he would speak the language of the *galants* like the *abbés* of the French Court, a language full of refined mythological allusions. He was not a creative genius. By careful study he obtained a perfect knowledge of his native tongue, which had then fallen so much into neglect, and handled it in masterly fashion. The purity, the charm and inexhaustible variety of his style have no equal in the literature of the entire century. His talent for languages was of great help to him in his work as a translator. Amongst other works, he translated a book of philosophical reflections by Graciano Baltazar, a Spanish Jesuit, entitled *The Courtier*. It was this book which became the favourite reading of Arthur Schopenhauer. It deals with the problem how to get on in life. The writer does not, however, treat virtue, honour and diligence as the foundations of success, but circumspection, knowledge of men, and a crafty use of opportunities. The book was really intended for the use of young courtiers who wished to advance to honour over the treacherous ground of Court life.

In harmony with the spirit of the times, Faludi wrote many stories, so-called *moral tales*, amongst which it must be confessed there are some piquant ones ; but at the end of these the author relieves the mind of the reader by assuring him that the story is merely an instructive allegory, and only written for the sake of the moral lesson to be drawn from it.

In the *Winter Evenings* (possibly after the Spanish) the members of a small gathering of friends are supposed to be telling stories to each other. One tale is about Mauritius, a powerful wizard and king, who flies with his daughter to a lonely island. It curiously resembles *The Tempest.*

Faludi's works may be divided into three groups. His translations of collections of *sententiæ* (Baltazar's work among them) form one group, and a second consists of translations of moral dialogues. The third is composed of his original works, songs which appeal to the heart, and are forcible in their simplicity, descriptions of scenes of nature, idylls written in more melodious language than that of any previous writer, one *morality*, and a collection of his own original *sententiæ*, or teachings, entitled *The Godly Man.*

Had Faludi been more extensively read, and his pure and refined language more carefully studied, it is possible that the great linguistic controversy which arose a few years after his death, the so-called Language Reform, might have taken a different turn.

VIII

THE NEW CLASSICAL SCHOOL

CURIOUSLY enough, GEORGE BESSENYEI (1747–1811), the man who was to cause a great literary revival in Hungary, happened to live in Vienna, the very centre from which Germanising influences usually spread towards Hungary.

The Queen-Empress, Maria Theresa, anxious to increase the dignity and splendour of her Court, and also to consolidate the empire, organised a magnificent Hungarian Lifeguard in Vienna. Every Hungarian province was requested to select two representatives, from the most distinguished young gentlemen, and to send them to Vienna. One of the two officers sent by the province of Szabolcs was Bessenyei, a strikingly handsome, stately and chivalrous youth, full of talent and of character, but somewhat lacking in culture. The moment he began to move in the polished circles of the Viennese Court, he became conscious of his shortcomings, and at once began to educate himself.

The new idea of rationalism, originating in Paris, had just begun to spread in Vienna. The cultured men who impressed the young Lifeguard officer, were devoted to the new ideas, and fervently admired Voltaire and the Encyclopedists. To be a *Voltairist* was the fashion of the day, and formed one of the requirements of *bon-ton*. No wonder that the impressionable youth was carried away, the more so as he soon acquired a thorough knowledge of German and French, and was able to read the German humanists and French encyclopedists in the original.

This new tendency of the human mind was so revolutionary in its nature, that it naturally hastened the coming of political revolution. The " rationalism " of which men were so enamoured was really a revolt against the authority of mediæval traditions. Religious intolerance, blind submission to authority, superstition, especially that most shameful superstition—the belief in witchcraft —mental and political slavery ; all found ardent and brilliantly clever adversaries in the French encyclopedists.

Bessenyei threw himself into the new movement, and in his day-dreams, saw a flourishing Hungarian literature, and a vigorous mental life, with himself, perhaps, as the Voltaire of Hungary, for its centre. In co-operation with a few other Hungarian Lifeguard officers, Bessenyei formed a small literary circle. It was strange that Vienna, the very centre of hostility to every national effort, should be the scene of the revival of Hungarian literature.

Voltaire used the stage as the platform for the dissemination of his ideas. Bessenyei resolved to do the same. His first work, which was published in Vienna in 1772, and which marked the commencement of a new chapter in the history of Hungarian literature, was entitled *The Tragedy of Agis*. The theme resembles that of a play by the German Gottsched, but Bessenyei follows the form of the French tragic poets. He observes the " three unities," and adopts a contemplative, argumentative style and a refined, courteous tone, but his tragedies lack the psychological basis and the brilliant oratory of the French plays. He imitates Voltaire even in such little peculiarities as putting speeches full of allusions to current events into the mouths of his characters. Attila, for instance, the ancient king ofı the Huns, speaks against the unlawful power of the priests.

Bessenyei's plays are weak, and he was not very fortunate in his choice of the drama as a means of regenerating Hungarian literature, at a time when there were neither theatres nor actors. Nevertheless he must be honoured as a pioneer, and since his time the history of Hungarian literature has been one of continuous progress. The modern era was inaugurated by him, though perhaps he effected more by his example and enthusiasm than by his talent.

Several other plays of his were published in Vienna. One is *Attila and Buda*, the theme of which is the hostility between the King of the Huns and his brother Bléda, or Buda ; the subject of another is *Ladislas Hunyadi*, the noble and chivalrous hero, beheaded in the flower of his youth. They are all more or less similar, written in a cold, somewhat stiff style. He was much more fortunate in a prose comedy, *The Philosopher*, which contains one successful figure, a good-natured, straightforward, but somewhat unpolished country gentleman, the type of a Hungarian landowner. This type, which afterwards figured so largely in Hungarian literature, was first introduced by Bessenyei, but later on greater writers made use of it, and enriched it with many original features.

Bessenyei imitated Voltaire in his prose writings even more than in his dramas. The eighteenth century liked novels containing the meditations of a traveller, where the hero was supposed to visit foreign countries and give his reflections upon their habits and laws. Bessenyei wrote a novel of this kind, *The Travels of Tarimenes*. The country visited is the empire of Maria Theresa, which the author praises as the realm of happiness. In the book we meet Maria Theresa and her enemy Frederick the Great, whose army is vanquished by that of the Empress. Voltaire had flattered Frederick the Great. Bessenyei exalted that monarch's adversary, Maria Theresa.

Voltaire was the first author who dealt successfully with the history of civilisation, and Bessenyei followed him along that line also. He studied English literature as well as French, and translated, though crudely, Pope's *Essay on Man*, while his brother, Alexander Bessenyei, translated Milton's *Paradise Lost*. Alexander had also been enlisted to serve in the Lifeguards, but the gigantic and powerfully-built man had to leave the service because no horse could be found strong enough to carry him.

One of George Bessenyei's merits was his strong advocacy of the foundation of a Hungarian theatre, and of a scientific academy.

There was a certain intellectual restlessness in Bessenyei's life, and his ideas fluctuated unaccountably. At first he determined to use his influence at Court on behalf of the Hungarian Reformation, then suddenly he became a Roman Catholic. This was, of course, highly appreciated by Maria Theresa, who rewarded him with a sinecure. After her death, however, she was succeeded by her son, Joseph II., and it is one of life's little ironies that this eminent and enlightened ruler deprived the apostle of rationalism of the post which he had gained more by his apostasy than by his activity and merits. What could Bessenyei do now, disgraced by his monarch, and an object of suspicion in the eyes of his fellow

officers ? He could not stay in Vienna, so he returned
to Hungary and retired to his estate, where he lived a
lonely life, shut up with his books. As a Voltairian, he
never went to church, and when he died, he was buried
without any religious ceremony. His tomb is not in the
churchyard, but in a garden under a tree. During the
last few years of his life, Hungarian literature had begun
to take a new direction.

Among those who were stirred into activity by Bessenyei
were the clergy, and their superior literary education made
them important factors in Hungarian life. Their studies
were chiefly classical, so that when once they began to
write, they naturally took the classical poets, and especially
Horace, for their models. It must be remembered that
during the eighteenth century Latin was so largely used
in Hungary that it might almost have been regarded as a
living language.

In the history of Hungarian literature, the poets who
followed Latin models are designated by the name of
"The Classical Poets." Their works, like most modern
works in imitation of the Latins, are stiff, cold, somewhat
too abstract, and naturally full of mythological allusions.
The most noteworthy of the group was a monk of the
Order of St. Paul, Benedict Virág, the "Hungarian
Horace." He was full of genuine enthusiasm for what
the Latins called *virtus*, but his poems impressed other
poets rather than the general public. Before poetry could
make any further progress, it was necessary to settle the
rules of prosody. Hungarian poetry, like that of all
modern nations, is based upon accentual rhythm, but
when, in the sixteenth century, John Erdősi (or, in
accordance with the latinising fashion of his day, John
Sylvester) tried to imitate Latin verses, which are founded

on length of syllable instead of accent, the result was surprisingly good. The Hungarian language has proved to be much better adapted to the rules of Latin prosody than any other European tongue. It is well known that Hungarian hexameters are just as melodious, and as perfect from the point of view of prosody, as the Latin verses. Just because the result of this first essay was so satisfactory, Latin metres and stanzas had been largely used before the poets of the classical school commenced their activity, but it was they who first elaborated the rules for this kind of poetry.

We have seen that Bessenyei and his followers imitated the French Encyclopedists, while Virág and the other classical poets chose Horace for their model.

But there was another group of writers who turned neither to Rome nor to Paris for their models, who wished to wear neither the Roman *toga* nor the French *culotte courte*, but desired to remain national in their taste and garments. Those writers formed what was called the "National School." The wars of Rákóczy, and later on the tyrannical germanising efforts of Joseph II., stirred the national feeling and awakened men to the need of that sentiment, and strengthened the love of liberty and independence. "Down with foreign fashions! Down with foreign models! Let us be national in all things. If we must imitate, then let us find our models among the old Hungarian poets, such as Gyöngyössi."

The most prominent member of the school was a valiant Hussar General, Count JOSEPH GVADÁNYI (1725–1801). His family was originally Italian (Guadagni) but he became thoroughly Hungarian both as patriot and as writer. As an officer in a Hussar regiment, he took part in the Seven Years War, and had a share in that brilliant and daring military adventure of 1757, when General Andrew Hadik suddenly made his appearance before Berlin with his troops, amongst whom were twelve hundred Hungarian Hussars, and so great was the fright occasioned by the unexpected attack that the terrified town consented to open its gates and pay tribute.*

Gvadányi wrote most of his works after he had retired from active service on a pension. The best-known, *A Notary's Journey to Buda* (1790), is a long narrative poem. It strikes the reader as entirely free from imitation, as sincere, and wholly national. The characters and the whole atmosphere of the poem are purely Hungarian. This accounts for the immediate popularity of the book. A country notary, an honest but inexperienced man, travels on horseback to Buda. After many amusing adventures he arrives at his destination, but to his great disappointment he sees that in the very capital of the country, which ought to be the fountain-head of the national spirit, everything is foreign, the language the people speak, the books they read, the garments they wear, and even the measures they dance. People recognised themselves in the various characters, for the reign of Joseph II. had greatly tended to germanise Hungary. The notary himself is a well-drawn type of the patriotic Hungarian of that day, with his fervent national feeling, Latin education, scanty experience and little practical knowledge.

The centre of the awakening national life was the town

* An anecdote tells us that when the General left Berlin he wished, as an act of courtesy, to take home with him a present for Maria Theresa. The present was to take the form of a dozen pairs of fine gloves, but the spiteful glover sold him twenty-four left-hand gloves.

of Debreczen. Debreczen is situated in the most purely
Hungarian part of the country. Its inhabitants are
Hungarian Calvinists. In the eighteenth century it was
the largest town in Hungary, and from the time of the
Reformation was the centre of Protestant theology and of
national intellectual life in general. It is often called
"The Calvinistic Rome." It was there that botany was
first studied scientifically, and that the best Hungarian
grammars were written. In the large, though village-
like town, there was a huge ugly building like a barrack,
the inmates of which wore long black *togas*. This was the
most famous high school in the country during the
eighteenth century, the college of Debreczen.

The most original poetic genius and the finest lyrist
of his time was MICHAEL CSOKONAI VITÉZ (1773–1805),
a student at that school. Strongly national in feeling and
at the same time deeply learned, he represents the town in
which he lived. His one shortcoming, a lack of elevated
taste, he shared with all the writers of his school.

Csokonai was born in Debreczen and died there, but
the greater part of his life was spent in restless wandering.
It would seem as if the Muse of poetry bestowed the
traveller's wallet on Hungarian poets. We have seen what
a wandering life Balassa led. Csokonai's life was very
similar. In his talents and taste, Csokonai resembles the
German poet, Bürger. His earliest critic points out the
similarity.

The ruling ideas and tendencies of the time had their
effect on Csokonai's mind, but it is interesting to observe
that despite all foreign influences, he remained thoroughly
national. The eighteenth century liked the playful,
pleasing, and sometimes yearning tones of anacreontic
poetry, and thus Csokonai wrote poems of that character.

But he did not copy the playfully amorous *galanterie* of the Greek poet ; he substituted his own strong, sincere feelings. Another feature of the age was a passion for solitude. Thoughtful persons, it is true, had always found pleasure in escaping from the noise and bustle of town life to the quiet and solitude of Nature, but in the eighteenth century, the influence of Rousseau raised that sentiment to the level of a cult, and some of Csokonai's finest poems are in praise of solitude. Undoubtedly stimulated by Rousseau, his inspiration, however, came direct from the beauties of Lake Balaton, which plays the same part in Hungarian poetry as the lakes of Westmoreland in English.

The public taste was also powerfully impressed by Pope's *Rape of the Lock*, and, influenced by the English poet, Csokonai wrote a comic epic entitled *Dorothy, or the Dames' Victory over Prince Carnival*. He did not, however, adopt the satirical style of Pope, but displayed the burlesque, and at times rude, comic character of the society with which he was acquainted. He travesties certain details of the great world-epics in an inimitably amusing way.

The goddess of strife, Eris, causes quarrelling among the guests at a ball, and they divide into two parties and attack one another. One party, that of the old maids, is headed by Dorothy. What is their grievance against Prince Carnival ? That the time of Carnival is too short, and there are not enough weddings. They also wish to obtain possession of the register of their births, and even the young women join them. In the course of the strife, Venus arrives, and rejuvenating all the old maids, reconciles them with the rest of the world, and they all marry.

Csokonai was the first to introduce the tone of the old

popular songs into literature at a time when they were ignored or despised by persons of culture.

Csokonai died at the early age of thirty-two. It is said of Correggio that one of his own masterpieces caused his death, and Csokonai lost his life through his activity as a writer and speaker. He had written a poem *On Immortality*, for the occasion of the funeral of a distinguished lady ; he read it himself in the churchyard during the ceremony, thereby taking a severe chill which soon proved fatal.

A curious controversy known as the *Arcadian Controversy* arose after his death, amusing on account of the naïve ignorance it displayed. Kazinczy suggested as an epitaph to be engraved on the poet's tombstone the words : " I, too, have been in Arcadia." The poet's fellow townsmen, the worthy, matter-of-fact burgesses of Debreczen, did not know what it meant. They looked up the name Arcadia in Barthélemy's popular *Le Jeune Anacharsis*, and there discovered the following statement : " In Arcadia there were excellent fields for the rearing of domestic animals, especially asses." They felt hurt, and the ensuing controversy would have furnished a suitable theme for Csokonai's muse.

Another of the burgesses of Debreczen was MICHAEL FAZEKAS (1760–1819). He took part as an officer in the wars against Napoleon and went to France. Once he and his victorious soldiers entered a French château, which they were entitled to pillage. But Fazekas went straight to the library, sat down, read there for a few hours, put back the book he had been reading, and left without taking a single thing.

The influence of French literature may be seen in his works. A comic narrative poem, though written in foreign-looking hexameters, became very popular. In this he made use of a well-known French story, which, in accordance with the new revolutionary ideas, sided with the serf against the lord. Two or three decades after Fazekas, Claude Tillier employed the same story in his humorous novel : *Mon oncle Benjamin*. A heartless landowner robs, with violence, a young peasant, takes his geese and sends them to market, and has the lad flogged. The peasant determines to pay back this flogging three-fold, and does so. First he disguises himself as a wood-cutter and induces the nobleman to follow him into the wood to select timber, and there flogs him. Next he gains admittance to his room as an itinerant physician and flogs him a second time. After this the nobleman does not dare to go anywhere without his attendants, but on one occasion a man whom he meets tells him that he could help him to capture the wicked peasant if the attendants were sent to a certain place which he points out. They accordingly go, leaving their master alone, when the man throws off his disguise and flogs the nobleman for the third time. The peasant's revenge has a moral effect. The heartless landowner confesses his fault and amends his ways.

IX

THE LANGUAGE REFORM

AT the commencement of the nineteenth century Hungarian literature presents a remarkable phenomenon. In the course of a few years the literary language was so entirely transformed, that practically a new tongue came to be at the service of poets. As culture and literary taste spread, and authors grappled with the theory of art and of poetry, it became more and more evident that the Hungarian language was neither rich enough, nor polished enough, to express all the new ideas which increased culture had called into being. Many new words and technical expressions were needed. The process of enriching the language by the instrumentality of literature, was called "the Language Reform." The effort was crowned with victory in the decade 1830–1840, when Count Stephen Széchenyi was endeavouring to reorganise the state, really to create a new Hungary. For the new country a new language was a necessity.

The greatest reforms are linked with the name of FRANCIS KAZINCZY (1759–1831). It is true that before his time some authors had invented and used new words in their writings, but the commencement of serious reform is marked by the appearance of Kazinczy. At first he had enormous difficulty in overcoming the opposition which he aroused. In some provinces, indeed, there was such strong opposition to his ideas that his works were burnt by the public hang-man. Hungarian authors were now divided into two hostile camps. The "orthologists" thought that the language should remain as it was, both in quality and in quantity, while the "neologists" joined Kazinczy in his endeavour to increase its range by introducing new words and expressions.

Before Kazinczy died the Reform had triumphed, not in all points indeed, but as a principle, and practice quickly followed. Many new words created during this period of word-manufacture have since entirely dis-appeared, but the fact remains that some six or seven thousand words, rich in meaning, were permanently added to the language through the efforts of the refor-mers. How many words were lacking in which to express even the commonplace details of the life of a cultivated society, can easily be understood when we find that in speaking of the theatre, for instance, a Hungarian had no native words for "theatre," "actor," "curtain," "part," "character," and had to employ foreign ones.

Other languages, such as German and English, had the same difficulty, but they simply took over some Latin or Greek word, and as these remained uninflected, the foreign nature of the word was less apparent.

Another circumstance which added importance to the work of the reformers, was that even the already existing treasures of the language had not been systematically collected and arranged. There were no good dictionaries and no works on philology. The valuable material of the popular idiom was not easily available, and the reformers frequently wasted time in creating words through their ignorance of existing ones. A third fact which gave impetus to the reformers was that many Hungarian words were too long to be easily used in verse, the length being due to the so - called "agglutinative" character of the language.

The reform entirely changed the language. In new books there were a great number of words of which the previous generation had never heard. As one author said, with little exaggeration, sometimes the reader hardly understood what he read, there were so many strange words in it. Of course this autocratic way of making words which people scarcely understood, was only possible with a language like Hungarian, where by means of different affixes any number of new words can be made. The mistake of the reformers was that they sometimes added syllables which had never before existed, and which they invented, as, for example the affix—*da*. Sometimes, again, they cut off one part of the word, and treating the remnant as a complete word (though often it was a mere meaningless stump) they used it as a basis for the fabrication of fresh words. In other cases they translated a foreign word literally, though this did not suit the genius of the Hungarian language at all, but Kazinczy hoped to transplant the beauty of foreign languages into his native tongue. The idea of collecting the obsolete but purely Hungarian words used by old authors, and bringing them into fashion again, was much more commendable.

The mistake, then, of these reformers was that they did not consider the natural laws of Hungarian etymology, while it was their great merit that they did actually succeed, within so short a time, in creating a complete literary language. The success of the reform was simultaneous with the intellectual and political progress which marked the early part of the nineteenth century.

By the middle of the century, however, it was felt that the transformation of the language had gone too far, and a salutary reaction set in. Of course, the best poets had always been moderate in their employment of new words. John Arany, the most consummate artist in language, was strongly opposed to exaggeration. But the event which, more than any other, served to establish a reasonable mean, was the appearance of a philological periodical, the *Magyar Nyelvőr*.

Its editor, Gabriel Szarvas, was not only a most profound student of philology, but he was endowed with a kind of sure linguistic instinct, which guided him in his judgment as to what should be excluded and what would really prove of value to the language.*

Gabriel Szarvas commenced his activity at the time when the great statesman, Francis Deák, was restoring the ancient Hungarian laws and constitution. What the statesman did for political laws, the philologist endeavoured to do for the laws of his native tongue. For this end he strove in his periodical, which became the chief organ of the reaction.

Francis Kazinczy, on the other hand, was a child of the eighteenth century, which was characterised by grand and bold ideas, but which lacked appreciation of lawful organisation or historical continuity. His ideas concerning language reform displayed the spirit of the time, the age of the French Revolution. The conviction that

* Gabriel Szarvas (1841-1895) was a touching example of untiring energy and fervent love of study. Though quite unable to read or write, in consequence of the increasing weakness of his eyes, he succeeded, with the assistance of his wife, in finishing the first half of a very large dictionary.

language must be freed from obsolete conventions and made a more rational and useful organ, for the benefit of all, had its origin in the rationalism of the eighteenth century.

Men's minds were dominated by a highly abstract conception of the equality of all human beings, an equality not only of rights but of nature. They were so entirely possessed with this notion that they would not concede the existence of deep-seated racial and individual differences. Neither would they acknowledge the strength of historical conditions, the power of habit and convention, or the modifying influence of natural environment. They ignored the fact that in the development of a people there is an unbroken chain of cause and effect, each event following naturally from the preceding one, so that a nation's present is but the fruit of its past. Since all men are equal, they thought, every law which does not recognise that equality must be altered.

In this work of reform only pure common sense or reason was to be consulted. Whatever conflicted with pure reason must be transformed. All the most weighty institutions, such as religion, the State, the constitution, and moral laws, they urged, were based on convention. But things created by convention can also be changed by a fresh convention as soon as reason finds it advisable. Was not religion invented by the priests, kingship by tyrants, the state by the aristocrats, and language by a few of our intelligent ancestors? Why, then, should not these obsolete institutions be replaced by others?

Kazinczy's language-reforming plans were based upon a similar highly speculative and rationalistic notion. He considered the whole of the existing language, with all its time-honoured rules of etymology and syntax, as a matter of convention, and felt himself entitled to alter it as he thought best on purely rational principles. "In respect to languages," writes Kazinczy, "the supreme law is not custom, but the ideal of the language." There is a subtle but undeniable resemblance between Kazinczy's treatment of language and the well-intentioned and humanitarian, but tyrannical, rule of Joseph II. In both we see the attempts at generalisation and simplification which marked the French Revolution. Both men wished to get rid of traditions, and to replace them by logical systems, based on common sense.

Francis Kazinczy, the leader of the language reform movement, was not great as a poet, but was cut out for a reformer. He was full of enthusiasm, perseverance, and persuasive eloquence, and surpassed all his contemporaries in respect of learning and good taste. Without possessing any great creative genius, he became the centre of the literary world of his day; and, although he lived far from the capital, was closely in touch with everything going on there.

His life was divided into two periods by the tragic events connected with the conspiracy of Martinovics. Ignatius Martinovics, an abbot and a man of energetic and restless disposition, resolved, with several other malcontents, to spread the doctrines of the French Revolution. The men were rather ecstatic enthusiasts than real conspirators. They gathered the revolutionary doctrines into the form of a catechism, and Kazinczy copied the book. This proved disastrous to him.

The Austrian Court heard of the little band, and imprisoned Martinovics with all his fellow-conspirators. On December 14, 1794, Kazinczy was at his mother's house, when suddenly twelve lancers drew up before it, took Kazinczy prisoner, and carried him to Buda in chains. The death sentence was passed upon all of them. Martinovics and the other leaders of the conspiracy were executed, but Kazinczy was spared, and his sentence commuted to imprisonment.

For some time he was confined in the fortress of Spielberg, near Brünn, which afterwards witnessed the sufferings of Silvio Pellico. Later he was taken to Kufstein, in the Tyrol, and to Munkács, where, some years later, Ypsilanti, the Greek patriot, was imprisoned. For some months he was denied writing materials. He therefore wrote with his own blood, or with the rust of his chains dissolved in water. At length, after a confinement lasting six and a half years, he was set at liberty. It was during the long years of solitude in prison that his schemes for the reform of the language ripened in his mind, and the moment he was free he went home to his small estate in the country, and commenced to labour for their accomplishment. His aim was twofold : he desired to raise the level of literary taste, and to embellish the language. He translated a great many of the master-pieces of foreign literature and began to write critical essays on the works of contemporary Hungarian authors. In a very little while he became the highest literary authority. All the writers appealed to him for advice and criticism. As he lived in the country, his activity involved a great deal of correspondence, and he is the most volu-minous letter writer among Hungarian men of letters. Except Voltaire, no literary man has written more letters than he. The collection of them, shortly to be published by the Hungarian Academy, will form twenty-five to thirty large volumes.

There were no literary magazines in his time, and their place was filled by his correspondence. It is said that the large sums which he spent on postage, then very dear, added greatly to his difficulties.

As a poet, Kazinczy was at his best in didactic pieces; and as a prose writer, in biography. He died in 1831, during the great cholera epidemic.

Kazinczy saw clearly the part which he was called to play in literature. He once wrote : "We have merely commenced the work of reform. Our life has had to be spent in clearing and preparing the path of progress. But the time draws nigh when the sons of the gods will appear and cover Hungary with glory. Still, if the path has been made ready for them, the merit is ours."

And Kazinczy was right. Soon after him the "sons of the gods"—the great geniuses—arrived. The nineteenth century was the *grand siècle* of Hungary. It was the century of Vörösmarty, Petőfi, Arany, Széchenyi, Deák and Kossuth. Hungary, as we see her now, is the product of that age, which was richer in its results than any other since the foundation of the state.

At the beginning of the nineteenth century, however, there seemed small hope of a better condition of things.

Herder, the greatest philosophical historian of the day, wrote in his principal work, "*Ideen zur Geschichte der Menschheit*" (1784-91), that the Hungarian people and language would probably die out. The situation in Hungary certainly appeared to justify that opinion, and patriots were sadly contemplating the possibility that the historian, who wrote without any ill-will, but merely as one expressing a philosophical conviction, might be right.*

* The words that so profoundly impressed the Hungarians were as follows : *Die Ungarn "sind jet unter Slawen, Deutschen, Wlachen*

The same fear, giving rise to gloomy forebodings, is to be seen in the writings of the poet Daniel Berzsenyi, who said, in one of his odes (*To the Magyars*), that "Hungary could not be destroyed by the wild hordes of the Tartars, nor by the world-subduing might of the Turks. Civil wars were not able to ruin her, because her ancient virtue remained alive. But now the slow, subtle poison of degeneration is paralysing her, and if virtue is utterly lost, then the realm, though mighty as Rome herself, is doomed to perish. With the Hungarians of to-day, Attila could not have conquered Europe, Árpád could not have won a home for his people, nor Hunyadi have driven back the Turks. When once degeneration sets in the end is not far off. On the page of history it is written in letters of fire, that a nation once stricken with that blight must perish, as Troy and Babylon, Carthage and Rome, perished."

John Kiss, an author of the same period, wrote to his friend Kazinczy, referring to Herder's words, "However sad it may be, I also prophesy the annihilation of my country."

A learned cavalry officer, Joseph Csehy (who was soon after killed by a Russian bullet during Napoleon's Russian campaign), was once sitting in a public library, reading Herder. Andrew Dugonics, University Professor and novelist, happened to enter the library at that moment and Csehy pointed out the words of Herder to him, adding with a sigh, "The sun of our nation's life

und anderen Völkern der geringere Theil der Landeseinwohner und nach Jahrhunderten wird man vielleicht ihre Sprache kaum finden."

Some decades later even (1821) Goethe said of Hungary, "A country wonderfully rich in blessings. 'Tis a great pity it cannot progress."

has set." To this Dugonics angrily replied : " Don't believe that stupid German, he lies ! " The dialogue is characteristic of the temper of the times, when a fraction of the people, more by virtue of temperament than of reasoning, believed in their country's future.

But a change was at hand. At the beginning of the century it seemed as if all was lost, but in fact all was won. The day of greatness had been silently preparing. An awakening and stirring were going on in the hearts of men. The sentiment of patriotism was slowly gaining strength and finally became irresistible. And as though Nature knew what high aims had to be attained, she brought forth a greater number of eminent men in a few decades than she had formerly produced in centuries.

To this age belongs Vörösmarty, the first great classical poet of Hungary. He was born in the first year of the century. But before him, others had begun their work, and in 1802 appeared the first of the poems which were to become known and enthusiastically loved by the whole nation, *Himfy's Love* by Kisfaludy. Nature brought forth her gifted children in quick succession. In 1803 Kossuth was born, and in the next year Deák. Soon after came Eötvös, Liszt, Arany and Petőfi. In 1825 Széchenyi, destined to be Hungary's greatest reformer since the time of St. Stephen, stepped forth upon the stage of public life. The year in which Arany's masterpiece, *Toldi*, made its appearance, saw the birth of Munkácsy, the famous painter.

Hungary's three greatest poets, Vörösmarty, Petőfi, and Arany, happened to be contemporary with her three greatest statesmen, Széchenyi, Kossuth and Deák. Those men together, by herculean efforts, managed to awaken the country from its torpor, and to fill men's hearts with

hope. They organised the population into a true nation.
By their wisdom they created a future for their country,
and by their poetry they surrounded it with glory. One
sign of the country's awakening was the rapid development of the capital, Pest, which had not yet been
amalgamated with Buda to form the present capital,
Budapest. At the commencement of the nineteenth
century Pest had no more than twenty thousand inhabitants, while at its close the population numbered more
than half a million.

The greatest transformations took place in the realms
of politics, literature and social economy. The chief
political reforms are linked with the name of Kossuth.
For many centuries, Hungary had not been a democratic state, for the nobles and landed proprietors possessed many important privileges which were denied
to the rest of the population. The people were divided
into different social layers, each endowed with its special
rights or burdened with its special duties. All this came
to an end through the activity of Kossuth. The various
classes were fused together into one great community :
the nation, with equal rights and equal duties (1848).

In one of the lectures which Kossuth delivered in
England he gave an account of this great national transformation. " Excepting the burgesses of the privileged
towns, the nobility and the gentry were the only classes
that fully enjoyed the political and social rights conferred by the constitution. But those privileges were
not reserved only for the eldest son as in England. In
Hungary, every member of a nobleman's family inherited all the rights and titles of his parents. Accordingly the privileged class had grown exceedingly, and
numbered from five to six hundred thousand persons,

nearly as many as the burgesses in England. But one day the Hungarian nobility, like the Phoenix in the fable, lit with its own hand the fire which consumed it as a separate, privileged class, and they rose from its ashes, as an integral portion of one large free community. Liberty, equal rights, equal duties for all citizens, without any distinction on account of race, language or religion, those were the fruits borne by the events of 1848. We gave up our prerogatives, our privileges and immunities, which we saw were harmful to the rest of the community, and declared that we would take upon our own shoulders our fair share of the duties and burdens of the state. By means of equitable laws we enabled all the people to share with us our rights, and all the blessings of our country and constitution. We called them to be our brothers, one with us in the enjoyment of personal, religious, social and political freedom; to be as entirely equal with us in these respects as we all are equal, whether king or beggar, rich or poor, in the certainty of death and in the common hope of a life beyond the grave."

When society had been reconstituted in 1848 upon this new basis, there yet remained one great task to accomplish, to secure the independence of the new state in the face of Austria and the other countries of Europe.

The work was done by Deák. His great achievement was the *Ausgleich* or Compromise of 1867. Amidst the labyrinth of circumstances he found the right clue. He was able to weigh the strength of the country against the dangers of the situation. His unrivalled power of judgment, his wise and perfect self-restraint, and his quiet but indomitable energy made Deák's work as great a masterpiece of statesmanship as the works of the poets, his contemporaries, were great in the realms of verse.

Literature sprang into life and grew with amazing rapidity. The different, and often antagonistic literary schools, the popular, the high-classical, and the national, became united. Whatever was weak or false in them vanished. All that was really valuable developed to a higher degree. Just as through Kazinczy a rich prose language was gained, so now, by the powerful creations of Vörösmarty, a brilliant and purely Hungarian poetical language was called into life. The poetry of the new era had two roots ; one drew the living sap from Latin soil, and the other struck deep into the native earth. Latin influence predominates in the earlier poems, but it yields to the growth of a distinctly national spirit and style.

Every modern nation has had to pass through the study of the classical poets before attaining to its own highest literary development. The Latin races completed that part of their preparation at the time of the Renaissance, and naturally had a flourishing literature long before the Hungarians, who took up the study so much later. In Vörösmarty, the first poet of the great age, classical influence is still predominant, but later, in Petőfi and Arany, we see the triumph of the new spirit.

The more fruitful source of the new poetry was purely national. The great literary transformation which is indicated by the poetry of Petőfi and Arany may be described by saying that they used and transfigured the popular traditions, folk-lore, and ballads, raising them to the highest level of poetry.

Hungarian literature is, in fact, the record of Hungarian patriotism. The ideas of nation, fatherland and race are much more pronounced in it than in other litera-

tures. It is quite natural, for we always cherish more
anxiously what we are in constant danger of losing,
than the most precious treasures which we can quietly
enjoy in the security of unchallenged possession.   These
features also are uppermost in the popular tales and
ballads, as we saw when considering the Kurucz poetry.
Every innovation in the way of culture was first looked at
from the point of view of the patriot, who asked, how far did
it strengthen the nation ?   Science, art, literature were all
estimated according to the probability of their developing
the national sentiment.   This was the one test by which
to try the value of everything.   In Hungary it was never
l'art pour l'art.   What in other countries were merely
refined pleasures, became in Hungary patriotic duties.
Art and literature ministered to patriotism, and patriotism
ministered to the preservation of the race.

No more touching example could be quoted than that
of Alexander Körösi Csoma, the learned explorer.   That
heroic scholar bade farewell to his fatherland for ever
and travelled from Transylvania, through Alexandria,
Nineveh, and Bokhara to India, doing a great part of the
journey on foot, and suffering greatly from hunger, disease and the deadly climate, in order to penetrate to the
Himalayas.   This task, in which he was generously aided
by England, was undertaken with the object of discovering the origin and cradle of the Hungarian race.

Széchenyi, the reformer, was the hero, and the martyr,
of one idea, that of the nation's advance. This great man,
who devoted his whole life to the service of reform and
progress, exclaimed once in Parliament : " I admit that I
would not value any advance which was not markedly
national in its character.   The national sentiment is the
foundation of the state.   Without it, we shall become a

mere conglomerate of populations. It may be that our wealth would increase, but this prospect does not attract me. Before all else, fidelity to my race !" Progress, in any department of life, was but a means to the preservation of the race. This appears to have been the central idea in Széchenyi's mind, as in the minds of his contemporaries, and when that idea came into contact with other noble ideas, it helped to strengthen them.

The rearing of the edifice of the new state demanded incalculable labour, enterprise, self-denial and self-sacrifice. It is an old idea, which exists in the popular legends, that to make the foundations of a building strong, the sacrifice of human life is necessary. True it is that the Hungary of to-day has been baptized with the blood of her children. The sacrifice which her establishment demanded, and which was ungrudgingly given, was the lives of her noblest sons.

So great a result could only be achieved by a combination of splendid talents and great characters. Sacrifice we see everywhere, from the time when Kazinczy was flung into the fortress of Kufstein, to the time when Madách, also confined in a political prison, wrote his immortal *Tragedy of Man*. Many a poet besides Kazinczy and Madách found his way into prison : Verseghy, Bacsányi, and Szentjóbi-Szabó, who died in his chains. Half a century later, Petőfi, Hungary's greatest lyric poet, died on the battlefield, laid low by a Russian bullet or the lance of a Cossack. The greatest statesman, Széchenyi, in consequence of mental strain due to excessive labour and anxiety, lost his reason. The noblest patriots were imprisoned or exiled.

Naturally the great sons of this great epoch were filled

with enthusiasm, and all that was finest and best in the mind of statesman or poet was condensed into the one ideal of serving the fatherland. We can hardly find another age in history which, during a time of peace, can show such splendid examples of exalted patriotism, as the period between 1810 and 1848. And the hearts of other men must have been great to have enabled them to understand and value these patriots.

The men implicated in the Martinovics conspiracy were executed at the Vérmező, in Buda. One by one they fell, Sigray, Laczkovics, Szentmarjay, who when preparing to place his head upon the block, whistled the Marseillaise, the noble dreamer Hajnóczy, and last, Martinovics. Next day, in the very ground which had drunk their blood, rose trees were planted, bearing sweet-scented flowers. Like these, the flower of Hungarian poetry sprang from the blood of the martyrs.

The present generation knew but one of those great pioneers in person, Francis Toldi, the first writer in Hungary on the history of literature. The veteran soldiers of England could not speak with more veneration of the victorious heroes of Trafalgar or Waterloo than Toldi spoke of his great contemporaries, the two Kisfaludys, Kazinczy, and Vörösmarty. Kazinczy, in spite of his keen critical faculties, was capable of great enthusiasm. A good Hungarian poem moved him to tears merely because it was Hungarian, and on seeing some new building erected to beautify his country, such as the cathedral at Esztergom, he burst out into exclamations of joy.

About the end of the eighteenth century a young Hungarian gentleman went to Transylvania, the part of the country which, though inhabited by many foreign

8

races, had kept its political independence the longest. He writes : " It was at sunset that I reached the summit of a hill where Hungary and Transylvania touch one another. I stopped awhile, for both before and behind me there opened a grand view, which nevertheless made my heart ache. To the west I saw my country, with her wide-stretching plains, which I had to leave. To the east lay Transylvania, with a line of dark blue hills in the distance, her undulating surface swelling like the waves of the ocean.

"My heart also began to swell at the thought of parting. To take in the picture around me, I threw myself down upon the ground, just on the frontier line ; my head and my heart rested on the soil of that dear fatherland which my next step would leave behind. Tears fell from my eyes upon the uttermost sods of my country, and at that moment I resolved that I, a descendant of those who had conquered this land, even though a nameless child of the middle class, would work with all my might, even if silently and unobtrusively—I would work like the silkworm, spinning from the substance of my own heart what might serve my ill-starred nation, if aught that I could bring of inspiring word or true deed might prove of service."

The youth, who was not less inspired by poetic genius than by fervent patriotism, did actually spin the silken thread of which he had dreamed, and weave it into fabrics of beauty. He was Alexander Kisfaludy, the author of *Himfy* and one of the pioneers of the nineteenth century.

In 1818, at Athens, a young Hungarian traveller (styled by the Greeks " the English lord" on account both of his wealth and his dress) was musing amid the ruins of the city. "Is this," thought he, "the fate of so glorious a nation?" And then he vowed that he would sacrifice all he possessed in order to raise his country, to inspire it with hope and confidence, and to lead it towards a prosperous future, even though he had to do it alone. A wonderful resolve, but yet more wonderful is it that the traveller fulfilled his promise. This young man's name was Stephen Széchenyi, the founder of modern Hungary.

Hungarian literature reached its highest level in the forties of the nineteenth century. The enthusiasm of the leaders gradually took possession of all men's minds, and in the middle of the century a new ideal—the democratic —suddenly appeared. Those two ideals, patriotism and democracy, seized and dominated the minds of leaders and people alike.

The voice of the leaders rang out and awakened an ever-widening circle of echoes. Literature was the first to respond ; then the Press, which was just beginning to be a power in the land, awoke. Great orators helped in the work of stirring the hearts of the people. No wonder if, from this hot, teeming soil, poetry suddenly sprang up, like a tropical flower of rapid growth and fascinating beauty. Such a fertile soil was needful for the development of the national poetry, which, in its highest phase, is represented by Vörösmarty, Petőfi and Arany.

The second great ideal was that of democracy, which captivated the mind of Europe. The peasant class came into fashion in politics, as well as in art and literature. The poetry of Arany and Petőfi had its origin in the popular tales and ballads, and it seems almost as if their poetry were but the ennobling of these.

"It is of no use denying it," writes Petőfi to Arany.

" Popular poetry is the true poetry. We must strive to assure its supremacy in literature. When once the people begin to reign in poetry, they will be nearer to that political power which it is one of the aims of the century to give them." Arany said " Amen ! " The same year in which Petőfi wrote this (1847), Edward Szigligeti's first popular play, *The Horse-Herd*, was performed. Szigligeti introduced the peasants on to the stage and showed them in dramatic conflicts as the centre of serious interest ; before his time they had only furnished the episodic humorous elements in a play.

JOHN ERDÉLYI (1814–1868) began a work similar to that of Bishop Percy in England. He studied folk-lore and collected a number of songs, tales and ballads, which had previously been disdained. In his preface he declared that the collection formed one link of the chain which would bind the different classes of the community together.

The two great currents, the democratic and the patriotic, united, and augmenting each other's power and rapidity, gave new direction and force to Hungarian genius.

X

LYRIC AND DRAMATIC POETS BEFORE 1848

FROM its very beginning the nineteenth century was favourable to literature. In the year in which Kazinczy left his prison, a little volume was published containing four hundred short love songs, all of them written in the same form. It was the first volume of poetry to captivate the reading public. Young men learned the poems by heart, ladies treasured the volume, and the pieces written in their albums were usually selected from it. The author of the book, ALEXANDER KISFALUDY (1772–1844), was a young man of twenty-eight, who a little while before had been fighting against Napoleon as an officer in the army. Fifteen years later, his younger brother, Charles, also commenced his activity as a writer. The two brothers occupy an important place in Hungarian literature. They were both leaders and pioneers, fond of embarking on great literary enterprises. Their talents were, however, very different in character, and their activity pursued different lines.

Alexander, the elder, was a lyric poet, while his brother was the first to write original Hungarian dramatic poetry. Alexander, who was of a tranquil and happy disposition, wrote sentimental poems. Charles, who was inclined to melancholy, wrote comedies. The elder brother was a type of the sensible country gentleman. The younger was of a restless, self-consuming, artistic temperament. Alexander outlived his brother, and to a certain extent outlived his popularity.

As a young man, Alexander Kisfaludy was an officer in the Lifeguards, like Bessenyei, but he belonged to a later generation, having been born in the year in which Bessenyei's first work was published. We read in some memoirs that when two English magnates, conducted by Duke Eszterhazy, visited the fine rococo palace in which the Lifeguard officers lived, they were much struck on seeing a young Hungarian officer seated at a table, busily translating Tasso. The young officer was Alexander Kisfaludy, on whose poetry the literature of Italy had a great influence. " The literature of love songs was born in the sunny vales of Provence," said Uhland, in a well-known poem. Kisfaludy's love songs were certainly born there. He was in northern Italy with the army during the war with Napoleon. At the conquest of Milan he was made prisoner and carried to Draguignan in Provence. It was there, not far from Vaucluse, the abode of Petrarch, that he began to write the work which made him famous : *Himfy's Love.*

The love songs which make up the volume are linked together by the thread of a love story. Himfy meets Liza, and falls in love with her at first sight. But his love is not returned. Himfy tries to forget his enchantress, leaves his country, and seeks the excitement and distractions of war. He even contemplates suicide, Kisfaludy here revealing the influence of the "Werther" epoch. At length Himfy returns, and finds that Liza loves another. Of course, the success of the book had no connection with the commonplace plot. Its immense and instant popularity was due to the songs in it. All at once the former " classic " poets seemed cold and lifeless. There was such an overpowering, southern warmth, the true Provençal atmosphere in these songs.   It was not only a small circle of literary men that took an interest in the book.   The whole population hailed it with enthusiasm.   The character of the songs, which Kazinczy called " lyrical epigrams," is shown by the following verse : *

> In the blue horizon's beaming,
>   Thee, sweet maid ! alone I see ;
> In the silver wavelets streaming,
>   Thee, sweet maiden ! only thee.
> Thee, in day's resplendent noonlight,
>   Glancing from the sun afar ;
> Thee, in midnight's softer moonlight ;
>   Thee, in every trembling star.
> Wheresoe'er I go, I meet thee :
> Wheresoe'er I stay, I greet thee ;
>   Following always—everywhere :
>   Cruel maiden !   O, forbear !

The first part of the book was entitled *Yearning Love*, the second *Blissful Love*.   The second part did not win so much appreciation as the first, nor did it, perhaps, deserve it.   Himfy had then married Liza, and as " Himfy " is practically a pseudonym for Kisfaludy, it means that the poet himself had married, and happy married love was not so moving a subject as the sorrows of the hopeless lover.

In Kisfaludy's time a new tendency manifested itself in the selection of literary themes.   Voltaire and his contemporaries had regarded the Middle Ages with contempt as a dark age of superstition and intellectual slavery, the very memory of which ought to be blotted out (*écrasez l'infâme*).   And yet, two or three decades after the death of Voltaire, the Middle Ages became almost fashionable.

* BOWRING, " Poetry of the Magyars."

Poets discovered new beauties in them and praised their religious and chivalric spirit. The new tendency was romanticism.

After the rationalism of the latter part of the eighteenth century, romanticism came as a reaction. In France, Chateaubriand was the leading representative of the new tendency, which restored the sanctity and veneration of sentiment. In England it was Walter Scott who threw open the iron-bound gates of the mediæval castles to his admiring readers. Authors began to drop their abstract ideas about man in general, and to lean towards the strongly national features of the Middle Ages. Alexander Kisfaludy went with the stream. His historical tales *From the past of Hungary* are chiefly tales of chivalry. Their psychology is imperfect, but they are told with much vivacity and charm. Kisfaludy spent many years of his life near the " Hungarian Sea " as Lake Balaton was then called. Many of the volcanic hills in that district are crowned with the ruins of fortresses, such as those of Csobáncz, Somló, and Tátika. The sight of them proved a great inspiration to Kisfaludy. But it was not altogether their religious or chivalric spirit that attracted him to the Middle Ages ; it was rather the fact that it was the time of Hungary's political independence. He was guided by his patriotic sentiments.

The life of Kisfaludy, judged by ordinary human standards, was a very fortunate one. He came of a respected, well-to-do, and influential family. Nevertheless, there occurred in his life conflicts in which he was beaten. He was a valiant soldier, but it unfortunately happened that his army had to contend twice with the genius of perhaps the greatest of military leaders, Napoleon. No wonder then that Kisfaludy's troops lost the day.

Later on, when an old national institution (the right of the nobility to raise troops themselves for the country's defence) was attacked in literary works and in the Press, Alexander Kisfaludy tried to defend it.   But unluckily for him, the writer with whom he got into controversy was the most brilliant publicist of the century, Louis Kossuth.

As an elderly man he saw a young man beginning to acquire a celebrity that put his own into the shade.   As that success was due to the drama, he also tried to write plays, but failed.   And the successful rival was his own younger brother, Charles Kisfaludy.

CHARLES KISFALUDY (1788–1830), the second of the great reformers of Hungarian literature, was the younger brother of Alexander Kisfaludy.   The two brothers differed widely from one another in character, in talent and in their outward life.   Charles was a thorough bohemian, of a dreamy yet light-hearted disposition. Alexander, on the other hand, had a well-balanced mind. As a gentleman farmer he managed his property judiciously, and he was an excellent husband and father. He was of a cheerful temperament, and it is only in his works that we find him sad and serious, for his life was tranquil and happy, while that of his brother Charles was restless and full of adventure.   Charles had a profound knowledge of human nature, while Alexander showed himself an indifferent explorer of it ; his own soul he could reveal in his lyric poetry, but he did not thoroughly understand the souls of other men.

The first troubles in Charles' life sprang from a quarrel with his father.   His vehement and unyielding disposition caused him to be disowned.   Charles, like his brother, became a soldier, and he, too, fought against Napoleon at the battle of Leoben.

But he soon left the army in order to devote himself to painting. He lived for some time in Vienna, gaining a livelihood by his brush, until some "hazy longing," as he describes it, lured him forth again into the wide world. For a year he rambled about in Italy, but in 1817 he returned to Pest, where he lived in very humble circumstances. An honest cobbler gave the young artist shelter, and helped him to sell his pictures. Even as a painter Charles Kisfaludy was a true son of his time; he painted fantastical landscapes, moonlight scenes, or Gothic ruins, in the style of the Viennese school.

But suddenly there came a change in his life; he ceased to work only with the brush, and took up the pen as well. While living at the house of the poor shoemaker he wrote a play, which was performed by a company that had recently arrived at Pest from the country. The effect was electrical. *The Tartars in Hungary* (1819) was the first Hungarian play that contained real dramatic action. From this time Kisfaludy's career was assured. He wrote one play after another, and they were all acted with increasing success. It was one of the great achievements of his life to create a public interested in the Hungarian drama, which had hitherto remained crude and undeveloped.

In Hungary the course of development of the drama was the same as in other countries. There, too, the Mystery play was the germ from which it sprang, and the drama was originally in the service of the Church— *ancilla theologiæ*. But in Hungary the development was not continuous, and the secular drama was slow in coming to maturity, because there were very few purely Hungarian towns in the Middle Ages; the greater part of the burgess class was German, and there can be no drama without town life.

After the Mysteries came the second stage in the history of the drama, the satirical plays, intended for reading and not for acting, dating from the time of the Reformation.

The Reformation, like every other revolutionary epoch, was highly favourable to satire. Authors found the dramatic form introduced into literature during Renaissance times the most suitable for these satires. The best of them is perhaps a play entitled *Meinhardt Balassa's Treachery*, probably the work of a Unitarian minister. Though a primitive production as a whole, it is remarkable for the powerful drawing of its chief character. Balassa was an unprincipled magnate, who sided with the Protestants and Catholics alternately in pursuit of his own selfish ends. The finest and most important scene is that in which Balassa confesses his crimes.

The third stage in the development of dramatic literature is marked by the Morality plays performed at the high schools. These were again a fruit of the Reformation. Their authors were the schoolmasters. They were at first written in Latin, but afterwards in Hungarian, and their subjects were taken from the Bible or from ancient history. In the eighteenth century these performances at the schools were all the acting there was. There was no regular theatre. Yet Bessenyei tried to reform Hungarian literature through the agency of his dramas at a time when there was no possibility of their being performed. At last, in 1790, the first theatre was built at Pest. Members of good families formed a company under the superintendence of Ladislas Kelemen, and then, for the first time, the regular stage was open for the Hungarian tongue. The actors were animated by a sacred enthusiasm; they considered themselves the priests of a cult, that of the national art and language. "What shall we play on the first evening?" asked an actor of Kazinczy, who then held a high post as superintendent of one of the educational districts into which Hungary was divided. "*Hamlet*, of course," answered Kazinczy. "But who will translate it?" "I will." "But who will play the leading part?" "I will," again replied Kazinczy. Though the performance did not take place, the dialogue is characteristic of the time, when the future of the theatre was considered of such importance that a prominent man in the educational world was not unwilling to appear on the stage. It is true that a few years later the first company was dispersed, but the theatre was founded, and the beginning was an accomplished fact. Several other towns followed the example of Pest. In 1792 the first permanent theatre, which exists to this day, was established at Kolozsvár. From that theatre there issued companies of actors to create new homes for dramatic art. One of them played at Székesfehérvár, and that company, coming once to the capital, first performed the dramas of Kisfaludy with marked success.

It is Kisfaludy's merit that he created a sympathetic audience for the Hungarian drama. But he not only created a public, he originated the true national comedy. Before his time, comedies were mere imitations or adaptations of foreign plays, but Kisfaludy introduced Hungarian types and real national life into his comedies.

In his plots, he used largely the machinery which was only too well known through Kotzebue, Körner, and other playwrights of the beginning of the nineteenth century, namely, misunderstandings and impersonations. One of his types is the genuine, good-natured, but somewhat unpolished and clumsy country squire, who cannot get into line with the refined habits of good society. The humorous element in Kisfaludy's comedies amuses without sinning against good taste, and their healthy moral tone is unaccompanied by pedantry. Although in some respects the plays are primitive, their attractive way of depicting middle-class society gives them a value even at the present day. The humour lies rather in the situations than in the characters.

The play of *The Rebels* is based on a misunderstanding of the intentions of an amateur dramatic society which desires to perform Schiller's *Kabale und Liebe*. The members intend it as a surprise for some one, and they accordingly come and go and correspond in a very mysterious fashion. That air of mystery draws upon them the attention of the country magistrate, and as in their letters referring to the play they speak of death and murder and poison, he intervenes, bringing on a succession of lively scenes.

In *The Suitors*, again, everything turns upon an impersonation, the selfish suitors of a rich girl being received by another girl whom they suppose to be the heiress.

The chief character in *Disappointments* is a selfish and cunning man who wishes his children, a son and a daughter, to marry for money against their inclinations, but whose plans all miscarry.

Though comedy was more congenial to Kisfaludy's temperament, he tried his hand at tragedy. His best known tragedy is *Irene*. The first suggestion of the plot was given to Kisfaludy by an incident of the Turkish conquest of Constantinople, told in a letter of Mikes. "When the town was taken, among other prisoners they brought a remarkably lovely maiden to the Pash , who gave her to the Sultan. The Sultan was so captivated by her beauty that day after day he neglected his duties for her sake. The viziers began to murmur and to remonstrate with the Sultan, who by way of reply showed them the beautiful maiden. The pashas and viziers found her a sufficient excuse for the Sultan's remissness, but he, wishing to give evidence of his strength of will, said, ' I will show you that although beauty has temporarily enslaved me, I am strong enough to tear myself away from my pleasures, and that, being able to command myself, I am fit to command you.' And with that he slew the maiden."

Kisfaludy's play reminds us but slightly of this anecdote, so entirely has he transformed it. His heroine, Irene, when she falls into the Sultan's power and sees his devoted love, sets her heart upon gaining the Sultan's favour towards her subjugated fellow countrymen, the Greeks. She sacrifices herself for her people. The sacrifice is the greater since Irene had been betrothed to Leo, a young Greek hero, whom she loves even while facing the task before her. But two things happen. The army begins to murmur and to doubt the Sultan's strength when it sees that he has become the slave of his slave, and the tyrant discovers the secret of Irene's love for Leo.

His jealousy and wounded pride urge him to break the spell which binds him, and he stabs Irene to the heart. Some of the scenes display in a striking manner the greatness of Irene's patriotism and self-sacrifice, though occasionally she is too passive for a tragic heroine. "I shall gladly wither on thy fiery heart," she says to Mohammed, and her fate is rather that of a helpless victim than of a powerful tragic character.

Another of Kisfaludy's merits was the conversion of

Pest into a literary centre by means of a successful literary enterprise. During the eighteenth century Hungarian literary life had no real centre. George Bessenyei lived in Vienna, the very camp of the enemy, like an Iroquois among the Mohicans. Francis Kazinczy lived in the country, and Csokonai at Debreczen, the largest town in Hungary at that time. In the nineteenth century, however, the population of Buda and Pest began to increase rapidly, that of Pest especially, and soon exceeded that of the other towns. But amidst all the activity there was as yet no true literary life. It was Kisfaludy who created it. He began a literary enterprise which was calculated to gather round itself all the most talented authors. His plans met the favour of the public. Kisfaludy and his colleagues published an Almanack which bore the significant name of *Aurora*.

Almanacks were very popular at that time. There were no magazines, and the finest productions of the poets found a place in those silk-bound year-books, illustrated with steel engravings and gay with coloured fashion plates. Round that centre Kisfaludy gathered young authors of promise, and the pages of those almanacks first made known the name of a youth who afterwards surpassed all his fellow-workers on the *Aurora* —Michael Vörösmarty. Several of the steel engravings were prepared by Kisfaludy himself.

This book was the first to devote itself exclusively to fiction, and it accomplished a great work by gaining sympathetic readers for the national literature even in those aristocratic circles from which it had formerly been excluded.*

* How entirely the national language was neglected by the aristocrats is clearly demonstrated by a little incident in the life of

The Almanack did indeed prove to be the dawn—the *Aurora*—of a better future.

Charles Kisfaludy was a lyric poet as well as a dramatic author, and his poems mark the commencement of two new *genres* in Hungarian literature, which were afterwards cultivated with great success by others. One was the style of the popular ballad or romance, developed to perfection by Arany and Petőfi; the other, the dignified, classical hexameter verse, which became the *genre* of Vörösmarty. In one of Kisfaludy's poems, entitled *Mohács*, where he sings of his country's great loss in the battle, we find hexameters of such classical perfection that Vörösmarty himself might have written them. It is this poem which brings us to the threshold of the new age of literature (1825–1881).

In the eighteenth century there arose a new poetical school, which copied the style and metres of the Latin classics. But its productions were cold, and lacked life and the true Hungarian spirit. DANIEL BERZSENYI (1776–1836) was its only representative whose work attained to excellence. Berzsenyi was a Lutheran country gentleman, who passed his whole life on his estate. He was of a strong physique and very spirited, yet inclined to sentimentalism and so swayed by his emotions that when he first kissed his fiancée he fainted ! He was Hungary's greatest exponent of the grand

the Hungarian Palatine, Archduke Joseph. When he once paid a visit to the town of Florence, with a group of attendants, all of them Hungarian noblemen, he was received at the gates of the town by a deputation, on whose behalf Cardinal Mezzofanti, the world-renowned linguist, greeted the noblemen in Hungarian. When however, thanks had to be returned, it was found that not one among the Hungarian magnates was able to reply in his own native tongue.

style in poetry, and his odes are the finest in Hungarian. Horace was his great model, but Berzsenyi remained national, although robed in a classical toga. Behind the ancient metres and mythological allusions we can detect the Hungarian poet of the nineteenth century, a man harassed by patriotic anxiety and a prey to melancholy, but one whose eyes were turned towards God in adversity and who found his consolation in religion. Berzsenyi was more emotional than Horace and shared more in the sentiments of his age. In a famous ode—*To the Hungarians*—he laments the decay of the nation, once so powerful, due to deterioration in morals and decline in valour. The foundation of every country must rest on morality. When that is lost ruin must follow. It caused the fall of Rome herself. He mused on the fate of Greece, Babylon, Rome and Carthage, and the lessons taught by the world's history. It is a curiously sad poem, but characteristic of the times in which it was written.

Berzsenyi's highest flight is in the form of a prayer wherein the poet declares that while no man can comprehend God, yet what we can learn of Him from His works should inspire us with perfect trust.

A PRAYER.*

O, God, whom no wise man in thought can reach,
 Thou whom his yearning hope can barely trace ;
Thy being, like the sun, pervades all life.
 But human eyes can never see Thy face.

The highest heaven and ether's Uranus
 Around thee in revolving order course ;
The very worms unseen beneath the sod
 Proclaim Thy wondrous wisdom and Thy force

* LOEW, " Magyar Poetry."

9

The myriad orbs from nothing Thou hast called,
 Thy glance brings worlds to life or sends to death,
And measures the swift flowing tides of time,
 Whose ocean-waves are even as Thy breath.

Zenith and Nadir glorify Thy name
 Strong tempests breeding strife o'er sea and land.
Thunder and lightning, dews and flowering boughs,
 Alike proclaim them creatures of Thy hand.

*   *   *   *   *

Of all Hungary's poets the most idealistic was FRANCIS
KÖLCSEY(1790–1838). He was a perfect type of the dreamer.
He came of a very ancient family, which had played a
part even in Árpád's time, but he was not rich, and his
friends endeavoured to persuade him to undertake some
employment in order to add to his income. " To my
small income," he replied, " I add the independence of
my soul, and am satisfied." He was so immersed in his
studies and reveries that sometimes he did not leave
the house for months, but spent all his time in reading
and meditation. He had lost an eye in his early childhood, and this gave a certain melancholy and spiritual
look to his pale face. He was so enthusiastic about
liberty, that in spite of his patriotism, he yearned to
go to America, which he looked upon as the land of
freedom, but where he would probably have been as
much disappointed as Lenau was, who went there a few
years later. Kölcsey, however, did not remain a mere
poet of the study. In 1832 he went to Pozsony, where
Parliament then sat, as a member, and soon became the
most famous orator in the House. His style, with its
poetical turns which caught the imagination, became the
model for Louis Kossuth. " The saintly man," as he was
called, died at the early age of forty-eight, but by that time
he had become equally famous as orator and poet.

Kölcsey, like other idealists, was rigid and unpractical. He lived in the clouds, creating a world for himself, and came more and more to regard the activities of mortals with something like contempt. His indignation as a patriot drove him to extremes of feeling which no other Hungarian poet had ever reached, even in his most embittered moments. It was natural that such a man should be profoundly conscious of the gulf between the actual and the ideal. In one of his poems, speaking in the character of Zrinyi, the poet lamented the decline of his country. He appeals to Fate to spare Hungary, or the hour of her doom will soon strike. But Fate answers relentlessly : " My law must be fulfilled and the star of the Hungarians will set because of their misdeeds. On the banks of the Danube and the Tisza will arise another nation, speaking another tongue, a better and a happier people."

We may imagine the sufferings of a sensitive nature, driven to take such despairing views. And it was not merely his own country that Kölcsey criticised so severely; he was equally dissatisfied with the whole of mankind, and yet he loved his fellow men fervently. One of his poems, *Vanitas Vanitatum*, is full of stoical spirit. " Here is the scripture ; read its pages, and you will find the truth taught by Solomon that all is vanity. Our earth is but an ant-hill and an evanescent phenomenon. The events of history pass like a sigh. The heroism of the legions was as a bubble. The greatest of battles is no more than a cock-fight. Self-sacrificing virtue is but a dream. The death of Socrates, or Cato, or Zrinyi was a kind of insanity. What are knowledge and philosophy but systematic ignorance and chimera ? Faith and hope are mere illusions ; our life is but flame of a candle, and death is the breath by which it is extinguished. Immortality is like the scent of a flower ; when the flower dies its perfume outlasts it for a short time only. We ought not, therefore, to attribute any importance to fate, life, virtue or knowledge. Be firm as a rock, and whatever aspect fortune may wear for you, know that all is vain." As in his contemporary, Alfred de Vigny, so in Kölcsey, this rigid stoicism was the result of hyper-sensitiveness.

The severity and rigidity of Kölcsey's idealism showed themselves also in his criticism. He passed the same judgment upon Csokonai, the author of *Dorothy*, that Schiller passed upon Bürger, namely, that his style savoured too much of the popular poetry. He also wrote a criticism on Berzsenyi in which he reproached that great poet for using dialect, inflated metaphors, and complicated metres.

Severe criticism was unusual at that time and Berzsenyi was very much hurt ; in fact, Kölcsey's strictures cast a shadow over his whole life. After Berzsenyi's death, Kölcsey sought in his funeral oration at the Academy to make peace with the dead. "Spirit of the departed," he said, "I utter above thy tomb these propitiatory words. But a little while, and I shall follow thee. We were both but human and why should we be ashamed of it ? The paths of life cross one another, but the tomb is the abode of peace ; our petty interests do not pass its threshold. The man has left us, but the poet is ours for ever."

The best known poem of Kölcsey is the *Hymnus*. This, and Vörösmarty's *Appeal* became the two Hungarian national anthems. Both poems owed their character to the political situation of the country. Both are full of sadness, yet they both express the hope that after so much suffering Hungary's lot must change for the better. The first part of the *Hymnus* recalls the many blessings for which the nation had to thank God : the fertile and beautiful country, the wheat-growing plains and vine-clad hills, The Hungarian arms had been victorious over the Turk and had taken the proud city of Vienna. But the nation's wickedness had aroused the wrath of God, and then came the Tartars and the Turks, as well as internal dissensions, and even from the blood of her heroes there sprang no freedom for the country. The poem ends with the words : " Have mercy, O God, upon the nation, so long bruised by adversity."

In Kölcsey's lyrics there is a great deal of sentimentalism and melancholy, but his splendid ideals break through the clouds like sunshine. In him all the tendencies of his age in literature and politics were clearly manifested. His life and poetry were the truest expression of the idealism which is so characteristic of Schiller.

To one of the theatrical companies which occasionally visited Pest, a certain young amateur, a law student, attached himself. He played under an assumed name, but his real name was JOSEPH KATONA (1790–1830), and it was his admiration for its leading actress, Mme. Déry, that induced him to join the company.

Katona was the son of a poor weaver in Kecskemét, and he studied law at the University of Pest. While playing from time to time as an amateur, he began to think of writing a drama. Among his attempts in that direction is the tragedy of the *Palatine Bánk*, or *Benedict*. Katona published it in 1821, when all the theatres in Hungary were ringing with the applause of Kisfaludy's comedies. Curiously enough, Katona's play, the best Hungarian tragedy ever written, had no success. Its author, who became Attorney-General, died in 1830, nine

years after the publication of his finest drama, and
nobody knew that the country had lost in him her greatest
tragic dramatist. Katona's play of *Bánk ban* (the banus
or palatine Bánk) is a tragedy of the finest type, and its
reception was due to certain curious coincidences.*

The censor forbade its production on the stage
because it dealt with the murder of a queen, a dangerous
example for subjects. Not long before, a queen had
actually been killed, Marie Antoinette, a relative of the
Austrian Emperor. Thus the stage was closed to Katona's
tragedy. But there was another circumstance which miti-
gated against its success. The character of the play was
opposed to the general tendency and taste of the times.
It was an age which liked the polished and graceful in
literature, and its taste was not satisfied by the rigidly
majestic character of the tragedy. Though the patriotic
element in it was likely to appeal powerfully to the public,
its overpowering tragical element was not duly understood
and appreciated. Katona's language displays remarkable
force and terseness, but he paid no heed to the innova-
tions of the language reformers, and that fact made an
unfavourable impression upon his critics. And finally
we may mention one other circumstance that had its importance for him, as for all other authors. Katona did
not belong to any literary group or clique, and consequently remained isolated.

The historical event which supplied Katona with his

* John Arany translated a few scenes of the play into English,
and they were found strikingly similar to the Shakespearean plays.
Katona's greatness lay in his power of analysis, which enabled him
to portray faithfully the growth of the passions. His picture of the
tragical development of the soul of Bánk, leading to the inevitable
explosion, with its ruinous recoil, will ever remain a masterpiece of
dramatic poetry.

theme is in itself strikingly tragic. Imagine a just and noble-minded king who is compelled to leave his country and fight in foreign lands, and therefore charges his representative, the palatine and chief judge of the country, with the safeguarding of his kingdom and his queen. While he is away, the over-indulged brother of the queen, with her consent and assistance, seduces the palatine's wife. Simultaneously the most ardent patriots, embittered against the foreign queen, who, for the sake of her foreign courtiers, neglects and oppresses the Hungarians, form a conspiracy against her.

What a conflict of circumstances for the Palatine! What contending duties! Which side shall he take? Duty points to his place by the side of the queen. But she is the enemy of his fatherland and the originator of the offence against his honour. On the other hand, how can he, the representative of the king, take the part of the conspirators?

This truly dramatic situation attracted many authors. As early as 1562 Hans Sachs discovered its dramatic possibilities, and wrote a play entitled *Ein tragedi, mit zwölff personen zu spielen, Andreas der ungerisch König mit Bankbano seinem getrewen statthalter*. Nearly two hundred years later the English writer, George Lillo, wrote a play on the same subject, called *Elmerick, or Justice Triumphant*. Both Lillo and Hans Sachs took their subject from Bonfini's Latin *History of Hungary*. Six years after Katona's play was published, the Austrian poet Grillparzer wrote a tragedy, *Ein treuer Diener seines Herrn*, also dealing with the story of the palatine. Grillparzer knew nothing of Katona's drama.

Katona rose far above all other writers in his treatment of the theme. His drama is a plastic image of the storm tossed soul of the noble palatine.

Since the time of Shakespeare, tragedy has become the representation of one dominating passion. Katona, however, in depicting his hero, does not describe the growth of one passion only, but shows how different passions clash with one another, how they lessen or augment each other's force. In the hero, the husband and the patriot contend fiercely with the knight and the palatine. The passion which is most purely human is victorious, but while it destroys every obstacle in its path, it involves the hero himself in disaster.

The historical event belongs to the thirteenth century. The noble-minded *banus*, a knight proud and jealous of his honour, was palatine of King Andrew II. The queen, the German Gertrude, was the mother of St. Elizabeth, who inherited her mother's strength of will without her arrogance. The king was called away to some distant region to put down a rebellion, and in his absence the country was ruled by the queen. Her rule was most disastrous. She was a gifted and ambitious woman, and had all the energy and determination of a man. Unfortunately, however, even the best of the Hungarians were merely foreigners in her eyes, and she favoured only her own countrymen, the Germans, and, above all, the members of her own family. On this account a feeling of animosity sprang up against her, and reached a menacing height as the Hungarians saw how they were impoverished, flouted and oppressed for the sake of foreign intruders. Illegal taxes crushed the people, as more and more money was needed for the riotous revels of the Court. Discontent and disaffection daily increased. The palatine, the representative of the king, had the greatest difficulty in preventing open revolution, and found equal difficulty in suppressing his own rising indignation.

Once, when on a visit in the course of his duties to some
of the country districts, where he was painfully struck by
the misery of the overworked and heavily taxed peasants,
and the manifold signs of political oppression, a message
reached him from home, bidding him return without
delay, and secretly. Bánk's soul became a prey to the
darkest forebodings and he returned with feverish haste.
This is the beginning of the drama. Why this mysterious
summons ? The reason was indeed a grave one. Not
only was the nation threatened, but the palatine's virtuous
and beautiful young wife Melinda was also in imminent
danger. The queen had a dissolute brother, Prince Otto,
who persecuted the lady by his advances in her husband's
absence. The queen, in other respects so energetic, was
weak in dealing with her brother, and instead of putting
an end to the intrigue, forwarded the prince's vile plans,
and gave a court ball in order that Otto might meet
Melinda without hindrance. The festivity was at its
height when Bánk appeared. He entered by a side door,
very few noticing the palatine's unexpected return, and
learned that there was a conspiracy against the queen
and that the conspirators were to hold a secret meeting
that very night. Their password was " Melinda." The
conspirators had heard of Otto's love for Melinda, and
Bánk was told of it by Petur, a masterly drawn type of
the Hungarian nobleman of that day, faultlessly honest,
perfectly loyal to the sacred person of the king, but
violent and embittered by oppression and the illegal rule
of the foreign queen. Two impulses strove for mastery
in Bánk's soul. One urged him, as the representative of
the king and as the knight whose duty it was to guard the
queen, to crush the conspiracy. On the other hand,
jealousy, and fear for his own and his wife's honour,

tempted him to leave the queen to her fate and to devote himself to the protection of his wife. As, however, during the festivities, he had been an unseen witness of the dignified refusal which Melinda had given to Otto, he thought his wife safe for the present, and thus found strength to attend to his duties. His first duty was clearly to put down the conspiracy : afterwards he would call the queen to account for her behaviour in the matter of Otto's intrigue. Accordingly he went to the midnight meeting of the conspirators at the house of the *banus* Petur. Petur, roused to passion, vehemently advocated the murder of the queen, but Bánk refused to take any part in such a plot. He answered in these characteristic words : " That Bánk should become a companion in your dark enterprise would need an offence as great as are his faith and loyalty." But his calmness only provoked Petur to a violent outburst : "Since no other liberator is left to thee, my fatherland, here I stand, all alone, ready to become the executioner of that sinful woman." The moment was a crisis in Bánk's life. He thrust aside his personal feelings and asserted himself as the palatine and chief judge of the country. His language breathed a kingly dignity. He knew Petur thoroughly, knew that he was violent, but also that in the depths of his heart he was a loyal subject, and that if Bánk stood up as the representative of the king's person, the rebel would bow before him. When, therefore, he heard Petur's words he cried: "Stay ! this traitor to king and country is my prisoner, and I order you to bind him. It is Andrew the king, in my person, who commands here." Strong as was Petur's rebellious mood, still stronger was the feeling of repentance with which he knelt before Bánk, and bowing his head, said " My king ! "

Bánk's victory was complete, the conspirators abandoned their purpose, and Bánk uttered the words, " Oh, Andrew, though thou shouldst conquer whole realms, thou wilt never gain such a victory as Bánk hath won for thee here !"

Bánk, as a true knight, saved the life of a queen and woman : he stands before us as a radiant image of Hungarian chivalry and truth. But darkness soon overspread the scene. Bánk learned that Otto, in spite of Melinda's refusal, still continued his attacks, and was devising a cunning plan to obtain his end by violence. He found, too, that the queen, whom he had just saved, had done her best to forward Otto's schemes. A feeling of bitter hatred towards the queen entered Bánk's heart. But perhaps it was not yet too late to save Melinda. The knight who brought the news thought it possible, so Bánk flew to the court.

But it was too late !

Melinda had fallen a victim to Otto's machinations and had lost her reason. Slowly an awful purpose shaped itself in Bánk's mind. He will himself demand satisfaction of the queen, the ministering demon of Otto. It is no longer the former Bánk, radiant in his loyalty and integrity, who stands before us, but the mortally injured husband, and the subject driven to desperation by the wrongs done to his country. He resolves to be the judge of the demoniacal queen who has robbed him of his wife, and his country of its freedom.

The great scene of the tragedy follows. Bánk proceeded to the queen's room, burning with suppressed indignation. The poet now has the difficult task of making us understand how so noble and chivalrous a man as Bánk could become the murderer of his queen.

As he made his way to the palace two circumstances added to his grief, the grief of the patriot and of the husband. He saw Count Michael, his wife's brother, together with his own little son, being dragged to prison, and in the queen's hall he met Melinda, whose mind was wandering. The queen discerned the storms raging in the heart of Bánk, and to cut short his reproaches, commenced the attack in order to drive him to self-defence. "Is this an honourable thing which you have done?" she asks. "You have left your duty and come hither secretly like a thief in the night. You have sinned against your own dignity and mine also. Is it honourable?" Bánk answered with bitter defiance. "No, it is not honourable. My honour has been destroyed by the destruction of Melinda. It has been taken from me together with my brother Michael and my son." And then, with growing vehemence, he reproached the queen for the evil she had done in the country. In vain Gertrude, who gradually began to realise the imminent danger of the situation, cried, "Subject! Bondsman!" Bánk retorted with dignity, "No! I am your judge and your superior here." Gertrude, seeing that her regal dignity had no weight with Bánk, appealed to his knighthood and demanded the consideration due to a woman. But her words merely awakened in Bánk contempt for a woman who had lent her aid to her brother in his nefarious intrigue. Otto appeared unexpectedly for a moment, but seeing Bánk, he fled. This added to the palatine's wrath. The queen, perceiving that she was entirely in Bánk's power, and divining his purpose, resolved to kill him. She grasped a dagger, intending to stab Bánk, and he, observing the motion, snatched it from her hand and stabbed her. The deed was no sooner done than Bánk fully realised its horror. He stood as though turned to stone, and the dagger dropped from his hand. The noise awoke Bánk from his stupor, and he said : " Do not applaud, my country, thine avenger is trembling." And the queen ? The proud, ambitious woman, so eager for power at any cost, on the threshold of death, forgot her crown, her glory, her dignity ; human feeling prevailed and she thought only of her children. On the verge of the grave, it is the mother who speaks. " My children ! Where are my children ? To die without seeing them ! Andrew ! My children !"

Now that the king's representative himself had murdered the queen, there was nothing to prevent the open rebellion of the nobles.

At length the king returned, to find embittered hatred, and revolution, around the dead body of his wife. What remained for him to do ?

He would fain have chastised the wrongdoers, but now could he punish, when the murdered woman had so many crimes to atone for ? The conspirators were imprisoned, and Petur, in accordance with the law of those times, was tied to a horse's tail and dragged to death. But the chief culprit was Bánk, the palatine. What was to be his fate ?

He appeared before the king, a stony expression in his face and the calmness of despair in his heart. " It is I who killed the queen. Petur and all the others are innocent." He felt the horror of his deed, but tried to justify it to his own soul. The justification gave him strength and pride. There follows an admirable scene, where Bánk is crushed because his deed is shown him in a new light. Hitherto he felt that he had acted as a judge and not as a murderer, and that every honest man would have done as he did, for he never doubted that the queen had a hand in Otto's crime.   But Bánk now saw all men turn from him as from a murderer.   He heard, stirred to the depths of his soul, Petur, even when dying, cry out, " Long live the king."

And at last Bánk learned that he was deceived after all. The queen, though formerly indulgent to Otto in his illicit courtship, was entirely innocent of the crime itself, Otto having given her an opiate to get her out of the way.

So all Bánk's fictitious notions concerning a just punishment were exploded.   He, the highest judge in the land, a cowardly murderer ! The king's representative a traitor to his king ! He, the blameless knight, the destroyer of an unprotected woman ! He was crushed to the earth.   But one more blow fell on him.   The dead body of Melinda, slain by the hired assassins of Otto, who had chosen this means of avenging Bánk's deeds, was carried in.   Bánk cried out, " My punishment is utter annihilation.   In the whole universe is no loss but mine, no orphan but mine own child."   At first the king contemplated punishing Bánk, but the others looked with pity on the crushed and broken man, and said, "O King ! Punishment would be but mercy to him."

The king recognised that a mightier Judge had taken the rod from his hand, and felt that he would not have dared to punish like this.

He became reconciled with the nation and declared, " Better that the queen should have fallen, if she were guilty, than that the country should."   The only mercy which Bánk craved was permission to bury his unhappy wife.

XI

MICHAEL VÖRÖSMARTY

THE dawn of the nineteenth century was bright with promise for Hungary. On December 1, 1800 was born MICHAEL VÖRÖSMARTY (1800–1855), the son of a steward of an estate in the province of Fehér.

Vörösmarty became the first member of Hungary's great literary triumvirate. He took his degree in jurisprudence, but never practised as a lawyer. He was the first Hungarian author to make a good living by his pen. The greater part of his life was spent in Pest, which in the third and fourth decades of the century was the centre of the country. During the war for freedom he was made a judge of the Court of Appeal, with the right of recommending to the mercy of the king, such a post being congenial to him both as a lawyer and as a poet. But during the latter years of his life, his hopeful and energetic spirit was crushed by the catastrophe of 1849. It was with profound sorrow that he beheld his country deprived of her liberty and even of the hope of future progress. He died on November 19, 1855, after years of grief and despondency, not however quite unillumined with hope.

Vörösmarty's first poems ushered in the golden age of Hungarian literature. His importance is due to three great achievements. The first was the creation of a new poetic language. Literature could not attain its zenith until it had an adequate organ at its disposal. Like Klopstock in Germany, so Vörösmarty in Hungary, was the first to employ the kind of language which afterwards became the language of all poets. If we read a poet who lived before Vörösmarty, and one who lived after him, we are struck by the difference between them. Vörösmarty employed a vast number of turns and words and poetical forms which were unknown before his time, but which appealed to the popular imagination and became a national treasure.

His second achievement was to unite the hitherto contrasted qualities of the different literary schools in his creations and so to form a higher and more perfect type. Before Vörösmarty's time there was one school of a well-marked national tendency. The subjects were chosen from the national life to serve a national aim, every allusion contributing to that end. We may cite Joseph Gvadányi, the author of *A Country Notary's Journey to Buda*, or Andreas Dugonics, who wrote historical novels in a somewhat uncouth style, and with too much of the didactic element in them. The works of that school were defective inasmuch as they were not sufficiently artistic. Then there was the classical school, the adherents of which imitated the Latin authors, especially Horace. Here no doubt there was enough of the artistic element— too much perhaps—for authors were too careful of the form, with the result that their productions were often stiff and lifeless and left their readers cold. But Vörösmarty combined the best qualities of both schools in his works, without their faults. He had the perfection of form and the lucidity of composition for which the Latin poets were famous, but he also possessed in full measure the sense for national subjects and vigour of expression in the national tongue.

His third great achievement was to become the poet of a really lofty style. No other Hungarian author ever soared so high. His voice is the noblest in the great symphony of Hungarian poetry. He was exactly what the ancients thought a poet should be, a *vates*, whose eyes turned from earth towards heaven in holy rapture. With this elevation of thought was combined a wonderful imagination.

Vörösmarty's first great work, which he finished at the age of twenty-five, was a grand national epic : *Zalán's Flight* (1825). It was inspired by patriotic enthusiasm and patriotic grief, the outcome of the political events of the day. In the second decade of the century, and at the beginning of the third, the Austrian Government silently and cunningly aimed a deadly blow at the liberty of the Hungarian State. Metternich and his party endeavoured to lull the Hungarian statesmen into such a condition of torpor that the very existence of the Constitution should be gradually forgotten. According to their Constitution, to which Hungarians cling as to their very life, Hungary possesses a national Parliament, which controls taxation and fixes the number of soldiers to be enlisted. The Austrian Government, aiming at absolute power, saw an obstacle in this Parliament, and the Emperor Francis neglected to summon it. Hungary was regarded as an Austrian province, having no claim to independence. The provinces in vain demanded the opening of Parliament and conformity to the existing laws. The Austrian Government did not stir a finger. Anxiety grew apace. "What will become of the country ? Is it *finis Hungariæ* ?" At last some of the provinces, the only

10

forum of State life, decided upon a stubborn resistance. They refused the supply of soldiers and neglected to collect the taxes. The country was in a state of fever, and revolution seemed imminent. The terrified Austrian Government endeavoured to overcome the difficulty by sending royal commissioners to the recalcitrant provinces with orders to act on the king's authority if the provinces refused to obey. But the provinces found a means of thwarting the efforts of the commissioners and of making their task impossible. Discontent and indignation grew to such an alarming extent that the Austrian Government thought it wiser to yield, and Parliament was opened in 1825, after an interval of sixteen years. Once again there was a national Parliament, though Metternich had thought it dead and buried for ever.

Such were the events which impelled the young poet to write his epic. His purpose was to recall to the people the grand scenes in their country's history, that they might be strengthened in the time of oppression and despondency. *Zalán's Flight* is in the style of Virgil, with the *deus ex machinâ* playing a part in it. Its subject was taken from the time when the Hungarians were con-- quering a home for themselves. The entry of the Hungarians into Europe a thousand years ago and their settlement on the shores of the Danube and Tisza was undoubtedly the most important event in the nation's history, and one worthy to form the subject of a great historical epic. We see two contending nations : the Hungarians led by the great conqueror Árpád, and the Bulgarians under their prince, Zalán. The war was the decisive one waged for the possession of the country, and it ended with the flight of Zalán before the victorious Hungarians, who took possession of the land.

The best possible translation could hardly enable a foreign reader to appreciate the importance of this work. He would find powerful descriptions of battles, much pathos, and fine pictures in it, but the characters would scarcely seem to him striking or interesting. The whole epic is really a long description of the war, in the well-known manner of Virgil, and as it deals wholly with battles it is somewhat monotonous. Another drawback is that Vörösmarty, wishing to be faithful to all the Virgilian traditions, introduced the mythological element. But the ancient Hungarian mythology was practically unknown, for Christianity stamped out every trace of it by persecution until hardly any tradition survived among the people. Vörösmarty was therefore obliged to invent a mythology for the purposes of his epic, and to introduce deities in which no one believed. The two principal gods are Hadur (the lord of battles) and the evil deity Ármány (Ahriman). It may be that these deities had never been worshipped by the people, and that none but the epic poets used their names. All this, however, is unimportant. The real significance of the poem lies in its language, which had the effect of a revelation. No other Hungarian poet had ever sung like this. None of the nation's bards before him had been endowed with such dignity and melody, such grandeur and pathos. Vörösmarty's hexameters flow so melodiously and with such force that it is universally agreed that since the time of Virgil no literature can show such perfect verses.*

Vörösmarty continued the work so successfully begun by his *Zalán's Flight*. The hero of his next epic poem,

---

* Hungarian prosody, like that of every other modern European nation, is based upon accent. But curiously enough the Hungarian language is just as suitable for the Greek and Latin verse forms, in which quantity is considered instead of accent.

Cserhalom, is the king, St. Ladislas (1092), who was the favourite character of legendary poetry. Cserhalom is the name of the battlefield where St. Ladislas vanquished the Kumanians. During the battle the circumstance happened which became so famous during the Middle Ages, that we find it depicted in fresco on the walls of old churches. According to the tradition, St. Ladislas, after his victory, observed that one of the flying Kumanians was carrying a Hungarian maiden on his horse. The chivalrous king rode after the Kumanian to rescue the girl, but since his charger was fatigued by the battle he could not easily overtake him, and the distance between the two riders did not diminish. St. Ladislas then cried out : "Fair maiden, take hold of the soldier's belt and throw yourself to the ground, that you may bring him down too." The maiden did as the king bade her, and the king soon came up with the soldier, disarmed him, and only spared his life at the maiden's request. Vörösmarty's poem is based upon the incident, which, however, he expanded and altered.

Vörösmarty's most famous but most terrible epic is entitled *The Two Castles*. The story is that of a family feud existing in the Middle Ages, between the owners of two neighbouring castles. Such ferocious events are narrated that a colleague of Vörösmarty, Daniel Berzsenyi, characterised the epic as "a cannibal poem." The feud had persisted for a long time, and once when Tihamér, a son of one of the noblemen, returned from the wars, a dreadful scene met his eyes. He found every member of his family slain, parents, brothers, all. Tihamér vowed an awful revenge. He would destroy his foe's whole family. He challenged all the members, one by one, to a duel. At last only two were left alive, the aged father and his young daughter Enikö. Tihamér challenged the grey-haired old man and slew him. Then arraying himself in his vanquished foe's helmet and coat of mail, he appeared before the last member of the family, Enikö. The maiden had passed the hours in dreadful agony of mind. Her family was slain. Her only hope was that her father might be victorious. All at once her hope appeared to be realised, and her anxiety ceased when she saw her father enter the hall. It was he, his helmet, his armour. She rushed joyfully to meet him, when Tihamér suddenly raised his helmet, and in a moment the maiden knew that her father was dead and that she was in the power of the victorious enemy. It was more than her overcharged heart could endure, and she fell like a flower before the sickle. The dreadful picture haunted Tihamér, who, unable to find rest in the castle, rushed away and was never heard of more.

Equally pathetic is the end of another poetical character, the heroine of a short, idyllic narrative poem entitled *Beautiful Ilonka*. The two poems differ greatly in character ; the one narrates stern, martial actions and the other shows us gentle resignation. It is easy to recognise the pre-eminently lyrical character of Vörösmarty's talent even in his dramas and epics, and often the parts in which this feature is the most evident, constitute the finest portions of both drama and epic, even though they are not in keeping with the *genre* itself. But where this lyrical element is in its proper place, as in an idyllic narrative poem like *Beautiful Ilonka*, there Vörösmarty excels.

> *A hunter sits still in the dark forest glade ;*
> *His bow and his arrow he ready hath made.*
> *The fleetfooted prey to surprise.*

But vainly he waits in his deep shady nook ;
The deer is asleep by the cool welling brook,
    Whilst the sun ever higher doth rise.

The hunter ne'er moves from his sure hiding-place ;
He will watch till the twilight hath moved on apace,
    Some stroke of good fortune to meet.
And see ! there is something at length comes in sight :—
A moth which a maiden, all lovely and bright,
    Follows after with light falling feet.

" O pretty gold butterfly, come to me, pray !
Or hence to thy distant home lead me away,
    Where the sun sinks to rest far below ! "
Thus saith the fair maid, as she hastily hies
Away o'er the sward in pursuit of her prize ;
    And she sports on her path like a roe.

The hunter exclaims : " What a true royal chase ! "
Then starts from his post to pursue in the race ;
    And follows the girl in her flight.
Forgetting all else, to o'ertake her he's bent ;
While she, unaware, on the moth is intent ;
    Both in hopes of a fairy delight.

" I've caught thee at last ! " said the maiden with joy,
And laid her fair hand on the fluttering toy.
    " Thou'rt caught ! " said the hunter, as well ;
And held forth at once his right hand to the maid,
Who let go the fly ; and, though greatly afraid,
    Won his heart by her eyes' magic spell.

II.

" Oh ! say ; doth the house of Peterdi stand ?
Its gallant old lord, lives he yet in the land ? "
    His house, though decayed, bideth still.
There sits by the wine-cup the vet'ran at rest,
The maid at his side, and the young stranger guest,
    Whose bright eyes soft allurement doth fill.

   *   *   *   *   *

' And now," saith the host ; " a full bumper we'll give :—
May my late leader's son as our monarch long live ! "
    But mark, how confused is the guest !

*   *   *   *   *

And thus in the course of gay converse and glee,
Fast flew the glad moments away from the three :
    But the maiden felt love's gentle flame ;
She gazed on the face of the noble young guest ;
And oft the mute longing her bosom opprest,
    To know whence he was, and his name.

" In this cup, ere we part, I will bid thee farewell !
Kind host, and thee, flower of the deep-wooded dell.
    Oh ! that Heaven to Buda may bring
Thee maid, and thy grandsire, at no distant day :
The hunter, who waits thee, compelled is to stay
    At the court of Matthias the king."

*   *   *   *   *

III.

The sire and his grandchild are now on their way,
Their long promised visit to Buda to pay.

*   *   *   *   *

" O, where shall we meet with our dear stranger friend ?
What favouring fate may his footsteps attend ?
    Dwells he here, or afar doth he stray
In the depths of the woods, by the fawns' cool retreat ?
Quoth the girl ; and her heart with emotion fast beat :
    Her blush came, and then faded away.

The Ujlaki onward come galloping now,
And laurel-wreath'd Garras, with war-hardened brow ;
    Whilst veterans their monarch attend.
Old Peterdi lifts up his voice with surprise,
His guest he can now in the king recognise :—
    " On his head may all blessings descend ! "

*   *   *   *   *

" *Shall we go to the court of Matthias, my child ?*
Or, rather return to our own Vertes' wild ;
To the home in our hamlet again ?
We may there," *said the worthy old man,* " *look for rest* "
But foreshadowing grief, as he spake, filled his breast ;
And sadly departed the twain.

As the flower, when blighted by inward decay,
Though lovely in aspect, must wither away :
So languished Ilonka the fair,
Avoiding the world, and absorbed in her grief ;
From deep hidden sorrow she found no relief ;
For memory fed her despair.

So soon to its limit her life's current flowed,
To the tomb fair Ilonka by sorrow was bowed,
Like a lily which droops to the ground.
Virtue's image she showed, and its too frequent fate.—
In the lone house the king stands ; but, ah ! comes too late,
For they rest 'neath the grave's hallowed mound. *

In his lyrics, as in his epic poetry, Vörösmarty was the
bard of lofty themes.

His lyrical poems fall into two more classes. Some
deal with simple themes in a simple style, and breathe a
spirit of serenity. Such, for instance, is the poem entitled
Bird Voices,† of which we give the first and last stanzas :

Thus saith the lark in upward flight
While circling to the heavenly height :
" *I greet thee, breeze, that sweeps the lawn ;*
I greet the beauteous golden dawn ;
The wintry snows are at an end,
Bright is the sky, glad fields extend ;
The grass grows green, and I will there
My little nest soon build with care.
Soon will the newborn earth appear ;

* BUTLER's " Hungarian Poems."
† LOEW's " Magyar Poems."

A well decked table set for cheer.
  O, joy and pleasure,
    Joy and pleasure,
    The meadow lands are ours for pleasure."

      *   *   *   *   *

" My sorrows and my joys are bound
To one who faithless roams around,
And on a light love's wing doth stray.
    Who now can hear
    My plaints so drear ?
    This spot so calm
    Brings my heart balm.
The rocky cliff re-echoes every tone
But I receive no answer to my moan.
Were I an eagle free
    And my heart burned so sore,
Soon on strong wings I'd be
    Up near the heaven's door.
And from the sun I would gain fire to burn
The callous leaves that coldly from me turn.
    I can but voice
    My dolorous cry ;
    Alas, poor bird,
    Can only die.
O, break, my heart, and cease as doth my song ;
What art thou but my song so sadly strong ? "

The nightingale, the forest's very heart,
Thus to the world her sorrow did impart ;
And when the wood thus speaks the world is still
And listens how with woe her heart doth thrill.

Other poems are of an entirely opposite character, full of emotion, exaltation, excitement. In them Vörös-marty treats of the highest subjects in the grandest style. His imagination passes all bounds, it gleams, it flashes, it rushes like a stream of lava. He soars to great heights and beholds visions which he enables us partly to see, grand yet gloomy visions, as though lighted by the ruddy flame of a torch wildly blown about by the wind. As an example let us take the first and the last two stanzas of the *Hoary Gypsy :* *

> *Come, gypsy, play : thou had'st thy pay in drinks,*
> *Let not the grass grow under thee, strike up !*
> *On bread and water who will bear life's ills ?*
> *With flowing wine fill high the parting cup.*
> *This mundane life remains for aye the same,*
> *It freezeth now, then burneth as a flame ;*
> *Strike up ! How long thou yet wilt play who knows ?*
> *Thy bow-strings soon will wear out, I suppose.*
> *With wine and gloom are filled the cup and heart,*
> *Come, gypsy, play, let all thy cares depart !*
>
> *The stars above this earth—all sorrows' home—*
> *Leave them in peace, their woes let them endure !*
> *From sin and stain by rushing of wild streams*
> *And tempests' fury they may yet grow pure.*
> *And Noah's ark of old may come again*
> *And in its compass a new world contain.*
> *Strike up ! How long thou yet wilt play who knows ?*
> *Thy bow-strings soon will wear out I suppose.*
> *With wine and gloom are filled both cup and heart,*
> *Come, gypsy, play, let all thy cares depart !*
>
> *Strike up ! But no—now leave the cords alone ;*
> *When once again the world may have a feast,*
> *And silent have become the storm's deep groans,*
> *And wars and strifes o'er all the world have ceased,*
> *Then play inspiringly ; and, at the voice*
> *Of thy sweet strings, the gods may even rejoice !*
> *Then take again in hand the songful bow,*
> *Then may thy brow again with gladness glow,*
> *And with the wine of joy fill up thy heart ;*
> *Then, gypsy, play, and all thy cares depart !*

What a profoundly sad picture he presents to us in his

* LOEW, " Magyar Poetry."

*Appeal,** a poem which became one of the two national anthems. Its leading idea is that a crisis is at hand, and either a brighter day must dawn or the whole nation must perish.

> Loyal and true for aye remain,
>   Magyar, to this thy home !
> Here, where thy cradle stood, once more
>   Thou'lt rest within thy tomb.
>
> No other land than this expands
>   For thee, beneath the sky ;
> The fates may bring thee bane or bliss,
>   Here thou must live and die !
>
> Thy fathers' blood for this dear spot
>   Hath often freely flowed ;
> Great names for full ten hundred years
>   Have hallowed this abode.
>
> Here fought, to found a native land,
>   Arpád against his foes ;
> Here broke the yokes of slavery
>   Hunyad, with mighty blows.
>
> *   *   *   *   *
>
> Magyar, to this, thy native land,
>   Ever devoted be !
> It nourished thee, and soon, when dead,
>   Its earth receiveth thee.
>
> No other land than this expands
>   For thee beneath the sky !
> The fates may bring thee bane and bliss
>   Here thou must live and die !

In *The Living Statue* he sings of subjugated Poland, for which unfortunate country Hungarian poets have always displayed much sympathy, for they see in her fate that which has long threatened their own country. Poland is the living statue, whose terrible lot it is to stand dumb and motionless while it sees and feels everything. The statue yearns for her spellbound limbs to be set

* LOEW "Magyar Poetry."

free; for a sigh that might relieve her marble breast; and for a word to escape her sealed lips. "It is but a brief word that I would utter to ye, oh mankind, world, nature, universe ! If on earth there is right, and in heaven mercy, look upon me and my agony."

Vörösmarty was a master not only of passionate and pathetic poetry, but also of the reflective epigram. His distiches, the form he used in his epigrams, are melodious, Hungarian being one of the few languages which are equally suitable for modern metres based upon accent and the ancient metres based on quantity. One of his reflective poems is entitled *Thoughts in a Library.* He begins by contrasting the subjects treated of in books with the material upon which they are printed. The paper was made of rags. On one page is written the praise of virtue, yet the paper itself may have been part of the garment of a murderer. Another book treats of innocence and purity, yet its pages may have robed the impure. Perhaps the book of laws was once the mantle of a tyrant or of an unjust judge. Then he goes on to ask whether on the whole books have been a blessing to mankind. It may be that they have widened the gulf between the cultured and uncultured, yet we must not undervalue them, for they pave the way to man's dignity. "What is our task in life ?" he asks at the end of the poem, where human feeling is blended with patriotic feeling. "To strive with all our strength for the noblest aims. The fate of a nation lies in our hands. When we have lifted this country out of its errors and misfortunes, we shall be able to say, as our eyes close in death, 'We thank thee, life, for all the grand opportunities of work which thou hast given us, and which have enabled us to play our part here manfully.'"

Vörösmarty was a great poet, but not a great dramatist, because he lacked two important qualifications. He had not enough psychological knowledge to construct real, life-like characters, nor could he invent probable incidents. Why then did he attempt to write for the stage? For both internal and external reasons. To take the latter first, it was while Vörösmarty was at the height of his activity that the drama began to assume an increasingly important position in the poetry of the nations nearest to Hungary, and in Hungary, where the stage was becoming an important factor, there was a great scarcity of original plays. But there was an inner motive too. Vörösmarty loved to give expression to grand passions for which the drama was the most suitable vehicle.

The influence of Shakespeare's historical plays can easily be detected in some of Vörösmarty's dramas, particularly those based upon the early history of Hungary. In *Csongor és Tünde*, he was very happily inspired by Shakespeare's *Midsummer Night's Dream*. Others again like *The Treasure Seekers* clearly show the influence of the German Fate-tragedies (*Schicksaltragoedien*). The most noteworthy, however, are the dramas which were modelled on the French dramatic school, like *The Bánus Marót*. The play of *The Bánus Marót* is based upon a pathetic incident. When Hungary was under the Turkish yoke the Turks carried off a number of young boys whom they trained to be soldiers. The Janizari army was largely composed of Christian youths. Vörösmarty wove around this a tragic plot, full of startling incidents. The drama is a story of revenge, crime and retaliation. A Turkish Bey in revenge steals the son of a Hungarian nobleman, brings him up as a Turk, and employs the youth in securing inmates for his harem.

The young man (Bod) returns to Hungary, having no remembrance of his country or of his family, members of which he happens to meet, though without recognition on either side. Such a situation could easily give rise to tragical incidents, but Vörösmarty, writing under the influence of the French school, heaped wonder upon wonder, introducing extravagant passions and improbable actions. Bod meets Ida, the wife of his brother Marót, and instead of stealing her for his master's harem, falls in love with her himself, and declares his love just as her husband returns home.

Then comes a common stage trick. Marót spreads a false report of his own death in order to deceive the lovers. A funeral ceremony is arranged, and Marót, unseen, hears Ida tell Bod that she loves him. The husband, embittered by his wife's faithlessness and especially enraged by her confession of love for a Turk, hands her over to the Bey and demands that Bod shall be beheaded. Soon, however, he discovers by means of a sword carried by Bod, which is a family heirloom, that Bod is his brother. He forgives him, and endeavours to free his wife from the Turkish Bey's prison. Bod undertakes the task of rescuing Ida ; he penetrates to the Bey's tent, but finding himself unable to deliver her, kills her, in order to put an end to the shame of his brother's wife. This costs him his own life, for he falls by the hand of the Bey. In the battle which follows the Hungarians are victorious, and Marót executes the Bey and swears the destruction of the Turks.

It is easy to recognise the influence of Victor Hugo and the French *école romantique* in this tragedy. Two brothers as deadly enemies, who recognise each other towards the end of the drama by means of a family token ; a man (Bod) follows a vile occupation, and is saved and ennobled by love ; a husband concealed within a suit of armour in the old hall of his castle witnesses his wife's treachery, spreads the report of his own death in order to confound the guilty woman by rising from his coffin, and, finally, in a frenzy of revenge, throws his once beloved wife into the arms of his most hated foe, the Turk ; these are all over-strained motives and reveal the influence of Victor Hugo and Dumas *père*.

The Vérnász (Bloody Nuptials) is still more terrible. Œdipus is surpassed. A father, believing his wife to be unfaithful, conveys his two children, a boy and a girl, to a forest and leaves them to perish. The children do not die, however, and many years afterwards the father meets the maiden and marries her, not knowing her to be his daughter. The boy has become an outlaw, and breaks into the castle of his father, who orders him to be executed. Soon after, the truth comes out, and the girl retires to a nunnery, while the father in a frenzy casts himself over a precipice.

The charm and melody of language, the lyrical beauty which we find in all Vörösmarty's dramas, reach their perfec-tion in a fairy play called *Csongor and Tünde*. Vörösmarty here dramatised an old fairy tale written by a sixteenth-century poet. Csongor, a young hero, and the fairy Tünde love one another, but an old witch opposes their happi-ness. The hero has to pass through many marvellous adventures before he recovers his loved one, who has meanwhile been banished from fairyland for allowing earthly love to enter her heart. Fairies and other fabulous characters influence the course of events, either favour-ably or unfavourably to the wishes of the lovers, as in the

Midsummer Night's Dream. The moral is, of course, that true love overcomes every obstacle.

Not the least of Vörösmarty's merits is that he was the first great translator of Shakespeare into Hungarian and the first Hungarian author to appreciate rightly the world's greatest dramatist. His translation of *Julius Cæsar* appeared in 1839.*

Vörösmarty urged others to translate his works well. " A good translation of Shakespeare," he said, " would be worth to any nation at least the half of its existing literature." Petőfi equally idolised Shakespeare. In one of his dramatic criticisms he said : " In the field of poetry Shakespeare has reaped all that is most beautiful. We can only glean after him what he did not find worthy of him." Arany was influenced by Shakespeare even when writing his ballads, and said of him : " We can best express our feelings by quoting the words of the psalmist, ' Thou art great in great things and great in small.' "

The three greatest Hungarian poets, Vörösmarty, Petőfi and Arany, arranged together to translate some of the plays. Their choice was in each case characteristic.

---

* The name of Shakespeare was first heard from the lips of Bessenyei. The first translation appeared in 1786. It was by Alexander Kun Szabò, after an adaptation by Weisse in German, and all the first translations were made from German variants. When the first theatre was opened, in 1790, Kazinczy translated *Hamlet* for it, but from such an altered version that the prince does not die at the end. In some cases managers even produced new plays, with the name of Shakespeare as author. For instance, a play was produced at Kolozsvár in 1812 entitled *Alexander Menczikov*, of which Shakespeare was declared to be the author. More absurd still, when a real Shakespearean play was given, it was advertised to be by Kotzebue in order to draw a larger audience. The finest of Hungarian tragic poets, Katona, was greatly influenced by Shakespeare's method of drawing his characters.

Vörösmarty, the poet of melancholy and grand passion, translated *King Lear*, Petőfi chose the proud, defiant *Coriolanus*, and Arany, the contemplative *Hamlet*.*

In the sixties, the Kisfaludy Society published the complete Hungarian Shakespeare, and to that work the best writers contributed.

Among the contemporaries of Vörösmarty whose work displayed similar tendencies, the most noteworthy was a Benedictine monk named GREGORY CZUCZOR (1800-1866). About the year 1848 he wrote a fiery poem entitled *The Alarm*, summoning the nation to revolt against the Austrians. For this he was put into prison, where he remained for nearly two and a half years, at first in chains according to the order of General Haynau.

Czuczor's chief epic poem is *Botond*, dealing with the pagan period of Hungarian history. Its hero is the chieftain Botond, who drove his mace through the bronze gates of Byzantium, and the poem tells of his love for a Greek girl.

Czuczor was the son of a peasant, and his songs brought with them into the realm of poetry the sweet fresh air of the country ; they at once found their way to the hearts of the people, and are still popular.

JOHN GARAY (1802-1853) was also an epic poet. One of his poems relates the deeds of the national hero, St. Ladislas, but his best known work is a ballad about the chieftain Kont, who was beheaded by King Sigismund. Very popular, too, is a tale of his about a soldier returned from the wars against Napoleon, who relates the most absurd and impossible adventures in a very amusing way

* Arany was the best translator of poetry, while the best prose translation in the Hungarian language, that of Cervantes' *Don Quixote*, was the work of William Gyröy (1838-1885).

XII

ORATORS

CONTEMPORARY with the literary revival marked by the advent of Vörösmarty, was an era of political reform which transformed the aspect of affairs in Hungary. In the year of the publication of Vörösmarty's epoch-making work, *Zalán's Flight*, the man who re-created Hungary as a modern State, Count STEPHEN SZÉCHENYI (1791–1860) came into prominence.

It rarely happens that one man exerts such a wonderful influence over a whole country as Széchenyi wielded. He had a deeply interesting and strange personality. His nature was at base romantic, but harassed by doubts and self-mistrust. His heart was torn by mental conflicts and self-condemnatory meditations, but he unquestionably possessed the genius of a statesman.

Count Széchenyi was born in 1791 in Vienna, the stronghold of Hungary's foes. His father, a highly cultured nobleman, suffered from religious melancholy, but retained a keen interest in mundane affairs and founded the National Museum in Budapest. His son inherited from him his restless, sensitive conscience, and also his interest in the nation's welfare.

At the commencement of his career, Széchenyi distinguished himself as a soldier, but throughout the term of his military service he was tormented by the vague discontent and yearnings of a man who has not found his proper sphere. He went abroad, and frequently visited Paris, London and Rome. Then he undertook a journey to Asia, and afterwards went to Athens, the ruins of which reminded him painfully of his own decaying country. He was troubled by some love-sorrow too, and his restlessness and dissatisfaction increased. Gradually a grand idea, that of saving his country, formed and ripened in his soul. Of this resolution he wrote in after years: "Oh, how often in my childhood I have seen my poor father stricken with sorrow, so that even I, child as I was, could realise vaguely that so much sadness was not caused by family cares alone. For my father was a truly Christian man, and was imbued with the stoicism of Epictetus, and he met all his private troubles with a calm philosophic smile. I could not then understand his sorrow, but I learned later that the decline of our nation was the cause of his grief. The hopelessness of the situation, foreboding speedy extinction, filled him with despair. Ever since my father, in whom shone so many of the virtues of a citizen, sank into his grave, I have unceasingly compared my country with other nations, to find whether there was any possibility of our resurrection. This was the task of my life. Other nations seemed to live in the present and to be cheerful and contented, while Hungary appeared to have no hope, and to think that all her fame and greatness lay buried in the past.

"Occasionally the clouds would break before my eyes, and my heart was thrilled with the message: 'Those for whose welfare you yearn are not dead, and there is hope for the future.' But all at once the sky again became overcast and I seemed to lie tossing on the waves of hope and despair, wearing out my own strength. My life was full of sadness, and hope seldom shone upon my youth.

"Thus it came about that in the year 1825, after passing through severe mental conflicts, and realising that no one shared my view, or, if he did, would dare to act, I swore to myself that I, relying not upon my talents, but on the purity of my intentions and on my constancy, would devote myself wholly to the work of calling my country back to life. I was cheered by a few hopeful signs, but I resolved that even if I remained alone or perished in the struggle, I would unhesitatingly tread the path which the spirit within me pointed out. After loyally serving my king during my military career, I would dedicate the rest of my life to my country, and I stepped out upon the field of public life, so thickly strewn with thorns, resolved that I, if no one else, would try to revive my country's former dignity, and would devote all my life and energy to the task."

Three main characteristics gave Széchenyi's work its epoch-making value. The first is that he directed the attention of the nation to financial interests. There had been eminent statesmen and politicians before Széchenyi and there were others contemporary with him, but they were chiefly jurists, and hardly any one recognised the importance of political economy, industry, commerce and means of communication, the very things upon which Hungary's future largely depended. Széchenyi's political faith was that Hungary must become more wealthy in order that she might become free and cultured. He awoke the nation from the torpor into which it had fallen and bade it cease to ponder over its rights and the infractions of them, and turn to the more important problem of reviving its prosperity.

He also insisted on the fact that the cause of the national decadence lay not in the Government, or in Vienna, but in the Hungarians themselves. Not Austria, but their own indolence, wrong-doing, and obsolete institutions were at fault. Reform must begin with themselves. He understood how to inspire the people with faith in their own future. Before Széchenyi, people had thought that their glory was a thing of the past and that the present meant only stagnation and decay. Széchenyi gave them as a new motto " Hungary was not, but is to be." He concentrated men's thoughts upon the building up of a great future, greater in every respect than the past. He cured them of the melancholy which had held the country's best workers bound as if by a spell, and braced them to earnest labour by his books, which acted upon them like powerful electric shocks. His influence was so great because he expressed, with the voice of genius, the inarticulate feelings and longings of the people.

Széchenyi's career as a reformer commenced with deeds, however, and not merely with words. Some persons were discussing and advocating, in his hearing, the creation of a scientific academy. Széchenyi stood up and offered a year's income (£5000) towards the cost of the project, and the Academy was founded. Then he established horse races on the lines of those held in England, partly to encourage the breeding of horses, and partly to provide amusement at home for the wealthier classes so as to induce them to remain in Hungary instead of living abroad. In order to cultivate a social spirit he founded the first political and social clubs in Budapest on English models, and the country towns soon began to imitate the metropolis.

His first great work, entitled *Credit*, was published in
1830. Arany called it "a pyramid on the boundary line
dividing Hungary's dead past from her living present."
The novelty of the book consisted in setting practical
aims before the nation. Széchenyi desired to create credit
in Hungary, and to make money easily accessible to the
agriculturalist. He drew attention to the cumbersome
methods of litigation, and the unpractical feudal customs
which obtained on many estates; to the need of improved
means of communication and of the abolition of feudal
services. In short he devoted himself to practical
problems in such a way that men woke up to the fact
that he was not the mere dreamer that they had taken
him to be.

Széchenyi's second book, *The World*, advocated amongst
other things the claims of the national language, and his
third, *The Stadium*, maintained the necessity of more
equitable taxation, of the abolition of monopolies, and
of equality before the law.

Széchenyi's treatment of his subjects was not sufficiently systematic. He leapt impulsively from one thing
to another so that his writings have something of the
character of a collection of aphorisms. His style, a
mixture of irony and deep feeling, is somewhat bizarre.
Passionate outbursts are often entangled amidst cum-
brous periphrases. Paul Gyulai, the critic, compared
one of Széchenyi's books to a dense forest, in which we
sometimes lose our way but where we are everywhere
surrounded by a sturdy growth of thronging ideas.
Here and there the growth is so dense as to bar our
way, the nettle of irony stings us, the thorn of sarcasm
wounds us, but when once we reach the height to which
our path leads, we see stretching before us a sublime

prospect, the future of Hungary. Throughout the time of his literary activity, Széchenyi vigorously prosecuted his various schemes of reform. He commenced important engineering works for improving the channels of the Danube and the Tisza, inaugurated a steamboat service, reconstructed the ancient road made by the Emperor Trajan, dug canals to facilitate commerce, and did much to develop and beautify the young capital. Nothing escaped his attention, whether great political problems or the desirability of an omnibus service, the planting of trees in the public squares or the culture of the silk-worm. He went abroad to discover the best model for a bridge to unite Buda with Pest, and it was at his instigation that the handsome suspension bridge was built under the direction of an English engineer, Thomas Clark. By means of this bridge, Széchenyi achieved a great democratic reform. In the time of the pontoon bridge a glaring injustice was continually perpetrated. The poor peasants, to whom the toll was a serious burden, were compelled to pay it, while the burgesses and nobles, who would not have felt it, were exempted. On the new bridge, however, a uniform toll of rather less than a halfpenny was levied upon all.

About 1840 Széchenyi's life became over-shadowed, and in time even his intellect became affected. His good luck and his popularity forsook him, while a new figure, that of Louis Kossuth, more and more filled the popular imagination.

Széchenyi's ideal, the gradual growth in wealth and power of the commonwealth and the development of culture among the people, came into conflict with the aims of a victorious democracy and its demand for independence.

"I read in the stars, blood, blood everywhere ! Alas, my wasted life ! On the firmament there shines in letters of fire the name of Kossuth. *Flagellum Dei*—the scourge of God," exclaimed Széchenyi once, his eyes filling with tears, as he foresaw the revolution which Kossuth was preparing.

And the revolution came. In 1848 Széchenyi, who was then a member of the first Hungarian Government, saw with growing excitement how the revolution was spreading. His mind was darkened. He accused himself. He imagined that he had roused the nation and started it upon its path and that now it could not be stopped. He felt like a physician who, in his anxiety to cure, had administered too strong a dose and saw his patient dying in convulsions. After enduring terrible mental sufferings Széchenyi lost his reason and was taken, in 1849, to an asylum at Döbling, near Vienna, which he never left. After some time, his health improved, and he wrote one more book entitled *A Glance*, this time in German, as it was directed against the Austrian Bach government. It was published anonymously in London, and is full of sound and weighty argument, vigorous onslaughts and biting satire.

In 1860, his excitement again increased. He imagined that Hungary stood on the brink of a new revolution, for which he was responsible, and on Easter Sunday he shot himself, and so, unhappily, did not live to see the success of Deák's efforts at conciliation.

Széchenyi's great aim was the salvation and advancement of his race, and to that end he employed means which his contemporaries could not rightly value or apply. His means were practical, and directed to the raising of Hungary to the level of the surrounding European nations. His journeys to England produced a great and decisive effect upon Széchenyi. His sensitive nature readily took every impression. He learned much and with enthusiasm. His great reforms were mostly suggested by English examples. He learned political economy from Bentham. It seemed to English visitors who stayed in his castle, that they were in the house of an English nobleman ; this may be partly accounted for by the fact that he was related to an English aristocratic family. " The more I learned to know the English " he wrote, " the more I was compelled to love them." In the diary of his English travels we read " The Germans write much, the French talk much, and the English do much." In 1832, when he visited his " beloved England " for the third time, he wished to study thoroughly the manufacture of machinery, and he entered a factory as a workman, and laboured diligently. He was often the guest of George IV., while the latter was Prince Regent. It was characteristic of him that his favourite poet should be Byron, whom he resembled in his capricious melancholy. It was to England, above all, that Széchenyi was indebted for a right estimation of the important part played by practical interests in the life of a nation.

After Széchenyi, whom Kossuth himself called " the greatest Hungarian," Louis Kossuth and Francis Deák became the nation's leaders.

Louis Kossuth (1802-1894) and Francis Deák (1803-1876) were Hungary's greatest orators. Kossuth's talents were in many respects in marked contrast with those of Deák. Deák was usually calm and moderate, while Kossuth spoke in tones of excitement and passion. Deák appealed to the intellect of his hearers, Kossuth to their imagination. Kossuth's fervour enchanted men ;

Deák's lucidity and wise moderation convinced them.
Kossuth's strength lay in his ability to rouse the
emotion of his audience more and more by his
inexhaustible fire and enthusiasm ; while Deák excelled
in linking one convincing argument with another. The
work of the former braced the nation to action on the
eve of a revolution, while the latter led the nation out of
a critical situation with wisdom and with dignity.

Kossuth's parliamentary career was very short, lasting
little more than twenty months, but it was brilliant and
effective.   In 1848 he was the leader of the Parliament
and captivated every one by his oratorical genius. At
that time he had well-defined aims, which he also proclaimed in his English addresses, namely the emancipation of the peasants and the defence of the Constitution.
To English audiences he gave the following explanation
of his aims. " Excepting the citizens of the privileged
towns, the only persons in Hungary and in the countries
under the Hungarian crown, who before the year 1848
enjoyed any of the privileges, social or political, of the
Constitution, were the nobles. Moreover the privileges
of a noble family were not confined to the eldest son, as
in England, but all the sons of a nobleman were themselves nobles, with the same privileges as their father.
Their numbers might grow without limit, and reached
about five or six hundred thousand, or about the number
of the enfranchised citizens of England. We should
not have been worthy of the name of patriot had we not
seized the chance of securing the constitutional freedom
and independence of our country. And Hungary must
be free and independent in accordance with her rights
and the terms of ancient contracts. Hungary is not
bound to any other country, but enjoys a separate

national life and a separate Constitution, and is not to be governed as an Austrian province, whether such provinces be governed well or ill, despotically or constitutionally, but is to be governed in accordance with her own Constitution and her own laws. This was our right with respect to the Austrian House and Empire, and was the duty of the Austrian House towards us. We had to safeguard this right and enforce the fulfilment of this duty. We had to take care that in every department of state life Hungary should be governed independently and be free from all foreign interference."

After the catastrophe of Világos, Kossuth went into exile. England, which had shown such magnanimous sympathy with those who carried on Hungary's war for freedom, gave him an enthusiastic welcome. He spoke with great effect on his country's behalf both in England and in the United States, and his speeches in 1859 were largely instrumental in bringing about the resignation of the Tory Government which desired to put a stop to the Austro-Italian war by England's intervention.

Kossuth did not approve of the reconciliation with Austria in 1867, achieved by Deák. He never saw his country again after 1849, and died far from her borders, in Turin, on March 20, 1894. When his body was carried home, indescribable scenes occurred everywhere along the route, all showing how the people idolised him, the hero of their struggles for liberty. Thousands of people travelled long distances to the railway line along which the body was to pass; and waited there kneeling.

But it was not only in Hungary that Kossuth was admired. Once when a Hungarian gentleman visited a family in Edinburgh, directly his nationality was known,

L

his hostess took him into a room which contained nothing but a portrait of Kossuth enshrined in a little chapel.

It was on May 2, 1833, that Deák first spoke in Parliament. His subject was the abolition of corporal punishment. Since that time there was no great cause or piece of legislation upon which his wisdom did not shed some light. In political controversy he was the country's acknowledged leader, who stated the nation's case in the clearest terms and defended it undauntedly. His most important achievement was the compromise with Austria in 1867, the fundamental conditions of which he had laid down in 1861.

The twelve years which followed the war of 1848–9 were years of great depression in Hungary. The Austrian Government had suspended the Constitution, abolished the ministry, the palatinate, and the provincial system, refused to summon a Parliament, and altogether dealt with Hungary as a conquered province. Those were the years of absolutism, when neither in Austria nor in Hungary, newly deprived of her independence, was there any Parliament or responsible Government.

Many believed that Hungary was ruined, that her future would resemble that of Poland, and that together with the Magyar language, the whole nation would be wiped out. But towards the end of the fifties despotism lost its strength, and it became more and more evident that it could not effectively administer the nation's affairs. The Austro-Italian war (1859), which ended in the defeat of Austria, demonstrated still more clearly the incapacity of Austrian rule, and the King decided to put an end to the old system of government and allow each country to have a Parliament. He therefore issued on October 1860 the so-called " October Decree," in accordance with which the Austrian Provinces, amongst which he included Hungary, had each to send representatives to the Reichsrath. This central Parliament was to decide all the most important questions, and each province, including Hungary, was to have a local Parliament to decide such matters as affected itself alone.

This new Constitution was opposed to the ancient Hungarian constitution suspended in 1849. Deák, in the Parliament of 1861, dealt with the question in his famous "Address to the King," in which he pointed out that Hungary was an independent country having a Constitution as defined in the contract made between the nation and the Habsburg family, the so-called Pragmatic Sanction. The nation therefore did not approve of the Constitution which Austria desired to impose upon them, and they refused to accept it, but demanded the complete restoration of their rights and independence.

As an answer to this address, which set forth with classical perfection the nation's rights and privileges, there came a document from the King addressed to the Hungarian Parliament, which refused the restoration of the old Constitution. On August 8, Deák read his second address, in which he refuted one by one the arguments contained in the King's document. He laid stress on the fact that the nation demanded no new rights, but simple conformity with the terms of the Pragmatic Sanction. He concluded his wonderful speech in these words : "With deep regret we have to state that in consequence of His Majesty's reply, we are obliged to consider Parliament as adjourned. It may be that the country will again have to pass through a time of suffering, but we must not try to escape it by neglecting our duty as citizens. The constitutional liberty of our country is not a thing of which we are free to dispose ; it was entrusted to our keeping by the nation and we are responsible for it to our country and our consciences.

"Whatever we are called upon to bear, the nation will endure in order to preserve for posterity the freedom inherited from our ancestors. We shall suffer without despondency, as our ancestors suffered, to preserve the country's rights, for what superior strength may take from us may be brought back by good fortune, but what we voluntarily surrender through fear of suffering is hard to regain, and the issue remains doubtful. The nation will be patient, hoping for a better future and trusting to the righteousness of its cause."

The Austrian authorities answered this second address by dissolving Parliament. Deák, on learning their intention, suggested that the nation should proclaim that, although Parliament could not oppose this act of violence but could merely protest against it, it was resolved to cling to its laws and to consider every breach of them an offence against the constitution. "Our only weapons," he said, "are the legality and the justice of our cause, and they support us against armed force. It is an ancient belief, and one which has never proved illusory, that truth always prevails in the end, and in this conviction lies our hope. If we would walk in safety we must under no circumstances abandon our laws, for they are the only secure territory on which we may stand without any armed force, and even in defiance of such force. Into the solitude from which I stepped forth I now retire with the clear conviction that we in Parliament have done our duty to our country, our constituents and our consciences, and that the example set by Parliament will be followed by our courts of law, and by all our citizens. They will cling to the law and never abandon it. Citizens must cherish their laws, for they give the soul peace, and enable them to face the most trying events with equanimity, and that leads to what is essential to the right endurance of suffering, to dignity, and dignity is born solely of a consciousness of the justice of our cause."

With the dissolution of Parliament the negotiations also came to an end, and it was not until 1867 that a reconciliation took place on the basis of Deák's first Address with a few slight alterations. That reconciliation restored their Constitution and independence to the Hungarians.

In all these struggles Deák was the nation's leader. He guided them towards their goal with the greatest wisdom and moderation, and at the same time with the greatest firmness. Deák had the genius accompanied by sound judgment, and fully deserved the title of " The Country's Sage" with which the people honoured him during his lifetime. On his monument was placed the inscription : *Victor sine sanguine.*

XIII

THE NOVEL

THE history of the Hungarian novel resembles, on a small
scale, the history of the novel in general. Its first form was
that of the heroic novel, a style that had flourished most
in Europe during the reign of Louis XIV. Romances were
full of the features most highly valued in that day, and were
brought to the highest degree of refinement by Corneille and
Racine, namely, courtesy and heroism. One of the representatives of this style in France was La Calprenède. He
wrote novels of from eight to ten volumes in length, and the
public read them eagerly. People then had more leisure
for reading. One of his stories, *Cassandra*, was translated
in 1784 by a Hungarian Lifeguard officer, ALEXANDER
BÁRÓCZY (1735–1809), a member of Bessenyei's circle.
He had a curious personality. Though a faithful disciple
of the matter-of-fact rationalism of Voltaire, he sacrificed much time and energy for an old superstition, the
manufacture of gold. When he translated *Cassandra*, the
language of Hungarian literature was still unpolished, and
it seemed a bold idea to try to translate a book full of refined
galanterie in its conversation, into a tongue so different in
character. But Báróczy tried, and his success influenced
the development of Hungarian prose for good. It must
be borne in mind that Báróczy was a Transylvanian, and
that in Transylvania there had been a Court life since

the beginning of the seventeenth century, when there had been no national Court in Hungary for ages. Báróczy made use of the language which he had heard in Transylvania, and was thus enabled to translate the novel as well as he did.

The sentimental novel was another phase in the evolution of the novel. Richardson, Rousseau and Goethe became world-famed for that kind of literature. The effect they produced has hardly ever been equalled. When *Pamela* was read aloud to a small circle of listeners in an English country town they set the church bells ringing when it became known that the beautiful and virtuous heroine was going to be married. When Napoleon went into exile, he left behind him all his power and his dreams of greatness, but he took with him Goethe's *Werther*. From no less a distance than China, Goethe received a teacup with Werther and Lotte painted upon it, dressed in Chinese garments. In Hungarian literature the sentimental novel is best represented by JOSEPH KÁRMÁN (1769–1795) in his book entitled *Fanny's Memoirs*. It is a story of the gradual pining away of a pure and delicate young girl. Her parents do not understand her. Her lover cannot be united with her, and she dies of grief. The delicacy and refinement of the author's prose were a revelation.

Kármán died at the early age of twenty-six. He was the editor of a magazine called *Uránia*. His wish was to create a literary centre and an organ for authors, and to provide the public with reading of universal interest. But his fate was that of so many pioneers, people did not understand him.

Kazinczy also wrote a sentimental novel, in imitation of *Werther*, entitled *The Sorrows of Bácsmegyei*.

12

The third kind of novel, which became fashionable everywhere in Europe, including Hungary, was the novel of the Robinson Crusoe type.

Readers in that age were fascinated by sea adventures and the marvels of tropical regions. General JOSEPH GVADÀNYI (1725–1801) wrote a story in verse, called *Rontó Pál*. His hero was the faithful follower of the bold adventurer, Maurice Benyovsky. The original of the story had lived a very adventurous life. He was a soldier in the Austrian army during the Seven Years War, but deserted, and joined the Prussians. The Austrians took him prisoner and resolved to execute him, but he obtained a pardon. Then he entered the service of Benyovsky, who afterwards became the king of Madagascar. After passing through many adventures, Benyovsky was imprisoned by the Russians in 1770, and exiled to Kamchatka. He escaped, and after incredible sufferings, and almost starving, he got on board a French vessel which carried him to Macao. He soon left it, and went to France, where his wonderful escapes created a great sensation, and Benyovsky became a favourite at the Court of Louis XV. In 1773 Benyovsky was sent to Madagascar to found a French colony. Some of the native races elected him their king. After some time, the king of Madagascar returned to Europe, and visited his native land, Hungary, where he occupied himself with great commercial plans. He was the first who urged that Hungary ought to aim at the possession of a sea-coast and to develop an oversea trade *viâ* Fiume. But he did not stay long at home ; his restless disposition drove him to become again what he always had been, an adventurer. He left Hungary, spent some time in England, and at length found his death in the same land where he had found a throne, Madagascar. He was killed by a

French bullet. The events of his life are faithfully narrated in *Rontó Pál*.

In the thirties of the nineteenth century two new kinds of novel became popular, which now surpass in importance and permanence all the others. They are the social and the historical novel.

By 1832 the society of the capital had begun to organise itself, and the first social novel appeared in that year. The author of *The Bélteky Family* was ANDREW FÁY (1784–1861). This story gave expression to the same ideas of progress, and of a great and prosperous future, with which Széchenyi was inflaming the souls of men. The old, inactive Hungarian nobles are contrasted with the new generation of workers, toiling at the foundations of Hungary's future greatness.

Andrew Fáy was equally esteemed as a man and as an author of didatic fables. He was a friend and fellow-worker of Széchenyi.

The historical novel sprang up almost simultaneously with the social novel. Its first exponent in Hungary was Baron NICHOLAS JÓSIKA (1794–1865). Jósika wrote under the influence of Sir Walter Scott. Like Scott, Jósika was born amidst mountainous and romantic scenery, at Tonda, in Transylvania, and gained his inspiration from old castles and ancient family chronicles. He was a soldier, and fought, like Alexander Kisfaludy, in the wars against Napoleon. On returning to Hungary he began to write novels. After the revolution he was condemned to death, but the sentence was only executed in effigy, and he lived in exile for some time in Brussels, and afterwards in Dresden, where he died.

Scott was his first model, but later on, during the time of his exile, he to some extent imitated the French writers.

His first novel, *Abafi*, is perhaps the most important of his works. Its scene is laid in Transylvania in the sixteenth century. We are shown the mental development of a young nobleman, whose life is finally crowned with the bliss of an ideal love. Abafi lives a somewhat loose and frivolous life, but one day he finds a little child abandoned in a wood, takes it into his care, and acts towards it as a father. The good deed gradually reacts upon his soul. He begins to reflect, to work and to cultivate his talents, and becomes a distinguished man. His evolution is aided by his love for a noble-minded woman, and also by the tyranny of the ruler, which awakens his courage and energy.

Jósika's chief merit was that he revived the past, although he was often superficial both in depicting character and the period. He was fertile in plots, and described a great number of historical figures and epochs. He took up, later, the social novel as well as the historical, but he wrote more than he ought to have written, in that respect also resembling Sir Walter Scott.

Another novelist, who succeeded Jósika, wrote with far profounder insight. This was Baron JOSEPH Eötvős (1813–1871).

One day at the boys' high school in Buda, the headmaster admitted a little boy of eleven to one of the classes and gave him a seat on the front bench. No wonder, for the boy was the son of the distinguished and powerful Lord Treasurer, Baron Ignatius Eötvős. But a curious thing happened. Directly the new boy sat down, the other boys all stood up and left the bench. There was only one opportunist little Jew who stayed on the same bench with him, as though guided by a presentiment that his neighbour was one day to be the legislator who would introduce the Bill for Jewish emancipation. When the master demanded of the boys the reason of their conduct, they declared that they were not going to sit on the same bench with the grandson of the traitor to their country. The traitor, whose name was known and hated even by the children of the land, was the grandfather of Joseph Eötvős, a man who had served the Court at the time when Francis, Emperor of Austria and King of Hungary, endeavoured to destroy the Hungarian Constitution, and refused to summon a Parliament. The provinces strove to defend the Constitution, and Eötvős helped the Court against them. But the little boy whom his schoolfellows treated so badly did not lose heart. Once when lessons were over, he mounted the master's desk and in brave words vowed before all his companions that he himself would always be a good patriot and serve his country faithfully, and make them forget the unpopular sound of his name. And what the boy promised the man fulfilled.

Baron Joseph Eötvős was one of the noblest figures in the world of Hungarian literature. He distinguished himself as a statesman, a novelist, a poet and a scientific writer. His literary activity, like his life, had an idealistic tendency. He was a man of reflection rather than of action, but his reflections were penetrated with feeling, and his logic was infused with warmth of heart. His personality presents the feature, so rare in authors, which is expressed in the words of Vauvenargues: *Les grandes pensées viennent du cœur.*

Though not primarily a man of action, Eötvős was twice Minister of Public Instruction, in the first Hungarian ministry and in the Andrássy ministry of 1867. As a statesman he was chiefly a highly intellectual and theoretical initiator of reforms. It was he who first gave an impetus to prison reform in Hungary, where, as in other countries, the prisons were dens of cruelty, in which the criminals became still more degraded. He also demonstrated most convincingly the advisability of Jewish emancipation. For years he pressed upon the people the need for a responsible Government, and for the introduction of a parliamentary system like that of England, and he vigorously exposed the obsoleteness of the autonomous provincial system. He was the most fervent advocate of compulsory education. In Deák's great task of reconciling Austria and Hungary, Eötvös was his chief fellow-worker.

Wherever profound thought and sound judgment were needed the people looked to Eőtvős, although the actual carrying out of his plans usually fell into the hands of other men.

His first novel was *The Carthusian* (1838), a work full of sentimental and melancholy reflections.

While Eőtvős was travelling once in France he visited the Grande Chartreuse, the cloister of terrible silence, and met there a pale-faced young Carthusian to whom a beautiful and passionate woman had written letter after letter urging him not to take the vows. This incident provided Eőtvős with his subject. *The Carthusian* is a novel of the type of Chateaubriand's *René*, or Benjamin Constant's *Adolphe*, that is to say, of the kind of novel in which we see the *mal de siècle* at work. But the novel of Eőtvős has a strong moral foundation lacking in similar works. " It is only the selfish for whom life contains no consolation." That is the fundamental idea of the book, and the hero Gustave wins a gradual victory over egotism.

The story is written as though it were the diary of a monk of the Grande Chartreuse. The hero is a rich young French count, who after experiencing much of the world's deception, renounces the pleasures of life and becomes a Carthusian monk. The novel is really the story of his two loves, both of which arouse great emotions and bring great disappointments.

Gustave loses his mother early, and thus the love for which he so greatly yearns is absent in his early years. At length he makes the acquaintance of a fellow student, Armand, to whom he becomes bound by a fervent and ideal friendship.

Then Gustave falls in love with a beautiful young widow named Julia, and he is in the seventh heaven of rapture, with love and friendship shining upon him. But soon the sky darkens. Armand proves a false friend and a duel ensues, while Julia is discovered to love another. Friendship and love have proved hollow, and the disillusionment generates egotism.

Gustave says : " Just as we gradually prepare a person for the reception of bad news, that he may not be overwhelmed by the weight of sudden sorrow, providence also gradually opens to us the knowledge of the human heart, that we may learn to bear the burden of our knowledge. First one man deceives us, and the wound, however deep, heals in time and makes our heart harder. Then we learn to doubt men more and more ; we lose our cherished ideals, but we bear it because we place less and less confidence in men, and the wound made by deception becomes less keen. Then our friends abandon us, our lover proves false, and we dare not trust anybody. A dreadful experience ! Yet time, which has robbed us of so many treasures, has taught us to retire into ourselves and thus, although we stand alone, we can endure it because we have become selfish."

A new pang is added to Gustave's sorrow. A society woman, out of revenge, spreads calumnies concerning him, and the world believes them although he is innocent. Disappointed and despairing, Gustave seeks consolation first in solitary studies, and afterwards in a dissolute life.

Whilst walking with his frivolous companions, Gustave sees a poor but remarkably beautiful and virtuous girl called Betty. One of his companions remarks that although the girl is very poor, no one can lure her from the paths of virtue. Gustave makes a bet of twenty thousand francs that he will make her his mistress. He becomes acquainted with her, pretending to be a poor student, and wins her love. Gustave might now be very happy, but when Betty hears of the horrible wager she sees her happiness destroyed and flies in despair. This stirs Gustave to the depths, he regards himself as Betty's murderer, and then begins that process of development which transforms the selfish man into an unselfish one. He learns that his father, whom he thought so heartless, is still fond of him. He receives news telling him that Julia is very unhappy, and that his friend Armand, having abandoned his life of frivolity, has gained peace of mind, and is living as a simple farmer. He sees Betty, who is dying. She tells him that she was happy with him, and is happy now she beholds him once again. Gustave sees that while he was selfish he could not but be unhappy, and that he has first found happiness in making others happy. " Do not abandon hope," he says at last, " and if the day should come when your heart is bruised by many painful experiences, and your strength seems exhausted as you tread the path the end of which appears to recede in spite of all your efforts, think of me and the memory of my life may save your soul from selfishness ; your dark days will cease; the pain caused by the world will be eased by the love of your dear ones, and the suffering caused by those you love will be forgotten amidst the approving smiles of the world. It is only the selfish for whom life contains no consolation."

The Carthusian is full of a noble fervour, but it is manifestly the work of a young author. The characters are fertile in fine sentiments and reflections ; but their actions are weak and purposeless.

Eőtvős' second novel, *The Village Notary*, was distinctly a novel with a purpose. It was really a vehement attack upon the autonomy of the provinces. In 1846, when Eőtvős completed the book, serfdom was not abolished and each province was a little kingdom in itself, its ruler, and sometimes its tyrant, being the *föispán* or lord-lieutenant of the county. If he committed any unlawful action it was practically impossible to resist it Eőtvős depicted the corruption and stagnation prevalent in the provinces with all the warmth inspired by his indignation. Deák, however, was right when, in speaking of this novel, he said : "On the title-pages of books treating of the ailments of horses there is often pictured a horse suffering from all possible diseases and infirmities at one and the same time, but in reality such an unfortunate animal does not exist. It is the same with the province presented to us in Eőtvős' novel ; so miserable a province does not exist."

The kind of persecution to which good men were subjected is shown to us in the career of the hero, the village notary. A noble-minded and idealistic thinker, finding that his schemes of reform are not acceptable, abandons the struggle and seeks a humble sphere of activity as a notary. More cruel still were the effects of corruption upon the peasants. Viola was a well-to-do peasant, a good man and perfectly happy with his family. But the provincial magistrate took a fancy to his wife, and as she indignantly repelled his advances, he began to persecute the husband Viola was taken prisoner, and although innocent, was condemned to be flogged. Unable to endure this humiliation and injustice, he tore himself from the grasp of the constables, and in a frenzy of rage and despair, killed one of them, severely wounded another, and rushed away into the forest and became a highwayman. Thus does bad administration create lawless men.

Next to *The Village Notary* came (in 1847) a historical novel : *Hungary in 1415*. In this he used as a basis one of the most terrible events of Hungary's past, the great peasant revolution. The pope had proclaimed a crusade against the Turks and eighty thousand Hungarian crusaders were assembled under the leadership of George Dósa. But suddenly the army (the cruciates or kurucz as they were called later) resolved not to march against the Turks, but to turn against the nobles, and they proceeded to do so with very great cruelty. Ultimately, however, the nobles were victorious and they took a terrible revenge. Forty thousand men were slaughtered. The leader, Dósa, was crowned with a diadem of red-hot iron, and the rebel peasants were punished by the loss of their sole remaining right, that of moving freely from one town to another. This fatal revenge divided the nation into two classes, the privileged and unprivileged, for centuries.

Eötvös depicted that terrible period with considerable historical truth, attained by arduous study. The story opens with the assembling of the crusaders and closes with Dósa's cruel punishment.

The social problem which engaged the thoughts of Eőtvős while writing this novel, occupied his mind as a philosopher too. His best scientific treatise is, " The influence of the leading ideas of the nineteenth century upon the State."* It is perhaps the most significant theoretical work in Hungarian. According to Eőtvős the nineteenth century was characterised by three dominating ideas : liberty, equality and nationality, which became powerful instincts in the nations. We accept them as mental guides which demand our allegiance, but when they seek to lead us in opposing directions they come into conflict with one another, and we see that we were wrong to trust in them. Eőtvős pointed out that these three ideas were really incompatible, that they would destroy every existing form of state life, and if either of them could be entirely realised, the result would not give satisfaction. For instance, equality is inconsistent with liberty, for complete equality becomes communism, and communism is a form of despotism exercised in the name of the people, and consequently opposed to liberty.

The idea of nationality again does not agree with that of equality, for the spirit of nationality aims at the supremacy of one nation over another, a spirit which is antagonistic to the notion of perfect equality. There is an impassable gulf between these ideas and their realisation.

What then can be done ? Only his concluding ideas can be mentioned. The state, he thinks, merely renders secure to each individual his material or immaterial possessions, but is not concerned with providing for his needs. The state is, in short, the individual's safeguard.

* 1851. Translated into German.

A state enjoys the right degree of freedom when the central power is duly balanced with local autonomy This proper distribution of power is the best preservative both against revolution and against despotism. The stronger the state the better does it bear local self-government and free association. We see that although Eötvös lived before Mill, his ideas were very similar to those of that great philosopher. In his conclusions as to the reforms that were desirable, Eötvös, like Montesquieu, drew his examples from England.

Eőtvős excelled in his funeral orations, surpassing in that respect even Kölcsey, whom he acknowleged as his model. His orations reveal a poetical nature and display one of his characteristic literary methods, that of explaining or illuminating Hungarian history by allusions to events in the history of other European nations.

The book entitled *Thoughts,* containing several hundred aphoristic utterances of a highly cultured and deeply religious mind, is of great value. One characteristic thought is that the heart is a better guide than reason. In the chapter on *Style* he says that a great ship floats as lightly as a cork. Buoyancy is due not to want of weight, but to proportion and a proper disposition of parts.

Eőtvős wrote a few lyrical poems, but he was not a sufficiently great master of language for us to count him among the best lyric poets. His finest poem is the *Farewell* * to his country :

> Land of the brave, my country dear, farewell !
> Good-by to valleys deep, to mountains high !
> Land of my hopes and where my sorrows dwell,
> I leave thee now—Farewell ! Good-by ! Good-by !

* Loew's " Magyar Poetry."

And if, my dear land, I return to thee,
May thy sons through thy bounds contented be.

    *   *   *   *   *

Quiet now reigns upon the Rákos plain,
   Too long the Magyar silent is, alas !
The fathers' traces fade away and wane,
   The winds spread over them fresh sand and grass ;
Silent expands the field !   Our trembling heart
And silent tear proclaim how great thou art.

And Buda must in sorrow now complain,
   No more does she of fame and glory boast ;
A graveyard of the land she must remain,
   Reminding us of all my country lost.
Time long before destroyed her ancient fort,
Her crumbling stones heroic deeds report.

And ancient Mohács stands, and higher grows
   The wheat upon her fields, the grass more green ;
Their roots spring from the dust of dead heroes
   Whose blood the irrigating dew has been.
No stone shows where the patriots were slain,
The silent field doth fill our heart with pain.

So long as on the Danube's silver face
   A Magyar's eye will gaze, upon her brink
Will live one of the sturdy Magyar race,
   So long our hearts with sorrow's pang shall sink.
Pray, tell me, Danube old, that floweth here,
Art thou a stream ?   Art thou my country's tear ?

I love thee in thy hallowed, silent grief,
   Unbounded is my love, dear land, for thee !
Thou art my heart's most cherished fond belief,
   Though stricken down with woe and misery.
Cheer up !   The future holds thy hope supreme,
Soon to dawn o'er thee in a golden gleam.

And now, good-by !   Farewell, thou blessed spot ;
   Farewell, forever fare thee well !   I go !
Whether again 'twill be my blissful lot
   To see thee happy—Well, who is't can know ?

And if, my dear land, I return to thee,
Throughout thy bounds may thy sons blesséd be.

Eőtvős was entitled to say of himself that his life was spent in endeavouring to realise his ideas. In his poem, *My Will*, he says : " If my name is to survive, may it be made memorable by no marble monument, but by the triumph of my ideas."

But it is to be feared that the reverse has happened ; he has obtained a statue on the banks of the Danube, but his idealistic and humanitarian ideas have not yet triumphed.

SIGISMUND KEMÉNY (1814–1877) was a contemporary of Eőtvős, and only one year younger than he, but he commenced his activity as a writer several years later. He too was a novelist, an advocate of the parliamentary system, and one of Deák's fellow workers. There was something ponderous and complex in his whole personality, but he had the great and promising quality of always going to first principles.

He, like Nicholas Jósika, was born in Transylvania. It is a curious fact that although he did not intend to become a doctor, but determined to be a writer, he took up the study of medicine. He wished to know both the bodies and minds of men. He came in time to play an important political part, and edited Deák's organ, the *Pesti Napló*. Towards the end of his life his mind became somewhat unhinged. He did not always recognise his friends, and would sometimes sit motionless for hours, murmuring to himself the sad truth : " Hungarian politics are a difficult business."

Kemény's best works are his historical novels. The chief feature of his activity as a writer was that he first amongst Hungarians employed the analytical method of Balzac. He considered the psychological analysis of his characters the most important part of his work, and always strove to discover the mental process which led an individual to decide upon a certain action.

In depicting love, he shows in each particular case what part is played by interest, sensuality, vanity, by the instinct of imitation, by the imagination and the mode of life. His desire was to penetrate to the depths of the greatest of mysteries, the human soul. Even in his historical novels it is no mere outward picture of the age which he presents to us ; it was not the daring adventures and multi-coloured events which attracted him most, as was the case with Jósika, but the inner man, and the ruling passions of the time. His guiding principle was that we cannot understand an epoch until we enter into the mental world of the people who lived in it. In one of his novels, *The Enthusiasts*, he gives the psychology of religious enthusiasm and sect formation. The enthusiasts were the Sabbatarians, whose followers may still be found in Transylvania, the original home of the sect. They received their name because, like the Jews, they kept Saturday instead of Sunday as their Sabbath.

The action falls within the seventeenth century. One of the heroes is a Sabbatarian minister. A powerful nobleman, Kassai, the Chancellor of the Regent, George Rákóczy, wishes to use this minister as a tool for the destruction of his adversary, Simon Pécsi, the leader of the Sabbatarians. The minister cannot consent to be so used, but unfortunately he was originally a serf who had fled from his master, and as Kassai knows this, the minister's life, and the fate of his young wife, are in his hands. Mental strain deprives the poor fellow of his reason, and towards the end of the story, Pécsi, the dreamer, is taken prisoner, but his grasping adversary, Kassai, does not achieve his aim. He fails to obtain the treasures of Pécsi, while on the other hand he loses the favour of the Regent. The novel is to be regarded as a study of religious enthusiasm and intolerance, displaying the fanaticism and inconstancy of the mob.

Kemény's most famous novel is *Stormy Times* (1861). There he not only presents the tragedy of a sect, but of a whole nation. The story tells of stormy times, the period, namely, in which the Turks occupied the fortress of Buda. During the reign of Queen Isabella, the Sultan Soliman transformed the cathedral of the great Matthias Corvinus into a Mohammedan mosque, and garrisoned the fortress with ten thousand Turkish soldiers.

Kemény explained this great disaster, and showed how the queen, the statesmen and the whole nation were deceived. Calamity swooped down upon the country like a dark-winged bird. Wisdom and right-mindedness were of no avail. Unselfish statesmen and cunning intriguers were alike impelled towards the catastrophe. Kemény was acquainted with the kind of fatality which compels a people in certain great crises. He witnessed a similar catastrophe in the Hungarian war for freedom. In this novel, Kemény sketches the interesting historical figure of George Frater, who from a mere stoker became a bishop and the first statesman in the country.

Kemény was the most tragic-minded of Hungarian writers : τραγικότατος as Aristophanes wrote of Euripides. In his books the atmosphere at the very commencement is like that which precedes a thunderstorm. We feel something heavy, close and oppressive all about us.

Fate appeared to him to be terrible indeed. It was
not their crimes alone which hurled men into disaster,
but sometimes even their virtues when not wisely
directed.

In his first novel, *Gyulai Pál*, Kemény also dealt with
a tragical event. Sigismund Báthory, the Regent of
Transylvania, had a powerful foe in his relative Balthazar,
whose growing popularity more and more threatened the
Regent's throne. But Báthory had a faithful subject
named Paul Gyulai, who desired to save the Regent lest
his beloved master should die either in prison or on the
scaffold. To save his master from Balthazar, Gyulai
invented a curious scheme. He caused an Italian
comedian named Senno, whom he believed to be closely
associated with Balthazar, to be assassinated, in the hope
that the spirit of revenge might prompt Balthazar to re-
taliate by some act of violence which would lead to his
own destruction.

Balthazar, however, took no such step, and Senno's
wife, whom Gyulai loved passionately, became the mistress of the Regent and persuaded him to execute
Gyulai. The woman he loved begged for his death from
the very man for whom Gyulai had sacrificed his honour
and committed a crime.

Kemény aimed at depth in his writing. Perhaps that
is why he is often heavy. He does not narrate lightly
and agreeably. He penetrates too far into the depths
from which spring our happiness and unhappiness and
all that gives life value—the depths of the human
heart.

MAURUS JÓKAI (1825-1904) was the most popular of
Hungarian novelists. At his funeral some one said : " If
all the persons whom he has called to life in his novels
13

were to appear—Hungarian peasants, knights of the Middle Ages, great magnates, honvéds, beggars, Roman senators, Greek sailors, Indian maharajahs, Turkish janizaries, nomadic Arabs and English lords, Assyrian kings and Christian martyrs and modern stockbrokers, negroes, Russians, Armenians and Gipsies—the multitude would line the streets for more than a mile."

The man who made all these various characters live, began his activity as a writer in the time of Petőfi and Arany, though he was younger than they. He was a student when he first met Petőfi and the two became firm friends. After the defeat at Világos the sentence of death hung over him and for some time he had to live in hiding. His flight was aided by Kossuth's secretary, who hired a carriage and horses, dressed himself as a coachman, and drove Jókai through the Russian camp. For months Jókai and his wife lived in seclusion amongst the wooded hills.

After the revolution he settled in Budapest as an author and editor, and from 1861 was a member of Parliament. In 1863 an article appeared in his paper, in consequence of which he was summoned before the military court and sentenced to a year's rigorous imprisonment in chains. His treatment in prison was not severe, however, in spite of the terms of his sentence, and after a month he was liberated.

Jókai's popularity became unbounded, and at his jubilee, among other presents he received from the nation a gift of 200,000 korona, or about £8,000. His first wife was a very celebrated Hungarian actress, and twelve years after her death he married a young woman who for a time was also an actress. He was a friend of the Crown Prince Rudolf, who died while still a young man,

Jókai's most striking talent lay in his wonderful power of invention. He wrote several hundred longer or shorter stories, but in every one he surprises us with a fresh plot and new ideas, so inexhaustible was his inventiveness.

His manner of telling a story is fascinating. His narrative runs so easily and interestingly that every incident is readily grasped. His style reminds us of the best novelists of the Latin nations, though it has many purely Hungarian features. We may say that just as Petőfi's poems were an exalted form of the folk-song, so Jókai's stories were a glorification of the anecdote. This accounts for his sparkling vivacity and fluency, but also for his superficiality.

The amiable character of Jókai's genius was enhanced by his humour, which was not so subtle as Kemény's nor so bitter as Thackeray's, but gay and agreeable, and created a pleasant atmosphere. His inventiveness was aided by a vivid imagination which coloured every plot and incident with marvellous richness. We may almost say that there has not been a more brilliant narrator since the time of the *Arabian Nights*.

But with his great qualities Jókai had one defect. Though a great novelist, curiously enough he had no real knowledge of human nature. He could not look into men's hearts, and his characterisation was often psychologically false. He always tried to discover something surprising and interesting, and to this end he frequently altered the character of his actors in an improbable way.

His best novels are those in which he painted the Hungary of his day. One of the finest is *The New Landowner*. This is a delightful and amusing picture of

Hungary during the "Bach Era," that period of absolutism following upon the revolution, during which Bach the Austrian prime minister endeavoured to germanise Hungary. The hero of the tale is an Austrian general who buys an estate in Hungary and begins farming, not very successfully at first, as he has brought with him Austrian methods and habits which are unsuitable to the Hungarian soil and temper. But in course of time he grows fond of the country and ultimately develops into a full-blooded Hungarian. In effecting this great transformation a part is played by the circumstance that one of his two daughters lies buried in Hungarian soil and the other becomes the wife of a brave Hungarian gentleman. The idea embodied in the novel was suggested to Jókai by the history of the Austrian general Haynau. This man, "the hyena of Brescia," after falling into disgrace, went to live in Hungary and bought estates there, and could not help feeling more and more respect and sympathy for the people against whom he had acted in such a dastardly way during the revolution. Many different periods are equally well characterised by Jókai in other novels. In *A Hungarian Nabob* he depicts the times immediately before the advent of Széchenyi, showing the aristocratic class in all its indolence and haughtiness, firmly entrenched behind its privileges.

The generation that followed, living about the year 1830, awakened and electrified by Széchenyi and yearning for progress, is shown in *Zoltán Kárpáti*. The glorious and feverish times of the revolution form the background of several of Jókai's works, for instance, *The Baron's Sons, Political Fashions*, and *Battle Pictures*.

His historical novels do not reach the height of the works just mentioned, for Jókai did not possess in any eminent degree the gift of making the past live again.

His power of imagination is conspicuously displayed in *The Novel of the Coming Century*, in which, amongst many other incidents, he describes a battle in the sky between airships.

Jókai once described his method of working, and said : " When I am writing a novel I try to be my characters, to live in them, whether murderer, traitor, voluptuary, or miser ; I try to make their feelings my feelings, so that I myself suffer, or despair, or am impelled by the inward promptings of the avenger. . . .

" At such a time, even the visit of my best friend is unwelcome, because it may be that he finds me in a tyrannical or an angry mood, or perhaps I am sentimental and tearful, or else in raptures.

" The door opens, and the state of mind which I have worked up is destroyed and I have to begin over again, for I can do nothing until I have warmed to my subject. I do not mean that no one can write in any other manner. It is possible to write with a cold heart, carefully calculating probabilities, but the work itself will suffer. It may be correct enough, but what I desire is that my readers shall feel the same warmth that I felt when writing.

" I never sit while working out my plot but always walk up and down. First I plan the whole long novel in my head, down even to the smallest details of the dialogue, but not including the descriptive parts. At such a time, imagination takes the place of memory, for I do not store up the details in my memory, but the course of events appears to unroll itself before me so that I seem to be describing what I actually see and could dictate the whole straight away. But I do not like dictating; while I am at work I do not wish to see a human face. When I sit down to write I am able to do as much as sixteen printed pages at one sitting, and sometimes even twice that number, without the need for any corrections, even so much as a single word. That imagination has taken the place of memory is shown by the fact that after a year I am able to read my own novel as if it were the work of another. I am quite ignorant of contents and very curious to know how my hero will get out of the scrape into which he has fallen.

" If my characters have many faults it is because I do not see them clearly enough. If I regarded them and moulded them as an outsider might, perhaps they would stand more firmly upon their feet, but what about their wings ? Well, this fault of mine I shall never be able to mend. I am growing older but not wiser, so my readers must just take my characters as they have done these forty years.

" I do not regard it as a merit that I have worked much, nor do I ask anything from the present or posterity on that account. I do not even ask that people shall read my works. I wrote them in the first place for myself and found happiness in the work. This was my world, my life's secret, the guide upon my path, my comfort in adversity and my defence in danger; it gave me hope for better times, resignation, and renewed strength for fresh efforts. All this have I gained from my desk. It has restored to me my lost fortune, has helped me to repel the attacks of my enemies and encouraged me to begin a new life. For forty years we two have been conversing together and we still have many thoughts to exchange.

" And now, ere I conclude, let me mention you, my most faithful fellow-workers, my helpers and supporters, you, my beloved green trees, that I have planted or grown from seed, and pruned and grafted, you, my companions, rising from earth towards the skies. You know how often you have whispered to me, and how many thoughts you have showered down upon me with your falling blossoms. Many are the quiet refreshing hours I have had amongst you, and many the dreams beneath the kindly shadow of your leaves. When tormented by my enemies you have sheltered me and allayed the agitation of my heart. If some day one should come hither and inquire why it was that I worked much more in summer than in winter, tell him that in the summer you were near me.

" The secret of my fertility as a writer was communion with nature."

CHAPTER XIV

ALEXANDER PETŐFI

IN 1841, a young actor stepped into the sacred bower of Hungarian poetry, and suddenly, everything became changed there. New flowers sprang up from the soil, and the very air seemed different. This revival of poetry, which occurred simultaneously with the political revival, was brought about by ALEXANDER PETŐFI (1822–1849). His personality was as extraordinary as his life and his poetry. At the age of eighteen he was a private soldier, and at twenty, a strolling actor leading a life of great privation. Yet by the time he was twenty-seven, he was the most famous poet in Hungary, and in the same year, on July 31, 1849, he died on the battlefield. His short life was one of restless wandering. For a long time the place of his birth was as little known as that of his death. As a boy we find him mentioned now at this school, and now at that. He was still a boy when he became a soldier, and in the course of a very short time, he had lived in three countries, Hungary, Croatia and Styria. Next he was an actor, and the wanderer's knapsack, though more like a beggar's wallet, fell to his share. He always put at the foot of a poem the name of the town in which it was written, and those names would furnish a list long enough to teach us the geography of Hungary. During the last year of his life, he was again in the army for the third time. Three times he left Transylvania to return to Hungary, and three times he went back to Transylvania, where, on the third time, he met his death. The swift movement of his life certainly helped to develop his talents. But in his career of wandering and excitement there was one period of rest : four years of peace and undisturbed happiness, of love and poetic activity. That time of quiet was like the one calm point in the centre of an ocean whirlpool. It is well known to sailors that when a ship has been caught by a cyclone and whirled round, it arrives at length at a central point where all is still. It seems as though the storm has ceased and the waves have become gentle. The sea appears blue and smiling. But soon the currents on the other side of the whirlpool begin to draw the ship into their clutches ; the merciless storm is renewed, and the ship is at last wrecked by the hurricane.

Petőfi was born in the central portion of the lowlands, and was brought up amid the surroundings which are so faithfully depicted in his poems. The wide plain (*puszta*), the roadside inns (*csárda*), the *fata morgana*, the storks and the stud-farms, were the first sights with which the child became familiar ; and the popular songs were the first poetry that he heard. And the impressions then received had a profound effect upon his whole life. Petőfi's father, Stephen Petrovics, was a butcher at Aszód in the province of Pest, like his father before him. He was a man of strong passions, of unpolished manners, but thoroughly good-natured and honest, and not altogether uneducated, knowing even a little Latin. He married a young peasant girl from the province of Turóc, who probably only learned Hungarian after her marriage. She was a lively, amiable and tender-hearted woman, with a gift for singing. It was at Kis-Körös, in the first hour of the year 1823, that Alexander Petőfi first saw the light. His parents often changed their dwelling-place, and when the boy was ten years old, they sent him to a school in the capital. From his class-room the young Petőfi could look out on to the square in which his statue has since been erected. At the age of twelve, we find him in Aszód, where for three years he attended the grammar school.

It often seems as if the story of our life were all written down beforehand, in the depths of our soul, in our inclinations and talents, and as though life itself were but the unfolding and development in time and space of what lay hidden within us.

Petőfi had, in boyhood, three marked characteristics : a love of independence, a desire to become an actor, and a genius for poetry. For three months he was at the high school in Selmecz, but his father stopped his allowance on learning that his son, in spite of repeated warnings, associated with actors.

Deprived of that support, Petőfi left Selmecz and went to Budapest, travelling on foot. This was his first pedestrian adventure, and was full of hardships, but it was not his last, nor his most arduous. At Budapest, quite by chance he met his father, but he escaped and went to the National Theatre, where for some time he served in the double capacity of supernumerary and messenger, carrying the various actors' parts to their houses. Then suddenly a brighter day dawned for him. A relative, an engineer, gave him shelter at his house, and here the boy, quitting his hard service at the theatre, lived the life of a gentleman's son, riding, driving, boating, and hunting. Here also he commenced to write, imitating the Latin poets, and made verses about a pretty girl who lived in the neighbourhood, whom, however, he never dared to look in the face. Petőfi was now sixteen years of age, of medium height, with a dark olive complexion and a thick and somewhat stubborn growth of brown hair ; his eyes were full of fire and indomitable spirit, and his long neck was usually bare of collar and necktie.

But his relative soon gave him up as hopeless. He declared that the boy would never become anything but a comedian. Petőfi sullenly, and despondingly, went to Sopron and joined the army. There never was a soldier who loathed compulsion more, or loved freedom more dearly than he, yet he remained in the army for eighteen months. In 1840 his regiment was ordered to Graz, where he was struck down with typhoid fever. His military life was full of hardships. Even in the severest winter weather, he had to do the roughest kind of work in the courtyard of the barracks. " It is only now and then," he writes in one of his letters, " that with the aid of sacred, heavenly poetry, I am lifted out of this hell. If it were not for this treasure enshrined in my bosom, despair would kill me." At last, through the intervention of a kind-hearted doctor, he was declared unfit for service, and sent home. In 1841 he left Zágráb, the capital of Croatia, for Hungary. Weak, haggard, his countenance of an ashen pallor, and in a worn-out uniform, Petőfi crossed the frontier of his country. Once more there stretched before the fevered, sunken eyes of the poor soldier the land of his fathers, which he was soon to leave again. Here, at this critical point in his life, Fate seems to have said to him : " I will give thee eight full and rich years, a time of vigorous youth ; eight years in which to attain the summit of genius. During this short time thou shalt express all that was slumbering in the heart of thy nation for a thousand years. Thou wilt have to feel in thy heart every thrill, each pang, multiplied a thousandfold in intensity, but *thy* joy and *thy* sorrow will live for ever. For thy sufferings, and restless wanderings, thy reward shall be supreme inspiration and an early death."

In the course of the following year he hesitated between two careers. Alternately, he was student at the College of Pápa, and actor.

The stage seems to have presented irresistible attractions. During the summer of 1843 he lived by his pen, translating French and English novels, but in the autumn he returned to his old love, and again became an actor. The winter (1843-44) he spent in great misery in Debreczen, for after rambling about the country as an actor, he became dangerously ill. At first he lived with a friend, and then he hired a little room in the house of an aged widow. Through the window of this room, if it was not thickly coated with frost, he could see the town gallows. A large clay stove was his writing-desk. The only ornaments were the portraits of Vörösmarty and Schiller. During his illness, Petőfi made a collection of his poems, and at the end of February, he went to Budapest. This journey, the last of those marked by privation, he describes in a letter as follows: " I went on foot, in ragged clothes, with a few coppers and a volume of poems in my pocket. All my hopes were centred in that collection of verses. If I could sell them, all would be well. If not, then it would also be well, for I should either starve or be frozen to death, and my sufferings would be ended. I was wandering alone. Far as I could see, there was no living being in sight. Every one had sought shelter, for the weather was terrible. The shrieking wind drove the icy-cold rain into my face. The tears forced from my eyes by the cold and the thought of my misery, froze on my cheeks. After a week's painful journeying I arrived at Pest. There I stood then, at the last gasp. The courage of despair entered my heart and I went to see one of the greatest men of Hungary, with a feeling not unlike that of a gambler who stakes his last coin, knowing that the result means either life or death."

The great man to whom he refers was the immortal Vörösmarty, who succeeded in finding a publisher for Petőfi

The year 1844 was the turning point in Petőfi's life. His wanderings ceased, his poems appeared, and he bade a final farewell to the stage. Petőfi certainly had some talent for acting, or he would scarcely have clung to it so long, seeing how much he was drawn towards a literary career. He rapidly rose to fame. The surprising originality and freshness of his poetry carried all before them. In a short time he came to be reckoned amongst the most renowned men of Hungary.

For some time he worked as a sub-editor. It was during this period, at the beginning of 1845, when he was twenty-two years of age, that he experienced his great love sorrow. The daughter of a friend, a charming being, half woman, half child, died, and the poet wreathed her tomb with his *Cypress Branches*, a series of poems written in her memory. It was partly to escape from his grief that he travelled for some months in the north of Hungary, the first journey on which he was not driven by necessity nor harassed by privations. In the autumn he returned to the capital, his spirit healed, his heart full of courage and inspiration, and confident in himself and his future.

The following year was a time of poetical enthusiasm and happy love. It was on September 8, 1846, that Petőfi first saw Julia Szendrey, and on the first anniversary of that day he married her. The early months of his married life were spent in the romantic castle of Koltó, with his high-minded and poetical young wife. From Koltó they went to Szalonta, to pay a visit to John Arany. A few months before, Arany's grand epic, *Toldi*, had won the prize in a literary competition. Petőfi had greeted his unknown fellow poet with a beautiful poem, and soon afterwards they met and became firm friends.

At the time of his visit, Petőfi wrote to a friend : " Do you know why I was longing to come to Szalonta ? Because it is the dwelling-place of a great man, who is at the same time my friend, John Arany, the author of *Toldi*. If you have not yet read the book it would be vain for me to try and describe it, and if you have read it, it would be superfluous for me to say one word. And this great book is the work of a simple country notary. The week I have spent with my new friend I reckon amongst the happiest of my life."

Next year, in 1848, his poems show a more marked political tendency. He felt in advance the revolution which was impending, "as animals perceive the coming earthquake." This presentiment is expressed in the poem, *The Country*,* of which we quote a few stanzas.

> *The sun went down, but not a starlet*
> *Appeared in heaven—all dark above—*
> *No light around, except the taper*
> *Dim glimmering, and my homely love.*
>
> *That homely love's a star in heaven*
> *That shines around both near and far,*

* Bowring, " Translations from Petőfi."

A home of sadness—sad Hungaria !
  Where wilt thou find that lovely star ?

And now my taper flickers faintly,
  And midnight comes, but in the gleam,
Faint as it is, I see a shadow
  Which half reveals a future dream.

It brightens as the daybreak brightens,
  Each flame brings forth a mightier flame ;
There stand two figures in the nimbus—
  Old Magyar honour—Magyar fame.

O Magyars ! look not on your fathers,
  But bid them hide their brows in night ;
Your eyes are weak, those suns are dazzling,
  Ye cannot bear that blasting light.

Time was those ancient, honoured fathers,
  Could speak the threatening, thundering word ;
'Twas like the bursting of the storm-wind,
  And Europe, all responsive, heard !

Great was the Magyar then—his country
  Honoured—his name a history
Of glory—now a star extinguished—
  A fallen star in Magyar sea.

'Twas long ago—the laurel garland
  Was round the Magyar forehead bound ;
Shall fancy—eagle-pinioned—ever
  See Magyar hero-brow recrowned ?

That laurel crown so long has faded—
  So long thy light has ceased to gleam ;
Thy greatness seems a myth, thy story
  A fable of the past—a dream !

Long have mine eyes been dry and tearless,
  But now I weep, and can it be
That these are dews of spring—the dawning
  Of brighter days for Hungary ?

> *And can it—can it be—a meteor,*
>   *That for a moment burst and blazed—*
> *Lighted with brightness all the heavens,*
>   *And sunk in darkness while we gazed.*

> *No ! 'tis a comet, whose returning*
>   *Is sure as is the march of doom ;*
> *Hungary shall hail it, blazing, burning,*
>   *It cannot, will not fail to come.*

It was on the 14th of March, 1848, that the first news reached Pest of the Viennese revolution, which forced the Cabinet to resign.

The event inspired Petőfi to write the poem *Talpra Magyar*, which he recited to a vast crowd, amidst tumultuous applause, on the following day, the 15th of March. The refrain, " And we swear that we shall never more be slaves," was repeated by the crowd as though it were a sacred vow which they were making before the bard. When he had finished, the crowd made its way to the printing office, which had formerly been under the yoke of the censor, took possession of the machines and printed the poem, the people waiting outside until it was ready.

It was the first poem printed without the license of the censor.

NATIONAL SONG.*

> *Magyars, up ! your country calls you.*
> *Break the chain which now enthralls you.*
> *Freemen be, or slaves for ever.*
> *Choose ye, Magyars, now or never.*
> *For by the Magyar's God above*
>   *We truly swear*
> *We truly swear the tyrant's yoke*
>   *No more to bear*

* Loew's " Magyar Poetry."

Alas ! till now we were but slaves ;
Our fathers resting in their graves
Sleep not in freedom's soil.   In vain
They fought and died free homes to gain
But by the Magyar's God above, etc.

A miserable wretch is he
Who fears to die, my land, for thee !
His worthless life who thinks to be
Worth more than thou, sweet liberty !
Now by the Magyar's God above, etc.

The sword is brighter than the chain,
Men cannot nobler gems attain ;
And yet the chain we wore, Oh, shame !
Unsheath the sword of ancient fame !
For by the Magyar's God above, etc.

The Magyar's name will soon once more
Be honoured as it was before !
The shame and dust of ages past
Our valor shall wipe out at last,
For by the Magyar's God above, etc.

And where our graves in verdure rise
Our children's children to the skies
Shall speak the grateful joy they feel,
And bless our names the while they kneel.
For by the Magyar's God above,
          We truly swear
We truly swear the tyrant's yoke
          No more to bear.

Petőfi served the cause of freedom as a revolutionary
poet, as an orator, and as a journalist. His soul was
burning with enthusiasm, and its flame was always pure.
" No sound of my lyre, no stroke of my pen, has ever served
a mercenary purpose. I sang and wrote as inspired by the

14

deity within my soul, and that deity was Freedom," he said of himself, and rightly. But his exaggerated ideas were certain to awaken a reaction. His poem *To Kings*, with the refrain, " There is now no king who should be beloved," met with great disapproval.

" A few weeks after the 15th of March," wrote Petőfi in an article, "and lo, I am one of the most hated of men. Here I stand, in the abyss, my wreath torn from me, but at least I stand erect." It was partly due to this reaction, that when, at the elections, he stood as a parliamentary candidate, he was not returned. It is true that his speech to the constituents was proud and imperious, reminding us of the manner of Coriolanus in soliciting votes.

" The time of speeches is over," said Petőfi, " and the hour for deeds has arrived," and the event proved that he was right. The decisive struggle came. Petőfi could not remain quietly at his desk while such events were stirring. There are noble natures in whom there dwells a certain self-sacrificing restlessness. They yearn to perform greater deeds than those of the common round. Such was Petőfi. He felt that revolution, war, and death were approaching, and longed to go to meet them. In 1845 he had wished to die where the trumpets of battle were sounding. " God did not create me for solitude. I am called to the battlefield," he said. "Oh that I might hear the brazen trumpets resounding, calling to war. My restless soul can scarcely wait for the signal."

He obeyed the inward promptings of his soul, and also the call of duty, when he joined the " Honvéd " army. In October 1848 he was promoted to the rank of captain, and in 1849 he asked permission to join General Bem's division.*

* When Bem and Petőfi met, the latter said: " I offer you my

Bem had been an eminent Polish general, who had distinguished himself in the revolt of the Poles against Russia in 1830. And therefore Louis Kossuth offered him the command of the army in Transylvania, where he would be opposed to the Russians.

Petőfi was Bem's aide-de-camp and favourite officer. Three times Petőfi left Transylvania, but each time he went back, as though drawn by an irresistible force to Bem, who understood him better than any other of his superiors ever did, and consequently was more ready to overlook the faults due to his impetuosity. When Petőfi returned for the third time, and met Bem, four days before the poet's death, the general embraced him with tears in his eyes, and exclaimed " My son ! My son !"

Petőfi had already given his nation the treasures of poetry, which will be cherished so long as the Hungarian language endures. Now there was but one supreme gift which he could bestow on it—his life. Petőfi has described in prophetic language the death he fondly hoped to die. It was to die young, on the battlefield, fighting for Freedom, and when death came, to be buried in one common grave with those who had given their heart's blood for the same sacred cause. Fate granted his wish. On the 31st of July he fell by the hand of a Russian Cossack, at the battle of Segesvar. The bard who had sung of the common feelings of his countrymen was buried in a common grave.

The two main themes of his poetry, to which he was faithful to the end, are indicated in the motto of one of his volumes of poems.

sword." " I shall not be satisfied with that," replied the great general, " I want your heart as well."

> *All other things above*
> *Are liberty and love ;*
> *Life would I gladly tender*
> *For love : yet joyfully*
> *Would love itself surrender*
> *For liberty.*

The poem in which he prophesied his own death is the following :—

ONE ONLY THOUGHT.*

> *One thought torments me sorely—'tis that I,*
> *Pillowed on a soft bed of down, may die—*
> *Fade slowly, like a flower, and pass away*
> *Under the gentle pressure of decay,*
> *Paling as pales a fading, flickering light*
> *In the dark, lonesome solitude of night.*
> *O God ! let not my Magyar name*
> *Be linked with such a death of shame ;*
> *No ! rather let it be*
> *A lightning-struck, uprooted tree—*
> *A rock, which torn from mountain-brow,*
> *Comes rattling, thundering down below.*
> *Where every fettered race tired with their chains*
> *Muster their ranks and seek the battle plains ;*
> *And with red flushes the red flag unfold,*
> *The sacred signal there inscribed in gold—*
> *" For the world's liberty ! "*
> *And, far and wide, the summons to be free*
> *Fills east and west,—and to the glorious fight*
> *Heroes press forward, battling for the right :*
> *There will I die !*
> *There, drowned in mine own heart's-blood, lie—*
> *Poured out so willingly : th' expiring voice,*
> *Even in its own extinction shall rejoice.*
> *While the sword's clashing and the trumpet's sound,*
> *And rifles and artillery thunder round ;*
> *Then may the trampling horse*
> *Gallop upon my corse,*

* BOWRING, " Translations from Petőfi."

When o'er the battle field the warriors fly.
There let me rest till glorious victory
Shall crown the right—my bones upgathered be
At the sublime interment of the free !
When million voices shout their elegy
Under the unfurled banners waving high ;
On the gigantic grave which covers all
The heroes, who for freedom fall,
And welcome death because they die for thee—
All holy ! world-delivering liberty !

Petőfi's place in Hungarian poetry is easily defined. He is the greatest Hungarian lyric poet. Song was the natural and spontaneous expression of his personality. Feelings were ever welling up in his soul and finding an outlet in song. He was an "impressionist" in the highest sense of the word. All his feelings—patriotism, friendship, love, anger, political sympathy—quickly rose to passion. "My heart," he once said, "is like the echoing forest, to one call it responds with a hundred cries." He never endeavoured to moderate his feelings or to suppress them. He followed the first impulse and unrestrainedly gave himself up to the impression of the moment. He enjoyed the gladness of his heart, and suffered from its sorrow, in a measure quite unknown to other men. "Though the earth were covered with snow, if I could but sow in it the seeds of my joyful spirit, a forest of roses would lighten the winter's gloom."

His great capacity of feeling naturally made him extremely sensitive and excitable. Sanguine by nature, and full of youthful fervour, he was easily impelled to rash deeds, but never to any course which deviated from the path of honour. He was content with no compromise, could endure no compulsion, and wished to enjoy freedom in all its fulness and perfection. In the intercourse of everyday life there was a repelling restlessness in him, some stiff pride, and occasionally a certain superficiality, but in the service of freedom he was thorough and faithful to the end. For freedom he was ready to give all, even life itself.

Petőfi, like his great contemporary and fellow-worker, Arany, based his poetry upon popular traditions and feelings. He embodies many of them in his verses, but always uses them with the conscious art of a cultured poet. It was as if he had grafted the cultivated rose of true poetry upon the wild rose of the popular imagination. The former gave the beauty, and the latter the sap and strength.

Both Petőfi and Arany were pupils of the people. Arany learnt from them his graphic language, the plastic simplicity of his sentences and his epic construction. Petőfi used the features of the popular songs, though altered in accordance with his own individuality.

The essential characteristics of the popular Hungarian songs may be discerned in his poetry. We feel while reading his verses that we are standing on Hungarian soil. Nowhere can we find the qualities of the people and the character of their daily life better portrayed. The characters that he introduces are typically Hungarian, and the sober self-consciousness of the people, their quiet dignity and their well-known discreet reserve, are as faithfully depicted in his poetry as their warm feelings are reflected in himself. In the mature poetry of Petőfi we see love as the Hungarians conceive it, full of strength and warmth, and without any touch of French frivolity or German sentimentalism. Petőfi's writings give us a glimpse of Hungarian life and the Hungarian soul, lighted up by the flame of poetical exaltation.

He often borrowed the subjects and the rhythmical beauty of the popular songs. Those songs, born of the people, never treat the feelings in an abstract way, never merely mention that in the soul of the singer this or that sentiment is present, for one reason or another, but place the whole situation before us in a little scene. They scarcely ever contain a general expression of joy or grief ; it is nearly always the joy or grief of a clearly outlined individual in certain well-defined surroundings. Hence the great plasticity of the scene. This dramatic power is one of Petőfi's most striking characteristics. Nearly all his songs make us the witnesses of some little drama. Another poet might say " Sweet maid, I loved thee at first sight. Our eyes just met and thy glance set my heart on fire." But Petőfi writes a charming little peasant song, *Into the Kitchen door I strolled.*

> *The cottage door stood open wide,*
> *To light my pipe I stepped inside,*
> *But, oh! behold, my pipe was lit,*
> *There was indeed a glow in it.*
>
> *But since my pipe was all aglow*
> *With other thoughts inside I go,*
> *A gentle winning maiden fair*
> *That I perchance saw sitting there,*
>
> *Upon her wonted task intent*
> *To stir the fire aflame, she bent ;*
> *But oh ! dear heart, her eyes so bright*
> *Were radiant with more brilliant light.*
>
> *She looked at me as in I passed*
> *Some spell she must have o'er me cast.*
> *My burning pipe went out, but oh !*
> *My sleeping heart was all aglow.*

Petőfi's lyrics possess a genuine freshness, which

is found in such perfection in no poetry outside the popular songs. It cannot be acquired; the more the poet strives after it, the farther does he drift away from it. The songs of the people, on the other hand, are invariably full of it. Those nameless singers composed their songs under the overpowering impulse of strong feeling and were impelled by no other motive. And if a popular song is not full of life, if it is not simple and genuine, it quickly perishes and fails to win the ear of all men. Poets by profession achieve the triumph of perfect sincerity and freshness much more rarely than the unknown authors of the songs of the people. But Petőfi's verses were very different from the oratorical compositions of his contemporaries. All he says is simple, and expressed with fervour and the instinctive sincerity of a just mind. Deep, strong feelings, put into the simplest possible words—that is the typical Petőfi poem.

Related to his freshness is his sincerity. He shows himself to us as he is. For him poetry is not a means of enabling him to assume this character or that, but an opportunity to lay bare his inmost soul. His poetry is an open confession. All the incidents of his life, the news he hears, and the books he reads, profoundly impress his heart and his whole being. It never occurs to him to pander with the truth, and he pours his whole soul into his poems.

Other poets reveal themselves most frequently in carefully chosen moods. Not so Petőfi. He pours forth like a torrent all he thinks and feels and suffers. He tells us that he has been hungry, and cold and penniless, or that his father struck him, or that he was a strolling player, and that his coat was ragged. Who would have dared to speak like this before him? The poets would have been ashamed to appear in such sorry garb before the public. They thought a holiday mood needful to their singing, and that a gala dress must commend their poetry.

The classical Berzsenyi, by the way, actually used to put on a Roman *toga* when he wished to feel in the proper mood for writing odes. With some poets we feel as if a barrier existed between them and us. Petőfi never makes us feel like that. He is not afraid of standing near us, that we may feel in close touch with him. He does not disdain to speak of subjects commonly thought trivial, and he allows us to see into the depths of his soul. How did he dare to do this? Because he knew that the depths of his soul could only reveal his absolute sincerity. He could venture to speak of trivial, every-day matters, because his personality turned even the grayest and dullest incident to gold. His imitators endeavoured to copy his sincerity, and tried to speak in his daring way. Apollo might appear unclad, yet not every naked Greek youth carrying a lyre was an Apollo. The mantle of Petőfi did not descend on his imitators.

Through his poems, the subjects he used to treat became fashionable. Every young poet, as a matter of course, must needs have the same kind of father, somewhat rough, vehement and uncultured, though before Petőfi's time young men would have been silent about that kind of father, and if he had been a butcher or an innkeeper, would not have mentioned him for their lives. Now all of them spoke of their mothers who silently loved them, and if their fathers had been too severe, secretly kissed them. They forgot that Petőfi had been kissed by the Muse as well. They suddenly became interested in stud-farms, and horse-herds and strolling players.

Petőfi was the first who dared to see, as the poet ought to see, and his observation is always sincere. He sees everything around him, and speaks of it, but he sees it with the poet's eye. He was the first whose eye discovered the beauty of the Hungarian Lowlands. Hundreds of poets may have passed through the Lowlands and have seen their plains and farms, their roadside inns, horse-herds and highwaymen, but no one detected the element of poetry in them. Petőfi discovered the Lowlands for poetry. He seems to have thought : "Why speak about the snow-capped peaks of Helvetia, or the 'melodious bowers of Arcadia,' or the sources of Tiber, when the Hortobágy is here ? Learn to *see*, and you may find poetry in the homely scenes around you." But it was not only that he looked at the Lowlands with other eyes. He differed from other poets in his attitude to Nature. Nowhere has Nature been reflected with more youthful freshness and dewy beauty, than in his poems. She was no mere spectacle for him, but the extension so to speak of his own mental self. The clouds were his brothers. The Lowlands were the symbol of freedom. On an autumn day he says to his wife : "When thou kissest me, touch my lips lightly, that we may not disturb the beginning of Nature's Slumber." In his songs, Nature is spiritualised and endowed with feeling. Hills and valleys find voice in his verses, but not to teach some moral lesson, as in fables, but to express their own joys and sorrows.

Petőfi not only feels Nature but describes her. His descriptions of scenery are remarkably clear and plastic. An artist could paint them or an engineer draw them on a map. And even these poems are not merely descriptive, but lyrical as well, because they are penetrated by the poet's strong individual feeling. When he describes a dingy, neglected roadside inn, in his *Kutyakaparó*, he not only draws a graphic picture of the scene, but he conveys that feeling of leaden dulness and tediousness which benumbs the traveller as he enters the house. We not only see a rickety, weather-beaten house, neglected rooms, and a morose inn-keeper, but we become a prey to the very feeling which overpowered the author. Another happy feature of his descriptions is that he does not depict an object as an isolated existence in space and time, but introduces it to us as the scene of a series of incidents.

He probes deeply into the mysteries of human existence, and displays an inclination to muse on the transient nature of things. For him, the present hour is filled with thoughts of the future. His poem *At the End of September*, reveals not only the happiness of the moment, his rapturous love for his wife, and the beauty of the castle garden around them, but also contains forebodings of the future, his early death and his widow's quick forgetfulness. Lyrics have three themes recurring : Love, Nature and Death. The three eternal motives are united by a melancholy presentiment in *At the End of September*.* He commences by musing on Nature, then dwells on the idea of Death, and finally arrives at the third motive, Love.

> *The lindens are scattering their fragrance like clover,*
> *While the gay flowers bloom in the garden below ;*
> *A fawn-coloured mist spreads its canopy over*
> *The earth, and the mountains are covered with snow.*

* The first stanzas are quoted from Bowring's *Translations from Petőfi*, 1866, where the title given to the poem is *A Longing*.

On the bosom of youth summer's brightness is glowing,
*   And the buds and the blossoms abundantly spread ;*
But the dews and the darkness my path are o'erflowing,
*   And the dead leaves of autumn are dropt on my head.*

For so our lives fade, like the bud and the blossom ;
*   But come to me sweet one ! in gentleness come !*
And lay thy dear head on my welcoming bosom,
*   That head which to-morrow may bend o'er my tomb.*

If I die, wilt thou shed tears of sorrow above me,
*   When my eyes shall be closed in the dark silent grave ?*
Ah ! May not the words of some youth who will love thee
*   Make thee willing to part with the name which I gave ?*

Then take thou the veil of the widow and bind it,
*   A dark-waving flag, to the cross o'er my tomb ;*
I shall rise from the death-world, beloved, to find it
*   A kerchief for tears in that far land of gloom.*

But thought of oblivion shall never, oh never
*   Weigh low on my spirit, or cause me to grieve,*
For my love will be with thee for ever and ever,
*   And live. while eternity's cycles shall live.*

Even in his epic poems, Petőfi was above all a lyric
poet. He was too subjective to become an impartial
narrator of events. Whenever the characters in his epics
speak, it is from the heart of Petőfi that the words rise to
their lips. His most popular epic poem is *János Vitéz*.
Petőfi wrote it at the age of twenty·one, in a fortnight, in
a mean, dingy little back room. *János Vitéz* is the most
truly Hungàrian fabulous story ever told. What other
poets tried to accomplish when their talents had attained
their fullest development, that is, to write an epic poem
thoroughly popular and national in its spirit, Petőfi did
with playful ease at the very commencement of his career.
There is no imitation, in his work, of the poets of any other

country. The characters are all drawn from the fountain-head of Hungarian life. The hero himself, a young peasant lad, a shepherd who becomes a soldier, is a typical Hungarian. The form of the verse and the language of the poem are in entire harmony with the popular songs. The way he relates an event is precisely the way a tale is told among the people. The miraculous element in the poem is also borrowed from the popular imagination. Petőfi did not, like Vörösmarty, laboriously explore the ancient Hungarian mythology to find his subjects, but with the good fortune of genius, grasped the treasures which lay stored up and ready to hand in the popular fairy tales. The poem is exactly like a fable told by the people, but with the superior and conscious art of a good story-teller. The hero is a brave, honest, and dignified young peasant lad, a shepherd, in whose manly breast there dwells a tender heart. He loves with all his soul a little orphan peasant girl, Iluska. Once when they meet in the fields and speak words of comfort to one another (for they both lead a rather hard life at home), János forgets to look after his flock, and the sheep go astray. His master's anger knows no bounds and he is dismissed from his service. The lad knows that he has deserved this, but his grief is very great, for he has to leave Iluska, who suffers much at the hands of her heartless step-mother. In the course of the wanderings of János, one adventure ollows another. First he is attacked in the dark forest oy highwaymen, but they are so struck by his calm, un-flinching courage (alas ! he is not careful of his life now, once he has lost his happiness) that they tell him he must join them, as he is cut out for a highwayman. During the night, however, he leaves them secretly, sets fire to the house, and although all the treasures of the sleeping highwaymen were at his mercy, he would not touch wealth which was stained with blood. He continues his journey, when suddenly he becomes aware of the approach of a gay cavalcade. A troop of hussars is passing along the road. János can hardly contain his excitement. He goes up to the captain and says : " I am a wanderer, without a home in the whole wide world, but if I could become a hussar, I would not change places with any one." " Remember," replies the captain, " that we are going to the war, to aid the French against the Turks." " My life," János answers, " is of no value. It is true that as a shepherd I have only ridden a donkey, but that doesn't matter, for I am an Hungarian, and every Hungarian is cut out for a horseman." He turns out a splendid Hussar. They pass through the land of the " dog-headed " Tartars, and the rosemary groves of Italy. They come to the vast mountains of India, amid which they wander at such altitudes that the sun is only an hour's distance above their heads. Thus the heat is very great and they suffer from thirst, but fortunately they can easily reach the clouds and squeeze the water out of them. At length they reach the rich country of the French. The French king tells them of his great grief. The Turks have devastated his dominions and carried off his daughter. The Hussars do not hesitate a moment, but set off on the track of the Turks, and destroy their army, and János has the good luck to rescue the princess. The grateful princess offers her hand to her gallant defender, but János remains faithful to Iluska and declines the honour. The French king then gives our hero a large sack of gold, and he turns homeward joyfully, for he is now rich and can marry his true love. He embarks on a ship, but suddenly a storm arises " and the sea moans in pain, beneath the lashing of the wind." The ship is wrecked but János, after a hair-breadth escape from drowning, reaches the shore and finds a roc's nest. The hussar throws himself on the back of the powerful bird, plunges his spurs into him, and is carried homeward, to Iluska. But when he arrives there he hears from one of the young girl's friends that she is dead. "Why did I not fall on the battlefield?" cries out János in the agony of his grief. "Or why did not the waves overwhelm me?" He goes to the churchyard, plucks a rose from the maiden's grave, and leaves the village, never to return. Two companions accompany him, wherever he goes— his grief and his sword. He seeks death in heroic adventures in order that he may soon rejoin Iluska.

Once, on the borders of a large forest, he reaches the frontier of the land of giants. Close beside a stream stands a giant, who cries out with a voice of thunder: "There seems to be something moving down below there, in the grass; it's a man; let me tread upon him." But János quickly holds up his sword, the giant treads upon it and tumbles into the brook. János uses his body as a bridge, and when he reaches the opposite bank, proceeds straight to the castle of the giant king. The family is at dinner, and swallowing huge pieces of rock. The king mockingly breaks off a piece weighing four or five pounds and hands it to the visitor for him to eat. János grasps the stone, and hurls it at the king, striking him on the temple and killing him instantly. The frightened giants do homage to our hero and ask him to be their king, giving him a little whistle, one blast of which would bring them to his aid.

At length, with the help of the giants, János reaches Fairyland, the realm of love and happiness. But he feels sad and lonely even here, for the sight of others' love and joy makes him feel the more keenly the greatness of his own loss. Once, weighed down with grief, he proceeds to the margin of a beautiful lake and throws into its waters his only treasure, the rose which he has kept all this while. He bids it show him the path to death, and he will follow. But, oh, wonder of wonders, the rose is suddenly transformed into a lovely maiden. It is Iluska who stands before him. The lake is the water of life, and revives everything which is thrown into it, and as the rose grew from the ashes of the maid, the magic water recalls her to life. She is so lovely that the fairy maidens elect her to be their queen, while the fairy knights want János for their king, so there they both live happy ever after.

Petőfi's last great epic poem, *The Apostle*, is a series of boldly drawn but exaggerated events and feelings. The hero is a man of the people, full of lofty ideas, which, however, cannot be realised in actual life. He ends his life as the murderer of the king. In the story of his love there are some of the features of Petőfi's love-story, but chiefly the sadder ones, such as the obstacles to his marriage. The account of the hero's cheerless childhood reminds the reader of Dickens's novels, which were so much admired by Petőfi. The bird which cheers the imprisoned apostle seems to have flown to his cell from that of the prisoner of Chillon. It is certainly reminiscent of Byron. In the pathos of the hero there is a resemblance to the *Girondins* of Lamartine, while his bold defiant attitude recalls the manner of *Coriolanus*.

Petőfi's conception of the world is based on strong democratic convictions. It might be summed up thus : Mankind is continually developing. Great men and great ideas have the greatest influence on the education of the race. Yet this education is the common work of all men, and each must contribute his share. Every life leaves some trace in its deeds. "A grape," he says, "is a small thing, yet it requires a whole summer to ripen it. The world requires much more. How many thousands of sunrays have touched one single berry. How many millions may the world need? But the rays which help to develop and ripen the world are the souls of men. Every great soul is such a ray," continues the apostle, "I feel that I am one of those who are helping to ripen the earth."

Petőfi once called himself "the wild flower of Nature." But it would be a mistake to think that he did not study poetry. Certainly, he was always true to himself, but his talents were not altogether uncultivated. In his selection of themes he was influenced by Lenau. His humour reminds us of Csokonai, his irony and his descriptions, of Heine. His boldly expressed love of freedom has much in common with the temper of Shelley and Byron, while some of his *genre* poems resemble those of Béranger. His thrilling oratory shows that he admired Shakespeare, and his dramatic style, full of striking anti-theses, recalls that of Victor Hugo. In some of his patriotic poems we seem to recognise the melancholy of Vörösmarty, and certain of his popular romances reveal clearly the influence of Arany. Many a river and brook flowed into that vast and deep ocean, the soul of Petőfi, and yet its most striking and characteristic features, and its peculiar colours, are all his own, and his are the pearls, too, which formed in its depths.

Petőfi's poetry is the poetry of youth. People say, there are no longer any children, and that youth is dying

15

out. If it were so, it could be reawakened by the poems of Petőfi. All that is great and bright in youth, its generous emotions, its ardour, and sensitiveness, its feverish energy and its purity, its recklessness and its exaggerations, are to be found in him. If we wish to estimate his talents, we ought to compare his poetry with the works which other great lyric poets have written before their twenty-sixth year. If we did so, we should realise how phenomenal was his genius.

Two personalities seem to have been blended in him. One resembled the brass statue in Budapest, which shows Petőfi as the brilliant orator and leader of the people, who by his eloquence awakened the wildest enthusiasm, the bearer of the banner of freedom and revolution. But there was another Petőfi, the contemplative poet of the old garden at Koltó, the poet of Nature and Love, who while he saw the early snow on the mountains, and the first touch of autumn on the trees in the park, carried summer in his heart—who felt all that is sweet and grand in life, and who expressed his mortal feelings in immortal verse.

XV

JOHN ARANY

In the summer of 1836 a company of actors arrived at the little town of Marmaros-Sziget, in the north of Hungary.

Actors were not very highly thought of in those days, and ranked with a travelling circus company. It often happened, however, and indeed in this particular case, that the members of these strolling companies came from various social circles.

In striking contrast with the remainder of the company was a dark-haired, dark-eyed, pale-faced young actor, whom they all called "the student." He was only nineteen years of age, a modest, shy youth, who had joined the comedians in response to an inward call.

Five or six months before, he had been studying at the famous college of Debreczen, where he was the favourite of all his professors and the most promising of the students. Then, all at once, he threw off his black gown, and to the amazement of his companions and teachers, left the town in the middle of a severe winter and joined a company of actors. He was led to take this step by some hazy desire to devote himself to art or poetry.

Inexperienced and enthusiastic as he was, this seemed to him the best way to serve the ideals of poetry. It was only after several months of wandering that he recognised his mistake and the uncongenial surroundings in which he found himself. He thought that the stage would enable him to realise his poetical feelings, but his experiences proved to be prosaic and sometimes repulsive. His past life, his education and his aims, marked him out for a different career. He was familiar with, and admired, the great Latin, Greek, French and German poets. His culture, therefore, was far above that of his illiterate fellow-actors.

His temperament, too, differed from that required for an actor's life. He was tender-hearted, timid, over-sensitive and contemplative, and his manners were awkward. Such qualities make it difficult enough to succeed on the stage of real life, and still more difficult on the theatrical stage. And yet, what efforts he made to be useful to the company! He copied the play-bills and carried them round to people's houses. He repaired the scenery, painted the curtain, and supplied the thunder by rattling sheets of iron, and the cannonade of the battles by thumping the floor with heavy sticks. During the day he went about borrowing furniture and other requisites, and in the evening lit the lamps of the theatre. At night, when the performance was over, he was left in charge of the theatre, which was really an empty store-room belonging to a manufacturer, and then, gathering up the remnants of the rushlights, and making a couch of odd garments from the wardrobe, he would commence reading Horace, the poet of the refined pleasures of life.

Sometimes, however, he was assigned a good part in one of the plays, and then he was much applauded by the not over-numerous audience (and how many even of them had free tickets!) for he recited well, with real feeling and warmth. It was on an evening such as this, that his name first appeared upon the play-bill, that name which was to become the pride of a nation—JOHN ARANY (1817–1882).

At length his doubts as to whether he had chosen the right career grew too strong to allow him to remain where he was. What was he to do ? Should he return to the college at Debreczen which he had left with such high hopes, confess that he was disillusioned and beg to be admitted again ? No ! That was impossible. Yet what other course was open to him. While he pondered, there arose before his imagination a picture of the little thatched cottage of his parents at Nagy Szalonta, which had always seemed to him like a temple, for he had never heard there a word that was ignoble. He seemed to see his father, the honest, God-fearing peasant, who had taught him when a child of three or four years, to trace his letters in the ashes, for lack of writing paper, and had even imparted to him the elements of Latin grammar. How proud his father had been of his boy. Could he dare to return to his parents now, after causing them so much grief by becoming a strolling player ? Stay longer with his free-and-easy companions he would not, yet there seemed to be nowhere else to go. In deep despondency he used every day to make for the outskirts of the town of Marmaros Sziget and seek for solitude in the dense pine forests on the banks of the Iza, undaunted by the bears which roamed the forest, and plucking the bramble berries for his food. During one of these excursions he fell asleep, worn out with anxiety. In a dream he beheld his mother lying dead. This decided him. He frequently acted under the impulse of dreams, and their influence is to be seen in his poetry, especially in his ballads.

As so often happens with very poetical natures, his acts were guided by his imagination rather than by his reason. His decision once made, he set off to Szalonta as though driven homeward by an irresistible instinct. It happened to be the actors' pay-day, and Arany waited in the street, until the manager came, when he asked for a small instalment of his monthly salary of twenty-five florins, but was ashamed to announce his determination to leave the stage for ever. He packed his few belongings in a handkerchief, bought for a few kreuzers a small loaf and some bacon, cut a staff in the forest, and started for home on foot. Noontide found him on the high road, and towards sunset he reached the beech forests, where he fell in with a long line of carts carrying salt from Rónaszék.

To those who questioned him he replied in Wallachian that he was making for home because he was ill. The carters halted for the night at the top of a hill, where they unharnessed their horses and made a large fire in the warmth of which they allowed the poor strolling actor to sleep.

At dawn he arose, and with a hasty farewell to his rough companions, resumed his journey. Next night he arrived at a roadside inn, and the landlord gave him permission to sleep on a wooden bench, beneath the bare branches of a tree, with his bundle containing the loaf of bread for a pillow. The succeeding nights were spent in a somewhat similar way.

Yet the roving student-actor did not despair amidst his hardships. His heart was full of songs of youth and love. He was conscious of the romance of his wandering, as well as of its fatigue.

Soon the hills were left behind and his way led through

the oak-clad plains. At length he reached the marshy district of Ecsed and crossed the bridge, where he met a gendarme, who looked with some suspicion upon the poor wanderer.

But Arany's troubles were not yet over. The way to his native village of Szalonta led across the hot, sandy plains straight to Debreczen. But he would not for the world meet any of his former professors or fellow-students. How condescendingly they would pity him if they knew that after surrendering his rank as a college student to become astrolling player, he had been unsuccessful.

He dared not go near the college but passed along the back streets. His store of food was exhausted, and bodily fatigue was added to the grief and shame which tortured him. When he came to the houses of country pastors, which were always open to travellers, he was afraid to put his hand to the latch lest the pastor should ask him, "What are you doing here, you tramp?" He felt keenly in his own person all the misery of home-lessness which he afterwards described so vividly in the story of Nicholas Toldi.

How strange is life! A few years later another young actor was wandering through the same district. He too had given up a college career and obtained in exchange a life full of privations. He tramped along, but although he was hungry, ill, and cold, a prophecy of future great-ness gleamed in his large bright eyes. This second actor, who later on became Arany's most intimate friend and his equal in genius, was Alexander Petőfi. At last, after two days' walking, Arany arrived at Szalonta. His relatives and friends met him either with reproaches or with sarcasm. His less intimate acquaintances regarded him with suspicion.

His father, a simple old peasant, had become blind while his son was roaming about the world. His mother, who received him with joy, died a few weeks after his arrival. Arany suffered the pangs of remorse. What was he to do ? What would become of him ? His whole life seemed destined to be a failure. In addition to the mental trouble, he had taken a chill during his ramblings, and the pains in his chest were so severe that he felt sure that he was about to die. This period was the first great crisis in his life. He sat opposite his poor blind father, in the cheerless house, with a crushed and hopeless heart.

And yet he lived down his troubles and overcame his difficulties. The people about him were mistaken in thinking him a degraded man. His gentle and beautiful nature, and his sincerity won the hearts of all who learnt to know him, while his sound knowledge and his industry gained him their esteem. The clergyman of the town had often said : "No strolling comedian shall be a teacher here," yet young Arany was soon elected teacher at the grammar school. Although he felt their reproaches to be unjust, he made strenuous efforts to amend the faults for which people censured him. He threw his poems into the fire, bade adieu to the Muses who had led him astray, and resolved to be an industrious, ordinary man.

Four years after his adventures as an actor, he was elected notary to the town. He was then twenty-three years of age. In the same year, following the leading of his heart as well as of common sense, he married, and his married life proved a very happy one.

But he was not able to keep his resolve of becoming ordinary. For some time he suppressed his poetic instincts. The only writings which came from his pen were carefully drawn legal documents. But soon after the entrance of good fortune into his house, another visitor pressed for admittance, and that visitor was Poetry. First he wrote a long satirical epic poem about the oddities of provincial administration and provincial life, entitled *The Lost Constitution*. He sent it anonymously to the Kisfaludy Society on the occasion of a literary competition, and to his intense astonishment he won the prize. Arany had not, however, found his true self in that work. The poem is full of brilliant but cold wit; it glistens like icicles in the sunshine.

In the next year (1846) he competed for the prize with another poem. This time it was the great epic, *Toldi*, and he was again successful. In addition to the prize, moreover, he won what he valued still more, the suddenly awakened sympathy of Petőfi. Petőfi was all fire and flame while reading *Toldi*. Though he did not know the author, he wrote him a letter in verse, saying that he was sending his own soul across the intervening miles to greet the creator of *Toldi*. "All other poets have gained their laurels leaf by leaf, but to thee we must give a wreath at once." What attracted him so powerfully in Arany was not only a kindred greatness, but also a kindred popular tendency.

In June 1847, Petőfi went to see Arany, and Hungary's two greatest poets spent ten happy days in the humble home of the notary of Szalonta. "The chords of my lyre were ardent in emulation, and flame was kindled by flame," wrote Arany. He read to his friend the continuation of his *Toldi*, called *Toldi's Eve*, dealing with the old age of the hero, Nicholas Toldi. But this perfectly constructed epic was not published until several years later. In the course of the same year, Petőfi went once more to see Arany, this time taking his young wife with him, six weeks after their marriage.

The epoch of the war for freedom (1848–49) formed a great crisis in Arany's life. For some time he was the editor of a revolutionary paper on behalf of the Hungarian Government. In 1848 he enlisted for a time in the yeomanry. Next year he was obliged to resign his position of notary, as in consequence of the war and the devastation it caused, the town was unable to pay its employees. For some time he obtained occupation as a clerk, but the catastrophe of 1849 and the bloody suppression of the revolution deprived him of that employment.

After Hungary's defeat, Arany was in the depths of despair. He had lost his position, lost his slowly but steadily increasing capital, lost his idolised friend Petőfi, and lost all confidence in himself. He no longer believed in the future of his country nor in his own. " I fled like one chased ; fled from my own soul," he said, " no hope was to be seen anywhere in the heavens, only despair, which withheld me from lifting up my hands to those heavens."

In 1851 he was offered a professorship at a college in the typical lowland town of Nagy Kőrös. He accepted it and filled the post for nine years. As a professor, he was conscientious and untiring, and he made some valued friends among the staff, but he did not seem to strike root in Nagy Kőrös. At first his heart drew him towards Szalonta, where he had spent his childhood, but later on he began to wish to go to the capital. " What a cheerless place this Nagy Kőrös is," he wrote in a letter. " Our only resource and amusement is to go to the cemetery. It is only there under the shady trees, that we can taste the freshness of spring. Among the graves—perhaps that is partly the reason why I so rarely feel cheerful here."

None of his more important works were written during his stay in Nagy Kőrös. His chief productions were lyrical poems, but his ballads belong to this period, the years 1853 and 1855 especially having been "two years of ballads," which have become famous in the history of Hungarian literature.

In 1860 Austria was defeated in her war with Italy. Then all at once the breezes of a new spring-time began to stir the political life of Hungary. Austria's frigid absolutism commenced to thaw. The frozen wells of the national life once more bubbled and sparkled.

Arany went to the capital, and became director of the Kisfaludy Society and the editor of a critical weekly periodical. He was full of activity and animation, and seemed to be endowed with a second youth. In 1864 appeared one of the greatest of his works, *The Death of Buda*, a heroic epic based upon the Hun myths and the story of King Attila; in the same year he was appointed secretary to the Academy.

But now a great blow fell upon him. In 1865 his married daughter, Juliet, died at the age of twenty-four. Arany had loved her more dearly than any one else in the whole world. When his daughter was quite a young girl he wrote the little poem, so full of deep feeling, *To Juliet*.

"Though autumn may seem sad, with its falling leaves and silent woods, yet it has its consolations and its melancholy charm. The fruit is falling, true, but it has ripened. True, the woods are silent, but they have had their summer-time, musical with the carolling of birds.

Though the meadow be covered with snow, yet it has had its time of grass and flowers. But if flowers die in the bud, and if the new-born hope of spring die without summer's fulfilment, then indeed is there cause for sorrow. Oh, be glad, bright youthful spirit. Be thy true self. Thou art not yet strong enough to bear the weight of winter's snow."

When the girl died, his friends tried to console the bereaved father by telling him that time would soothe his sorrow, but years afterwards he said : " My grief is like a great weight, the longer I bear it the more it oppresses me." For nearly ten years he did not publish a single poem.

Then his fame rapidly increased. He became wealthy too, from the numerous new editions of his works, and his lucrative appointments. The king presented him with the Order of St. Stephen, a distinction which confers a rank equal to that of a baron. But after his daughter's death, Arany was never the same man that he had been before. Amidst the turmoil of the capital, he lived like a stranger. Although he was in the foremost ranks of the men of genius and learning, in the magnificent building of the Academy he was always dreaming of his little native village, and " of a cottage which my fond fancy is ever building there."

Three years before his death, Arany published *Toldi's Love*, the central portion of his great trilogy, dealing with his hero's manhood. Thus, at the age of sixty-two, he completed the work which he began at twenty-nine.

Once, in the spring of 1882, he scribbled on a slip of paper in his quietly humorous way : " In the sixty-sixth year of my life, God will reap me like ripe corn, and lay me in His barn that is awaiting me, and will sow new seed in my place."

And so it was. The ripe corn was garnered on October 22, 1882.

Arany's work had its roots in the Hungarian popular poetry, and reflects the life and thoughts of the people. His writings, and those of Petőfi, may, in fact, be regarded as a glorification of the popular ballads and tales. Petőfi took the character of his songs and his lyric style, while Arany owed to them his rich language and epic style. Petőfi possessed a thoroughly lyrical nature; he was always swayed by his feelings and could look on nothing in a calm, dispassionate manner. Arany, on the other hand, concealed his feelings and appeared tranquil even when deeply moved. He observed the world accurately on the whole, but he saw all things in a somewhat gloomy light. The chief features of his poetry are its realism and its pondering over the past. It is remarkable that so much objectivity and sobriety should be blended with such strong and deep feeling.

To gain a glimpse of his inmost soul we should turn to his poem called *Epilogue*, written towards the end of his life while looking back over his past career. He had struggled for perfection in poetry and had often felt defeated. " The secret blight," he said, " which mars my efforts is my eternal doubt, and the results I have achieved burn me like the blood of Nessos."

Arany wrote two great epics. The hero of one is a man of the Middle Ages, the mighty Nicholas Toldi. The other deals with the Hun kings, Attila and Buda. Each poem consists of three parts, but only the Toldi trilogy was completed.

The first part of *Toldi* is only concerned with a few

days in the hero's life. The subject was taken from an old sixteenth-century rhymed chronicle, but Arany greatly improved it, giving the events their psychological basis, and linking the fragmentary incidents of the chronicle by an inner thread of motive. In the old narrative of Ilosvay the hero is a peasant lad of immense strength. Arany's hero is the younger son of a country family of some standing, a noble-minded youth, but brought up to work almost like a peasant on the family estate. Through his trials and sufferings, he is ennobled and made a true knight. There are two brothers, George and Nicholas Toldi. The elder, George, who lives at the Court of Louis the Great, keeps his younger brother on the estate in order that he shall always remain a farmer ; otherwise he does not treat him harshly. George comes with his retinue to visit his mother, and in a masterly scene the two brothers are brought face to face, and passionate words pass. George scoffs at his brother until the youth maddened by insults, seizes the mill-stone on which he has been sitting in a remote corner of the courtyard and flings it among his brother's servants, unfortunately killing one of them.

Nicholas then leaves the house, feeling that he must atone for this action by noble deeds. After several days' wandering he arrives at Pest, where, at a tournament, he defeats a Bohemian knight who has been victor in many combats during the previous days. Louis the Great knights him for winning back the country's trophy, while the elder brother is punished for certain misdeeds.

The struggles of a noble nature, the pardonable fault, and the final triumph of the youth, are symbolical of the poet's own life, for he had to endure many a hardship before success was attained.

Toldi was the first epic, in which subject, language and characters were all popular. It made a great stir in the literary world and was awarded the Kisfaludy Society's prize. Every one admired the simplicity of the means by which Arany produced his remarkable poetical effects. There was none of the elaborate grandeur of the old classical epics ; there was no artificial rhetoric and no invocation of the Muse.

The language of *Toldi* far excels the flat and lustreless diction of most contemporary scholars and poets. It was as though Arany had discovered an idiom previously unknown. He was profoundly versed in his mother tongue. When we read his writings we seem to hear the rippling of the hidden sources of the Hungarian language. His native tongue, like every other language, was full of old and hackneyed figurative expressions, to which he gave new life and colour.

The second part of *Toldi*, which came third in order of publication, appearing only towards the end of the poet's life, shows us Nicholas Toldi as a man in the prime of life. We read of his chivalric adventures, of his one great love, and of his inward conflicts, more strenuous even than his feats of arms.

His love for Piroska is the chief subject of this part of the poem. The hand of the fair Piroska is offered as the prize at a tournament, and Toldi, out of thoughtless good nature, consents to aid a companion in arms by fighting in his place, with visor down, and carrying his friend's shield and colours. In this manner, contrary to all the rules of chivalry, he wins Piroska for Lorincz Tar. From this deed springs the great tragedy of Toldi's life, for too late he learns to love the lady and to repent the deceit which made her the wife of another.

Toldi's misery, the death of Tar and of Piroska follow in dramatic succession.

Arany wove into his poem the campaign of King Louis the Great against Naples (1347–1350), a classical example of the campaigns of the Middle Ages, full of incident and romance. Joan, the beautiful but immoral queen of Naples, had had her young husband, Prince Andrew, the brother of Louis the Great, murdered. Louis marched into Italy to avenge his brother's death, and occupied Naples, and Nicholas Toldi, in order to forget his own love-sorrow, accompanied the King.

The third part of the trilogy is *Toldi's Eve*, or old age. Nicholas Toldi lives in retirement in his decaying house and weedy garden. His king, Louis, who is an Angevin, feels resentment against him because he despises the polish and specious splendour of his Court. Toldi is out of favour and forgotten, and his only companion is his faithful old squire and servant, Bencze. In the opening scene old Bencze is helping his master to dig his own grave. Suddenly, a visitor arrives at the house, a thing which rarely happens now. It is a herald, who has come to tell the old hero that an insolent Italian knight has defeated all the Hungarian champions at the tournaments, has taken possession of the country's shield, and scoffs at Hungarian valour, boasting that he will carry the trophy home. That is enough for Toldi. The old lion becomes young again, as if by enchantment, and is eager for the fray. He sets out, disguised in the habit of a monk. The lists are surrounded by a vast concourse of people, all of them in terrible suspense since no new champion appears against the Italian. But all at once the heralds give a signal as a gigantic old monk arrives on horseback. He is a curious apparition, and his squire still more so. The squire's horse is as old and as gaunt as his rider's weapons are rusty, and his garments are old-fashioned and shabby. When the people see his rusty weapons they mock him and ask him if he sells them as old iron. The boys tease the old horse, which soon comes to a standstill, and on turning round the poor squire finds that they are holding on to its tail. When the old monk hears the laughter, he turns round and shakes his huge lance at the crowd, whirling it above his head as though it were a lath, so that mockery gives place to awe.

Some whisper that this apparition can be nothing but the ghost of Toldi. The unknown monk conquers the Italian in a masterly fought combat, and then suddenly disappears with his squire by some by-way, and makes for an old house of his in the town. His skill in fighting had made it evident to all the knights and to the crowd, that the monk was no other than Toldi. They stream to his house to bring him in triumph to the king, who is willing to be reconciled with the old hero. But the excitement proves fatal to the old man, who is one of those who "die of their own temperament."

In the king's ante-room some pages sing an ironical song about some old adventure of Toldi. Excited and indignant, the hero whirls round his mace and kills one of the singers. The king is grievously offended, and when Toldi leaves the Court, sends soldiers after him to take him prisoner. The messengers, however, find that he is dying, and the king, much shaken by the news, hastens to Toldi's house.

The aged monarch and aged hero are face to face. Toldi knows that to the ambitious but luxury-loving king his advice was often "a bitter medicine given in a rough wooden spoon," but even now he counsels him to love

16

the nation but not to weaken it by too much planing and polishing. He dies reminding the king of his sacred trust, the future of a people ; and soon the plain and strong iron coffin of the hero rests in the grave dug with his own hands. Toldi feels that he is out of place in a world filled with new thoughts and sentiments, and so the last, venerable oak of a vanished forest falls.

Toldi's Eve is a "humorous" epic in the best sense of the word. It possesses the kind of humour which is akin to pathos and tears. Over the whole poem there broods something of the smiling melancholy of autumn, of slow universal decay, in the strength of the hero as in the season, and although we cannot help smiling at the old squire, and even at Toldi himself sometimes, yet we honour and love them.

An important feature of Arany's work is his creation of typically Hungarian characters. If the true Hungarian type were ever lost, it could be revived with the aid of Arany's poems. He touched the very depths of the Hungarian character in creating Nicholas Toldi. Just as the sculptor of the Laocoon selected a powerfully built figure in order to exhibit pain in all its intensity, Arany chose a man of gigantic strength as a means of depicting the convulsions of passion. Every impulse awoke a more powerful response in Toldi than in other men. Toldi is eminently fiery and impulsive and his great physical strength adds to the force of those characteristics. Yet withal he has the most delicate sense of honour and the kindest heart. When roused to fury, he grasps a millstone and hurls it at his tormentors. When living for a time in a monastery, he threatens the prior and his fellow monks because they mock him.

His gaiety, like his wrath, is unrestrained. Even when

he is an old man the same features may be still discerned, although they are toned down by age. The
old hero who, at the Court of Louis, chastises the pages,
reminds us of the young Toldi who punished his brother's
squires. A man who is easily roused and is moreover of
a full-blooded habit, is very likely to suffer from over-
excitement, and to die of a fit of passion. The knight
Toldi who seeks to forget his bitter grief in revelry, recalls
the young lad whom we saw drinking in the inn on the
eve of his first combat. How natural it is that Toldi
could not appreciate the Italian culture of the Court, and
the dawning of the Renaissance. He, who had been
brought up as a farmer, was not likely as a soldier to
educate himself and take to ultra-refined Italian habits,
especially as in his early years he had fought against the
Italians, so that to his naïve soldier's mind it seemed impossible to make friends with a former foe. The polished
surroundings of the king tamed the lion from time to
time, but the last stab goaded him to wildness again.
However, like the lion, he can be noble as well as
formidable. He is one of those in whom proneness to
anger is linked with great sensitiveness. How tender
and faithful he is to his king, to his mother, to the lady
he loves, and to his old servant. In the soil of his nature
everything grows to great proportions, like one of our
plants in a tropical region. What is a small rose-bush
with us becomes there a huge tree.

Toldi is a perfect knight. His strong Christian feeling,
his loyalty to his king, his respect for women, his kindness towards the oppressed and the defenceless, in short,
all that made up the duty of a knight in the Middle Ages,
had not been learnt from masters of chivalry, but was
native in him. Wherever there is trouble, an instinct

prompts him to help. When he sees a widow, weeping at her murdered husband's tomb, he promises to avenge her. When a wild bull tears along the street, Toldi steps forth calmly to meet him as though merely performing an ordinary duty. He pursues a knight who has carried off a lady to the innermost recesses of his castle. On meeting a carriage which has fallen into a ditch, he puts his shoulder under the wheel and lifts it up.

He is always ready to risk his life for his king, even after they have quarrelled. Altogether he is one of those who do everything with their whole soul. Toldi the soldier belongs body and soul to his duty. Toldi the lover is penetrated to the centre of his being by the bitter-sweet feeling of his love.

Every man possesses the qualities which belong to him as the member of a particular nation, as an individual and as a unit of humanity in general. In Toldi, not only the national and the individual interest us, we are attracted by the universal human element in him. We are not merely touched by his loyalty, and love and filial affection ; his career may be regarded as a symbol of human life in general. Paul Gyulai referring to Toldi, asked, " Which of us has not experienced in youth that same restless desire to achieve something, driving him from the family circle out into the wide world ? Who does not remember a mother who watched him with an anxious heart, and felt an uplifting sense of triumph at his first success ? Who has not, on the threshold of manhood, been guilty of some indiscretion which has caused suffering to others, all unintended it may be, so that a hidden wound pains him even when he is otherwise happy ? And when we are old, and our hopes have become remembrances, and the burning flame of desire has died out in ashes ; when death has torn our loved ones from our side and we begin to feel out of place in a world which either has forgotten us or mocks us in the pride of its new ideas, do we not all resemble in some respects the aged Toldi ? "

But what perhaps attracts us most in this noble-minded giant is his highly sensitive conscience. Every fault finds its merciless judge in his own soul. In the first part of the epic the young Toldi unintentionally commits a crime, and then goes straight to the king at Buda, to receive either punishment or pardon. He cannot rest while there is a stain upon his character. In the second part, when Toldi breaks the rules of chivalry by fighting under another's colours and winning the hand of a lady for his friend, and when too late his own passion awakes and gives him infinite pain, it is still the pangs of an uneasy conscience from which he suffers most. Alike in his ballads and in his *Toldi* conscience is king and judge.

Piroska, the most charming of Arany's characters, and drawn with most love on the poet's part, is thoroughly Hungarian. A German poet, in depicting the heroine of so sad a love story, would have made her sentimental, but Arany paints her as a woman of deep feeling, strong and never sentimental.

Arany's work is characterised by its realism. The poet never lost sight of reality even in the highest soarings of his imagination. Whatever he described is so exactly depicted even in its details that we almost fancy he actually saw what he described. Here is one instance among many. Toldi listens sorrowfully to the news brought by his faithful servant. Another poet might have merely said that Toldi's eyes were full of tears, but Arany tells us that " A warm, heavy tear trembled in his eye, and as he, ashamed of his weakness, tried to wipe it away unnoticed with the palm of his hand, it trickled down his little finger."

Another characteristic is his way of presenting a mental phenomenon by means of its effects upon the body. He describes the impotent wrath of George Toldi, for example, as follows : " All the blood rushed to his head, so that he could only see indistinctly, although it was broad daylight. The statues seemed to dance around him as he nearly fell in his giddiness. Then a cold wave seemed to run down his body. How cold he was ; and yet how the beads of perspiration stood out upon his forehead. Then slowly his face became ashy pale, as if there were not so much blood left in him as would furnish one sip for a gnat." That description offers a concise physiology of anger.

The Hun kings form the subject of another trilogy. *Buda's Death* is the title of the first part. In this, Arany combined the fragments from various old chronicles into one great whole and described the combat between the two brothers, Attila and Buda. What the Arthurian legends were for Tennyson, an inexhaustible fount of inspiration, the Hun and Magyar chronicles were for Arany.

According to those chronicles, the Huns were the ancestors of the Hungarians, so that when the Hungarians entered Europe in the tenth century and occupied their country, they were really taking possession of their Hun inheritance, and Arany accepted this theory of the relationship between Huns and Hungarians. After Attila's death, say the chroniclers, his two sons Csaba and Aladár struggled for the crown, the Goths siding with Aladár and the Huns with Csaba.

In the Hungarian traditions the historical Bléda, who appears in the *Nibelungen-Lied*, under the name of Bloedelin, is called Buda. This King divided his kingdom into two parts and gave one to his younger brother Attila. The folly of this policy soon became apparent, for the energetic, chivalrous and able Attila rapidly acquired power and fame, while Buda became the mere shadow of a king.

These differences were accentuated by their respective queens, for Ildikó, the wife of Attila, offended Buda's wife, Gyöngyvér. Their quarrel poisoned the relations between the two brothers, until the sword was invoked to settle the matter. Attila attacked the town which the king had built and which had been named Buda after him, and slew his brother, thus gaining the throne for himself.

The second part of the trilogy is called *Ildikó*, and the third, of which there are but a few fragments, is *Prince Csaba*. The background of this epic is one of the greatest events in history.

The crisis in the war between the Huns and the Germanic races was the battle of Châlons. Had the result of that battle been different, it might have altered the course of European history. Eastern races instead of western would probably have been the masters of Europe.

The whole plan of Arany's epic, had he completed it, would have been as follows : Attila kills his brother, but he himself is soon murdered by his wife, the German Ildikó (Krimhield). In the battle between his two sons, Csaba conquers Aladár, but later on he is compelled to leave Europe and return to the original home of the Huns in Asia.

The Huns leave behind them the Székely race, however,

as a kind of guard over the country. At the end of the poem Arany intended to cast a glance into the future, when the Hungarians should return and enter into possession of the legacy of the Huns, the present kingdom of Hungary.

Arany created a great variety of poetic atmospheres in his epic poems. In the first part of *Toldi* we are wrapt in the golden sunshine of the broad, wheat-growing Lowlands. Everything is boldly drawn and clearly outlined. The second, *Toldi's Love,* is full of the mystic silver moonlight of romance, and the subjective feelings of the poet are revealed. The third, *Toldi's Eve,* is bathed in the melancholy light of an autumn sunset.

The whole tone is different in *Buda's Death.* The poem has a kind of antique *patina* over it ; its style is concise, and archaic, as though written by a contemporary of Attila, and yet by one who possessed the culture of the nineteenth century. Arany's epics do not differ in style only, but also in the drawing of the characters. Arany made an innovation in the epic by his introduction of minute psychological analysis. He not only gives us the deeds of his heroes and their motives, but he points out clearly what feelings and what passions have led them to act as they do. He shows what these feelings are, how they shape themselves, and what elements are mingled in the soul of the hero.

Arany's poetry reached its highest perfection, perhaps, in his ballads. A famous critic called Arany the Shakespeare of the ballad. Here, too, the poet's work was based upon the popular poetry and tales, and he took as his models both the Scottish and the Transylvanian ballads. The dialogue form prevails in the popular ballad, it is not the poet who tells the story, but the characters themselves, and thus the poem is invested with a dramatic interest. A dim, mystic light pervades everything, and the action is strongly tragic. In each of Arany's ballads some great crime is portrayed, with an equally great punishment resulting from the working of the offender's own mind or conscience.

This led Arany to the frequent description of madness. His ballads show many examples of insanity, all accurately drawn in their physiological and psychological aspects.

Arany's ballads answer to the definition of a ballad as a tragedy told in song. Here is an example :

BOR THE HERO.

Shadows of the dying day
  On the quiet valley fell,
Bor the Hero rode away—
  " Sweet and fair one, fare thee well."

Shadows on the valley fell,
  Wind-swept branches stir and strain,
' Sweet and fair one, fare thee well,"
  Bor the Hero rides amain.

Wind-swept branches stir and strain,
  Lo ! a lark is singing near,
Bor the Hero rides amain,
  Silent falls the maiden's tear.

Lo ! a lark is singing near,
  Whither wends its soaring flight ?
Falls the maiden's silent tear,
  Bidden now her troth to plight.

Whither wends that soaring flight ?
  Darkness mingles earth and sky,
" Daughter, haste, thy troth to plight !
  There is none to make reply.

Darkness mingles earth and sky,
  Ghostly shapes the forest fill,
There is none to make reply,
  " Come ! " 'Tis Bor that whispers still.

Ghostly shapes the forest fill,
  Forms that beckon and invite,
" Come ! " 'Tis Bor that whispers still.
  The beloved, the phantom Knight.

Spirit lips a chant intone,
  Ghostly whispers stir her blood,
" My dear spouse, O ! mine alone,
  Take me wheresoe'er you would."

See ! a train in bridal weeds
  Nears a fane of hoary stone,
Now the marriage rite proceeds,
  " My dear spouse, O ! mine alone."

Near the fane of hoary stone
  Gleams a light transcending day,
Spirit lips a chant intone,
  Festal robes the priest array.

With a light transcending day,
  Ruined aisle and altar shine,
Festal robes the priest array,
  " Now, Beloved, thou art mine."

Gleams a mystic, radiant light,
  Darkness folds the world beside,
Deathless vows the twain unite,
  Ah ! how deathly pale the bride.

Darkness mingles earth and sky
  Hark ! a frighted owlet cried !
Cold in death, the altar nigh,
  Lay the young and lovely bride.

The origin of some of the ballads may be explained by
the circumstances of his life. After the war for freedom, the
grief of the patriot was added to his natural melancholy

While that state of mind prevailed he had not perseverance enough to write a long poem, yet he was full of inspiration, and being thus urged in the direction of epic poetry, he composed his short epics, the ballads.

Arany's ballads are amongst the masterpieces of Hungarian poetry. Their subjects were all taken from Hungarian history, with one exception, *The Bards of Wales;* and curiously enough, although the subject is English, it had a distinctly Hungarian significance. It was inspired by an incident characteristic of the time of absolutism (1849-1860), called after the hated Austrian minister, *The Bach era.* Despotism made a bid for popularity and desired laurels which only a poet can bind into a wreath. Its instruments wished for an ode in praise of the absolute monarch. They secretly approached the chief Hungarian poets, promising them large sums of money, as well as favour, but all declined the task. They went to Arany, who was a professor in a country town, but he rejected their offer with scorn. This attitude of the Hungarian poets is idealised in *The Bards of Wales.* The subject of the poem is briefly as follows :

King Edward visits Wales after it has been subjugated by means of terrible bloodshed. Here the owner of Montgomery Castle entertained him in princely fashion, but no bard is found willing to extol the tyrant in the banqueting-hall. Moved to wrath the King gives orders that every bard who refused a song in his praise shall be executed. Five hundred bards lose their lives. But the King, on arriving home, is tormented by visions, and is unable to sleep. The death songs of the martyr bards resound in his ears until he is at last driven to madness.

The most dramatic of Arany's ballads is his *Call to the Ordeal.*

The Captive Stork, though not a ballad, is also an allegory belonging to the same period.

THE CAPTIVE STORK.*

A lonely captive stork doth stand,
With courtyard walls on every hand ;
*　Fain would he wing his flight afar ;*
Across the sea
His way would be,
*　But pinions clipped his soaring bar.*

He stands upon one foot to dream ;
Then shifts it ; weary he doth seem.
*　Thus changing he the time doth spend—*
Naught else to do
The whole day through,
*　Save shift and change without an end.*

His head beneath his wing he lays ;
Into the distance he would gaze ;
*　In vain ; four walls are round about.*
Four walls of brick,
So high and thick,
*　'Tis vain to strive to pierce without.*

True, he could look up to the sky,
But no desire directs his eye ;
*　Free storks above fly far away,*
Fair lands to see,
While vainly he
*　Both long to end his doomed stay.*

He waits, waits ever, still in vain,
That his maimed wings may grow again,
*　So he can high in heaven soar ;*
There, where his way
No limits stay,
*　Free homelands he can travel o'er.*

The country glows with autumn sheen,
But no more storks at all are seen,

* LOEW'S " Magyar Poetry."

Save one poor loiterer, who doth dwell—
A captive left,
Of freedom reft,
  Immured within a narrow cell.

The cranes have not yet made their start.
But even they will soon depart.
  He sees them not : he only hears
Too well above
The notes thereof—
  The birds of passage in his ears.

Once and again he even tries
Upon his crippled wings to rise.
  Ah ! they would raise him up on high,
Nor hold him low
Were it not so
  That they were clipped so cruelly.

Poor orphan stork, poor stork, 'tis vain ;
Thy pinions ne'er will grow again,
  Even though winter should be o'er,
For if they grew
False men anew
  Would clip them even as before.

Arany and Petőfi stood side by side in life, and together they stand in the history of Hungarian poetry as the most striking incarnations of the Hungarian spirit. The world of Hungarian sentiment and character is revealed in their works, but purified in the sacred fire of poetry. The sun of the nation's literature, which dawned so brightly in 1825, when Vörösmarty's *Zalán's Flight* appeared, attained its zenith in them.

This was the case with the public estimation of Tompa. Tompa began to write at the same time as Arany and Petőfi, the latter of whom was his friend. His writings were of a similar tendency and his talent was of the same genus. It is not surprising, therefore, that he was considered the equal of the other two members of the triad. Yet, though a significant and powerful writer, posterity has come to recognise that he was not so original as Petőfi or Arany.

MICHAEL TOMPA (1817–1868) spent his life as a Calvinistic minister in the small country town of Hamva. He was by nature remarkably sensitive and his meditations were of an elegiac turn. His life was full of trials. Poverty and loneliness sat by his cradle. His father was a poor shoemaker and his mother died when he was a baby. The boy could only enter the high school by means of money earned by serving as fag to a wealthy youth. At school he once suffered a deep humiliation, for at the age of twenty his professor ordered him to be caned, and as a consequence he soon left the school. Both his sons died early, and he himself suffered from a lingering disease. His lyric poems reveal a soul refined and exalted by suffering.

During the fifties, the years of absolutism, the allegory was very much used, for poets dared not say all they meant, and so they concealed it in allegory. Tompa's most famous poems were of this character, and he was threatened with imprisonment on account of them. In a poem entitled *To the Stork*, he says : " Spring is here and the stork has returned to her old nest. But thou art deceived, oh bird, for here with us there is no spring. Fly back again to happier skies. Seek not our meadows, for they have become cemeteries. Stand not in the waters of our lakes, for they are mingled with blood. Dwell not upon our roofs, for fiery brands are on them. Return to the south, for thou art happier than we. To thee God has given two countries ; we had but one, and have lost even that. Fly away, and if in those southern regions thou shouldst chance to meet those who have had to leave this their fatherland, tell them that we are decaying, diminishing, falling to pieces like an unbound sheaf."

In another allegory Tompa makes a bird speak to her young ones, thus symbolising the country's appeal to her poets.

THE BIRD TO ITS BROOD.*

How long, ye birds, on this sere bough
    Will ye sit mute, as though in tears ?
Not quite forgotten yet are now
    The songs I taught ye, surely, dears ;
But if for aye are vanquished quite
    Your former cheer, your song so gay,
A sad and wistful tune recite—
    Oh, children, sing to me, I pray !

A storm has raged ; our rocks apart
    Are rent ; glad shade you cannot find ;
And are ye mute, about to start
    And leave your mother sad behind ?
In other climes new songs are heard,
    Where none would understand your lay,
Though empty is your home and bared—
    Yet, children, sing to me, I pray !

In memory of this hallowed bower,
    Shady and green, call forth a strain,
And greet the time when soon in flower
    These barren fields shall bloom again ;
So, at your song, anew shall life
    Over this plain, with ease, make way,
Sweetening the day with sorrow rife,—
    Oh, children, sing to me, I pray !

Here in the tree is the old nest
    Where you were cherished lovingly ;
Return to it, and therein rest,

* Loew's " Magyar Poetry."

Albeit among the clouds you fly ;
Now that the storm has laid it bare,
Would you the traits of men display ?
Leaving this place, your home transfer ?
Oh, children, sing to me, I pray !

Tompa wrote many simple and charming songs, some of them too closely resembling in style the popular songs, but that is easily explicable by the fact that during the forties, when he commenced to write, the popular style was in fashion. He extolled the Lowlands, as Petőfi did, but he felt, as Petőfi did not, that much of their romantic glory had departed. The Lowlands of the chivalrous highwaymen, the lowlands over which a deep peace seemed to brood undisturbed, have gone, and we see railroads, cornfields, plantations and farm-buildings everywhere. Petőfi, Arany and Tompa treated the Lowlands like painters who hasten to sketch an interesting old house, full of romance, before it is destroyed. They immortalised them in their primeval state, before they had changed their character. " Ye Lowlands," says Tompa, " but a little while and your wild poetic beauty will have vanished. Where the vast herds of cattle were wont to roam and untamed horses scampered at large in the waves of the mirage, the shepherd's fires will soon be extinguished and his pipe be mute for ever."

In Tompa's lyrics, besides the allegorical and popular features due to the age in which he wrote, there is an element of sadness due to the vicissitudes of his life, and a religious element emphasised by his occupation as a minister.

A separate class of his poems consists of " flower tales," tales in which flowers act like living persons according to the characters with which the imagination generally endows them—*fleurs animées.* This is a charming *genre* both in poetry and in painting, but if overdone, gives an impression of artificiality and affected sweetness. Tompa is much more fresh and bracing in his versified narratives, in which he takes an anecdote and transforms it into true poetry.

XVI

TELEKI AND MADÁCH

COUNT TELEKI (1811–1861), a distinguished statesman, whose life was occupied by political duties, wrote, however, an extraordinarily fine tragedy, *The Favourite*.

Its scene was laid in Rome under the Emperor Valentinian, during the period of her decay, and the subject was taken from Gibbon's history. The drama is really the story of a terrible vengeance. Petronius Maximus, in a game of dice, loses his wife to the emperor. The winner lures the lady, who is ignorant of what has occurred, into his palace, but she escapes and saves her honour. Petronius, however, does not believe her to be innocent and resolves to be revenged upon the emperor. First he gains his confidence and then compels his wife, whom he regards as guilty, to become the emperor's mistress. Then he poisons the emperor's mind and stirs his resentment against his friends, and when several of these have been unjustly put to death, Petronius heads a rebellion against him, degrades and slays him. Having achieved his aim, Petronius desires to become reconciled with his wife, but she shudders at his touch and takes poison. The unhappy avenger is elected emperor and he hears the crowds shouting his name, but the only response evoked by the plaudits is : " Do not mock me, O Rome !"

Curiously enough the author's own life was an even greater tragedy than his drama. In 1850 Teleki was an adherent of Kossuth and one of the leaders of the emigration. In 1860, in defiance of all right, the Austrians took him prisoner in Dresden, and conveyed him to Vienna and straight to the palace where Francis Joseph, emperor but not yet king, received him and made him promise that he would take no part in politics for the time being.

He was then set at liberty, but soon found himself unable to resist the force of circumstances and of his own traditions. In the next year, Hungary's fate was at stake, and Teleki became the admired leader of the opposition, whether he would or not.

The opposition was strongly hostile to Deák's scheme and Teleki was chosen to speak against it. He was torn by conflicting feelings. Hungary was looking to him and expecting much from him, but on the other hand there was his promise to the emperor to take no more part in politics. He escaped from the dilemma by committing suicide when his fame was at its zenith.

In the year 1861, when John Arany had risen to fame, and established his leadership in the world of literature, he received a visit from a wealthy country gentleman who left with him the manuscript of a dramatic poem having the peculiar title, *The Tragedy of Man*. Arany, as secretary of the Kisfaludy Society, was usually overwhelmed with manuscripts, and merely gave the work a rapid glance, noting chiefly, here and there, an occasional fault of style. As he read, however, his interest became more and more aroused, and the wonderful power and originality of the poem revealed themselves to him.

The author, IMRE MADÁCH (1823–1864), was at this time

thirty-eight years of age, and had gained some reputation as a member of Parliament by his speeches, the fiery character of which was congenial to the temper of that stormy epoch. *The Tragedy of Man* was the first of his dramas to be published (1861), and it was also the last he wrote, for he died in 1864.

The Tragedy of Man is a poem of the type of Goethe's *Faust* and Byron's *Cain*. It is not one man, nor even a group of men, that the poet has chosen as the subject of his theme, but, boldly enough, the whole of mankind. His hero is Adam, the eternal type of humanity. The work displays the whole history of man, not merely his past, but his present, and even his future. We witness the whole process of man's development, up to the time when the human race will be extinguished, and its earthly home become frozen and uninhabitable. Seen through the eyes of the poet, that history appears a huge, grim tragedy. The problem for the poet to solve was, how to compress such an immense subject within the narrow limit of a single drama.

The opening scene is laid on biblical ground, in Eden. Adam yields to the temptation of Lucifer and tastes the fruit of the Tree of Knowledge. After losing Eden, the fallen man and his mate have to endure the hardships of exile, and they long to cast a glance into the far-off future to see what is to be the outcome of their toils and sufferings.

Lucifer, whose aim is to destroy the newly created human race at the very outset, causes the pair to sink into a deep sleep, and evokes a succession of visions which reveal the future of humanity, and in which Adam beholds scene after scene of the world's future, himself taking an active part in each.

The hero of each vision, or of each epoch, is Adam himself, the eternal Man, in whom are embodied the most characteristic features and the leading ideas of each age. The visions represent for Adam, and, in consequence, for the whole human race which he typifies, a long series of what the French call *illusions perdues*. In each vision or each part of the drama, we see new aspirations, only to be followed by fresh disillusion. Mankind for ever pursues new ideals, but is for ever deceived and baulked.

In the first vision Adam appears as Pharaoh in Egypt, while Eve has the form of a slave. Adam sees clearly that the fundamental conception of the Egyptian State is, the millions for the one—the ruler. Adam wishes to destroy that conception, and he longs to free both himself and his fellow men from the fetters in which it binds them.

The next vision shows the realisation of his hope. Adam reappears in the personality of Miltiades, in democratic Athens. But alas, his faith in the power of democracy is vain. His ideal is realised, yet its realisation brings only disappointment. The Athenian mob cannot make a worthy use of freedom, and proceeds to pass judgment upon its great leader Miltiades, demanding his death. In the soul of Miltiades, smarting beneath the cruel defeat of his hopes, bitter thoughts arise. He mocks at his own aspirations and calls that age alone happy which denies virtue and does not dream of or struggle towards lofty ideals.

And such an age does arrive, when man's one purpose has become the pursuit of pleasure. We find Adam at a bacchanalian feast in the sensual, dissolute world of the late Roman Empire. All at once, at the orgies of the insane revellers there appears an awful guest, the Plague. The Apostle Peter holds aloft the Cross, and preaches to the terrified Roman world the gospel of Christianity and asceticism.

What fate awaits the new ideal is shown in the next vision, where Adam, as Tancred the Crusader, sees how a perverted religion exalts celibacy and stigmatises pure love as a crime ; he sees how in the Byzantine Christian world Christianity has degenerated into a religion of petty dogmas, ridiculous controversies and brutal intolerance. Men have lost the spirit, and heed but the letter. What has become of the sacred religion of love and self-sacrifice ? Adam (still in the vision) yearns for something altogether different from this, which has filled him with nothing but bitter disappointment. " I am exhausted and long for rest."

In the following scene Adam is the astronomer Kepler, absorbed in his studies, and keeping aloof from the world. But science alone cannot yield him satisfaction : in his quiet laboratory he yearns for great reforms, and heroic deeds, which should fashion the world anew.

And the age of colossal events arrives, the age which sees the ancient world totter to its foundations and sink with a great crash into ruin. The day of the French Revolution has dawned, and Adam reappears as Danton. But the prediction concerning the French Revolution, that, like Saturn, it would destroy its own children, is fulfilled. The Revolution turns against its heroes and Danton dies on the scaffold.

Then we come to the present age. Adam, who had wished for a State founded on liberty and order, finds himself in such a State : he has become a citizen of London. Yet disappointment awaits him even here. The world has indeed become wide, but of a dead level of mediocrity. Love itself is to be bought and sold. The whole world is an immense market, in which none of the higher impulses find play, and the soul of Adam is possessed with the idea that this stream of people, this crowd filling the streets of the great metropolis, is engaged in the one task of digging its own grave. Adam sees the vast grave, but sees above it, while all the rest sink into its depths, Eve freed from all that is base, radiant in her purity, flying heavenward as the genius of Love.

The ninth scene is laid in the future, in the new socialistic world that is to be. Adam, as a travelling scholar, visits the State of the future, the Phalanstère, established in accordance with the ideas of the French socialists. The whole world is one vast settlement; the individual has no power or initiative, for everything is determined by the common will. The idea of Fatherland has long ceased to exist. Every man is but a part of a huge machine, the Phalanstère. No man has a name, but merely a number, like a prisoner. Every action is in conformity with the common good, but this conformity has the lifeless perfection only to be found in a machine. Art and poetry have become superfluous, it is only the useful which has a right to exist. The horse and the dog are only to be found in archæological museums : their place has been taken by machinery.

The heads of babies are carefully examined by phrenologists, in order that their careers may be judiciously chosen. The divine Plato himself is considered insane here, and fit only for prison. Adam, however, is repelled by such a world, so like a vast automaton, uninspired by a single grand idea, and illumined by no lofty virtue.

And at length the end approaches, the dreary, sad,

inglorious end. Adam sees mankind rapidly nearing the time when the last feeble spark of human life will be extinguished. The globe of the sun, shorn of its rays, so that Adam takes its blood-red disc for the moon, sheds its dim light upon a frozen world. The last men of the race, a few degenerate Esquimaux, are dragging out a miserable existence. When Adam arrives among them they take him for a god, and request that he would see that there were fewer Esquimaux but more seals.

So this is the goal to which all his struggles and aspirations are to lead, Adam thinks. His wretchedness is increased by the sight of Eve, as the mate of an Esquimaux, who humbly offers his wife's love to the stranger in accordance with the custom of the land. "I—I embrace this woman," cries Adam in horror, "I who once held Aspasia in my arms!"

La farce est jouée. Adam, who has stood beside both the cradle and the tomb of mankind, awakes from the awful dream. Was this to be the future of the race, his race? At the moment of waking, the visions just seen appear so terrible to him that he decides to put a speedy end to the long, painful struggle, of the dreadful issue of which he been warned by those prophetic dreams—yes, to put an end to it, or, rather, to prevent its ever beginning by stopping the stream of human life at its source—by his own self-destruction. But just as he is stepping on to the brink of a precipice, to carry out his fatal resolve, Eve approaches and whispers in his ear a secret, the first secret of the young world : she is going to become a mother. Adam sinks into the dust crying, " Lord, Thou hast vanquished me ! " And the skies open, and God looks down upon the kneeling Adam and strengthens him for the coming struggle, in which he is not to be left without help. In the face of life's adversities God bids him "Strive and Trust!" and with these words the drama ends.

THE TRAGEDY OF MAN.

SCENE III.

A beautiful landscape beyond the bounds of Paradise. Small shapeless huts. ADAM, EVE, LUCIFER. ADAM *is knocking stakes into the ground to make a fence.* EVE *is arranging an arbour.*

ADAM.

So this is mine. Instead of the wide world this spot is my home. I hold it and have it. I guard it from wild beasts and I compel it to nourish me.

EVE.

And I am building an arbour like that which we once possessed and so am restoring the Eden we have lost.

LUCIFER.

That is a mighty utterance. Family and property: these are the main springs of this world. They bring you pleasure, and torment. The two thoughts germinate, grow apace and are known as labour and fatherland. They generate what is great and noble and devour their own children.

ADAM.

You speak in riddles. You promised me knowledge. In the impulse of my joy, with some struggle, I renounced greatness. And what have I gained?

LUCIFER.

Don't you feel what it is?

ADAM.

I feel that as God has forsaken me and thrust me out helpless into the wilderness, I, too, have forsaken Him. I will be a God unto myself and what I gain by my own labour shall be fully mine. That is what gives me strength and pride.

LUCIFER (*aside*).

Dost thou indeed defy the shining skies? Behold the flashes of their lightnings will reveal the inner workings of your heart.

EVE.

One thing makes me proud, that I am the future mother of mankind.

LUCIFER (*aside*).

That's the woman's sublimest ideal—to make guilt and pain ever-lasting on earth.

ADAM.

What have I to thank Him for? That I exist? Is not the fruit of my own labour my reward for the pains of this existence? I must win the delight of a cooling drink through torturing thirst. I must pay for the ardour and glad sweetness of kisses with weariness and heaviness. Have I torn off the bonds of gratitude, and am I free to build my own fate—and sometimes, groping, to destroy what I planned—you were indeed not needed to help me in this. I could have done as much by my own strength alone. You have not torn away the chain that bound my body to this earth. A mere hair it is—oh! the infamy of it!—that hems me in and fetters my soul. I long to soar but I sink down. My eye and my ear refuse their service when I boldly attempt to solve the enigma of space. And when imagination draws me into higher spheres, hunger gnaws me and drags me down again full of shame, to the earth on which I wander.

LUCIFER.

Yes, those fetters are stronger than I.

ADAM.

Then you are indeed a poor weak spirit. What if this gossamer, this nothing, which myriads of beings scarcely notice—in whose web they revel joyously thinking they are free, but which a few chosen spirits only divine—defy your power.

LUCIFER.

Indeed, 'tis only this which can defy me, because 'tis spirit like I am. Do you imagine that because a power works secretly and silently that it is not strong? Believe me, there rests in darkness that which can shatter, can create a world and every head would turn giddy at sight of it. Only what limits the span of earthly time, only the work of men roars and glows.

ADAM.

Then let me—I feel the strength within me—for one moment

behold this power that rules me, so that I am in myself a separate entity and yet part of the whole.

LUCIFER.

" I am ! " Idle words ! You were and you will be. Existence is an eternal becoming and decaying.

*　　*　　*　　*　　*　　*　　*

ADAM.

Show me the future. Show me clearly and fully why I strive and wherefore I suffer.

EVE.

And show me also, if in all this renewing and creating my charms shall not fade and decay.

LUCIFER.

So be it ! So be it ! Enchantment cover these two. Show them clearly in a vision the dimmest, most distant, future. And lest they lose heart and flee ere they venture on the conflict, show them how sterile their goal, how hard the struggle, how artificial the game. In the clouded sky, I will leave one bright glimmer which shall delude them—the illusion, the palpable image of the future—hope.

FROM SCENE VII.

ADAM (AS TANCRED).

I should like to cast away my sword and repair to the shady forests of my northern home where pure morals and a man's worth still count, a spot as yet untouched by these false ages, did not an inner voice warn me that I am destined to create them anew.

LUCIFER.

Vain toil ! You will never succeed by yourself alone in conquering the spirit of the time. The stream rushes on—who can stand against it ? You must swim with it or perish. He who does great things, and is called great, is only he who understands his age. He does not create it, he finds his ideas in it. The crowing of the cock does not bring the dawn. The cock only crows because day dawns. Those despised ones yonder who go out to meet a martyr's death are an advance guard in the course of the ages. New ideas have dawned in them and they are dying for beliefs which their children will some day breathe in, like the very air. But enough of this. Look to your camp ! What is happening there ?

Critics have commented on this work from two different points of view. Some say that the dreams were recognised by the poet himself not to be in accordance with historical truth, and were deliberately chosen by Lucifer with the diabolical aim of driving Adam to despair and suicide, and so destroying in him the whole human race. Others explain the drama by saying that the great events and epochs of history appeared to Madách himself in the gloomy light in which he depicts them. According to those commentators, Madách, the poet of disillusion, who even in his lyric poems generally lamented some disappointment, saw in the history of the world nothing but a constant shattering of the hopes which spring up from generation to generation. Every age has its ideals, but even when reached they prove delusive.

Is man's history then really what Petőfi said of it, in a dark hour of doubt and hopelessness? " We are like the tree which flowers and fades : like the waves which rise and fall : like the traveller, who mounts a hill only to descend again. And so it goes on to all eternity, up and down, up and down."

If we take that view of *The Tragedy of Man*, its teaching is that the alternation of hope and disillusion, of ardent enthusiasm and bitter disappointment, which in other of his works is Madách's favourite theme, is the inevitable lot of mortals, and the whole drama may be regarded as an expansion of Schopenhauer's well-known dictum, that history is a painful nightmare weighing down the mind of humanity.

But is there then no consolation in this long series of disappointments? Does no stray, cheering sunbeam break through the darkness? The poet answers in the words of God, words which, in my opinion, express the main idea of the book : "Search not for the secret which a divine wisdom has mercifully hidden from thy sight." God points to love and spiritual aspirations for consolation, and sets the happiness of individual life against the unhappy fate of the race. Even if the history of mankind as a whole should prove sad and disappointing, God has blessed the life of the individual with many joys and hopes.

This book of Madách is the first in Hungarian literature which deals not with the life of one man, or of the nation, but with mankind as a whole. But *The Tragedy of Man* marks a new departure in other respects as well. There are two contending elements in it, imagination and reflection. The author's ideas do not always rise to the poetic level, and we sometimes have metrical prose rather than true poetry, though as prose it is undoubtedly of high quality. This peculiarity in its language makes the poem a characteristic product of its age.

The same transition from imagination to philosophical reflection which we find in it, is to be traced on a larger scale in the whole of the literature of the period. It is one of the defects of Madách's poems that his philosophical reflection is not beautified by imagination, but remains abstract and logical. Another imperfection is in the drawing of his characters.

The plan of the poem demands that at each epoch of the world's history a complete transformation should take place in the soul of Adam, but as such a change is only conceivable as the result of a long process of development, it could not possibly occur as abruptly as it is made to do. For instance, we see that in the mind of Adam, as the Egyptian Pharaoh, the conception of a thoroughly democratic state springs into being instantaneously, but this is manifestly impossible, for at that period all the psychological conditions and historical precedents which could engender such a notion were lacking. Whereas mental growth is really a gradual modification of existing ideas, in the poem there are nothing but sudden and startling contrasts. Adam sets his heart upon the exact opposite of the conditions which have proved so unsatisfactory.

As regards the other important character in the drama, Eve, the eternal woman, it must be confessed that in all her various transformations she is more like an abstraction than a real living woman. Yet in spite of these imperfections, the conception of the whole wondrous course of the human race is very grand, and the genius displayed in every detail very great.

Madách's pessimism had a two-fold origin. It sprang partly from the condition of his native land, and partly from calamities in his private life. In the fifties of the past century, after the war for freedom, Hungary was pining beneath the tyranny of Austria, during what is known as the Bach Period. At the same time the poet's life was blighted by private misfortunes. The Wallachian insurgents had atrociously butchered the whole of his sister's family, and in 1854 his wife deserted him. Imagine a man such as his poems and letters show Madách to have been, a man highly sensitive and contemplative by nature, and inclined to torture himself with all kinds of doubts and to take a tragic view of life; then place him in a period when the national aspirations have been stifled, an age of oppression and despair, in a society doomed to inaction and impotent resentment ; add to the grief of the patriot the sadness of domestic bereavements and the pang of the injured husband, and we shall then understand the state of mind in which Madách wrote his drama. Let us glance for a moment at the age whose doubts and griefs and longings found an interpreter in Madách.

In 1849, when the Austrian bayonets and Cossack lances had finished their work, the hangman began his. There followed a stillness as of death. The intellectual leaders of the people were either exiled or imprisoned, or dumb with sorrow ; the nation mourned its greatest poet, Petőfi, slain upon the field of battle ; its grandest statesman, Széchenyi, had lost his reason. The whole country was sunk in a heavy torpor. Those who loved her asked in agony, " Will she ever wake again ? " " It may be that they will not succeed in destroying the nation entirely, but the wounds they have inflicted will perhaps never be thoroughly healed," said Széchenyi. The effect of all this upon the mind of the people becomes clear when we read the poets of those times. For is not the poet always the truest exponent of his age ? Vörösmarty's poetry in the fifties is like a glowing furnace in the depths of which most precious metals are at white heat. In his poem *The Hoary Gypsy*, he imagines himself to be listening to a gipsy's weird music, and in each tune his gloomy fancy seems to hear nothing but the echo of sad events. And when he thinks of the sufferings of Hungary, it seems to him as though he " could hear the rushing wings of the vulture that comes to renew the immortal pains of Prometheus."

Another poet, Bajza, says, " Where there is no justice, only oppression and tyranny, freedom becomes a term of irony, and prison, which shuts out the sight of woe, becomes merciful."

Arany, the most cultivated and tender-hearted of all the poets, saw his country lying crushed and ruined, and as there is no kindness in telling the felled tree that it may revive and flower again, he abandoned his old poetic ideals, and with mocking laughter on his lips, but with bitterness in his heart, wrote a travesty of the great events of the time in his satirical poem, *The Gypsies of Nagy Ida.*

Mild Tompa himself broke out into wild, uncontrollable grief. "The young wife prays that she may not bear children ; parents do not bewail their infant's death ; only the aged rejoice, gladdened by the thought that they have not long to live."

Everything in Nature itself is interpreted in terms of a gloomy symbolism. To Charles Szász it seems as if "the clouds floating above were born of the vapour of tears and blood, but some day they will send down their lightnings upon the earth."

The works of Paul Gyulai bear the same note of bitterness. One of his characters, a farmer, grieves most of all because his dear ones, slain in battle or by the hangman, died in vain.

We may imagine what influence this environment had on Madách's naturally pessimistic disposition. And then, while other men found some solace for their grief as patriots in the joys of home, it was there that he received the cruellest blow through the faithlessness of his wife.

Madách wrote several dramas which were published after his death, but they may all be regarded as "studies" for his great work, which raised him to the rank of Hungary's greatest philosophical poet.

The great democratical movement of the years around 1840 brought the peasant into fashion, not only in politics, where the emancipation of the peasant became a battle-cry, and in the lyric and epic poetry of writers like Arany, Petőfi and Tompa, but also upon the stage. A new dramatic *genre* arose, known as the " popular play," in which the life of the Hungarian peasant was represented, accompanied with national music and dancing; it made an agreeable change from the raving villains of the romantic dramas. Its creator was EDWARD SZIGLIGETI (1814-1878) who was for some time an actor and was consequently well acquainted with stage technique. His first production was *The Deserter*, in which a large part was still played by the upper classes, but later on the humbler classes played a more and more important and exclusive part in his dramas such as *The Pistols*, *The Horse-herd* and *The Gypsy*.

In the Hungarian peasant world there were many poetical figures of which Szigligeti made use. There were, for example, the proud, hot-headed and somewhat pert peasant lad, who was yet full of deep feeling, and was equally sensitive to the sorrow of disappointed love and to the joys of life, with its song and dance; the highwayman (*betyár*), that long-since vanished king of the puszta, violent but generous; and that well-known figure of Hungarian village life, the cowardly, sly, and always comical gypsy.

Szigligeti was the chief provider of the Hungarian actor's repertory. During the first thirty years of the existence of the National Theatre, one third of the plays it produced were by Szigligeti. It was he who wrote the best Hungarian farce, *Liliomfi*. Among his serious dramas the best was *The Pretender*, in which he gave the story of Borics, the Hungarian Demetrius, who thought himself the lawful son of King Kálmán and claimed the throne until he learned the terrible secret of his illegitimate birth.

The chief follower of Szigligeti as a writer of "popular plays" was EDWARD TÓTH (1844-76), who was a poor actor when he wrote *The Black Sheep of the Village*,

18

in which he expressed the poetry of village life even better than his master had done. The hero is a peasant lad who in consequence of his unhappy love for a fickle-minded girl becomes an idler and a *black sheep*, but who is ennobled again by his newly wakened love for a gentle, true-hearted maiden.

In the social drama, the most important follower of Szigligeti was GREGORY CSIKY (1842-1891). His literary activity was of a curious character. He wrote a book on canon law, and one on Catholic matrimonial law, and also some very successful plays. For some time he was a Catholic priest but later on left the order.

Csiky was more a man of logic than of sentiment; he had a genius for discerning the characteristic features of his subjects and for constructing powerful plots. His characters often remind us of Dickens, so full are they of life and individuality. He achieved his first great success with the play : *The Proletariat* (1879). When the play was over, and the audience clamoured for the author, some one shouted to him : " Forward ! You are on the right path." In this drama the most successful feature was the *milieu*. Every one who has lived in a large town knows such a society of parasite adventurers and broken-down creatures, and these all stand before us, drawn with striking realism. The central figure is the " saintly widow," who gives herself out as the widow of a martyred hero of the revolution. People believe in her and help her pecuniarily, so much so that she is able to maintain an entire office in which her petitions for assistance are prepared. In reality, however, the " saintly widow" is neither a saint nor a widow, but quite the reverse.

At her side we see a friend who is worthy of her, a

Transylvanian nobleman who has spent all his money and now helps the "martyr's widow" to live at other people's expense, and to do all manner of shady business. In addition to this ruined landowner, there is a broken-down lawyer whose diploma was cancelled by the authorities some twenty years before, and who now works in the widow's petition office. In this society we find the widow's daughter Irma, a white lily amid all this foulness. She bears everything patiently as she believes the widow to be her mother, but at an evening party the widow drinks a little too much punch and betrays the secret that Irma is not her daughter. This is the turning-point of the drama. Irma escapes from the house to avoid a humiliating business-like marriage to which she cannot consent, and there is a striking scene when the lawyer's better nature awakes and he helps the girl to get clear of her evil associates and marry the man whom she loves and who is worthy of her.

The play owed its success to the realistic and almost too bold drawing of its characters. Similar in its tendency is another drama by Csiky entitled *Gilded Misery*.

A much more tragical play is *The Iron Man*, in which there is a truly dramatic conflict. The man of iron is a rich manufacturer, stern, obstinate, and implacable, who demands absolute obedience from every one. He has a son who is an "iron man" too in a calm strong way, and who falls in love with the daughter of a poor nobleman. But the manufacturer, who owes all his fortune to his own industry, scorns the idle aristocrat and will not hear of the marriage.

He has his way, and extorts from the girl a promise to give up her lover, on the threat that otherwise he will declare to the world his reasons for opposing the match and every one shall know that the baron has forged some bills of exchange. But now an unexpected catastrophe occurs. All at once the baron sees his crime in all its hideousness ; he was not strong enough to live honestly but at least he feels strong enough to die, and he thinks that his death may clear the way for his child's happiness. But feeling that in honour and dishonour she is one with her father, she too commits suicide. The son, who has inherited the unyielding nature of his father, is irrevocably estranged from the man whose hardness has caused these deaths, and kills himself amidst the ruin of his hopes. The tyrannical "iron man" stands before us, cut off from every source of consolation.

A very interesting tragedy is Csiky's *Spartacus*, dealing with the slave rebellion in Rome. The crisis is brought on by the circumstance that the slave Spartacus carries off a patrician lady, but he is in turn enslaved by the majestic purity of his captive, so that he dares not claim her love, and by his homage to her kindles the suspicion of his fellows.

XVII

RECENT WRITERS

THE Fiume express which rattled into the station of Károlyváros at noon on Sunday, November 5, 1899, did not leave it again until after some delay. A disturbing incident had occurred. Someone had committed suicide in a second-class carriage just before the train reached the station. A crowd quickly gathered, and when the body was removed from the train, they saw that the dead man's hands still grasped a revolver, a shot from which had penetrated his right temple. By means of documents he was found to be EUGENE PÉTERFY (1849-1899), a professor at the high school in Budapest. No one at the station was acquainted with the name nor knew that it was one of Hungary's most talented and cultivated writers who had thus flung his life away. Three days later this Hungarian author, for whom his own country was not to provide a grave, was buried in a little Croatian village in the presence of a few of his friends who had come in haste to show him this last mark of their affection.

On the sea coast, when the waves wash ashore the bodies of the unknown dead, the fishermen's wives are accustomed to say a prayer and light a candle over their grave. So, too, did the Croatian maidens, who, moved by pity, twined their wreaths around the grave of the stranger, cast up by the ocean of life. "What then is the value of life," asked his friends, "if one who has all his life laboured for his own education and perfection, like an artist engaged upon some master-work, finds it so easy to throw it away?"

Eugene Péterfy lived the most virtuous and most intellectual life. He had a healthy body but an ill-disciplined will. He was one of those problematical natures of whom Goethe said that in spite of their great talents they are not able to meet the varying demands life makes upon them. To him Pascal's well-known saying was applicable: "L'homme est un roseau pensant."

Péterfy was the best of Hungarian essayists. His great susceptibility to impressions, which throughout his life brought him much suffering, was the cause of his excellence as a writer. The qualities which essay writing demands were just the qualities which he pre-eminently possessed. He was above all an impressionist, and his essays may be defined as glimpses of great poets seen through Péterfy's temperament. The world's great authors thrilled his sensitive soul, and his essays were interpretations into language as refined as his own soul, of the feelings which they awakened. But of course this sensitiveness to each momentary impression was united with vast knowledge and sound logic or his work would not have value.

His essays are sometimes on Hungarian and some-times on foreign authors. The best among them referring to Hungarian writers are those dealing with the novelists. It would hardly be possible for any essayist to understand an author better than Péterfy understood Kemény, in whom, with his great love for the tragic element, he found a kindred spirit. The superficiality of Jókai in the psychological conception of his characters was seriously reproved by Péterfy.

Among his essays on foreign authors the best are those on Dante and Aristophanes. Florence and Athens were the two cities he admired and loved most, not merely as a poetical idealist but as a psychologist interested in every aspect of life.

The first writer who worked seriously at the history of literature in Hungary was FRANCIS TOLDY (1805-1875). He collected and arranged a vast amount of material and published in German a work entitled *Handbuch der ungarischen Poesie* in 1828. His reason for writing in German was that he wished to give some idea of the treasures of Hungarian literature to other nations. He worked very hard, and towards the middle of the century, wrote a more elaborate history of Hungarian literature chiefly embodying the results of his own thorough studies and painstaking investigations. In Toldy, untiring industry was united with vast knowledge and fervent patriotism. He was the good genius of Hungarian literature for half a century.

The country is indebted to Toldy for a mass of historical details concerning authors and their works, but for a critical estimate of the literature of the past, it is indebted to Paul Gyulai, who succeeded Toldy in the chair at the University.

The Hungarian philosophers who treated of aesthetics based their work upon the same foundation as the Germans, chiefly following Hegel, but differing from their German models in their pursuit of national aims.

In small nations criticism does not develop readily, for with them literature requires to be encouraged rather than severely criticised. The first real criticism containing no flattery and displaying remarkable power of analysis was that of Kölcsey. Besides Kölcsey, JOSEPH BAJZA (1804-1858) became important as a critic. He was a poet as well, whose poems are of an abstract, sentimental and impersonal character, a kind of drawing-room poet, with culture and a refined taste. Bajza started the first critical journal in Hungary, realising that instead of the prevailing friendly eulogies, serious and just criticism was needed. He was twenty-seven when the journal first appeared, and he continued the work in the supplements of " The Athenæum."

JOHN ERDÉLYI (1814–1868) was much less polished in his style than Bajza, but possessed more insight. He too was a poet, and became the Percy of Hungary by his compilation of Hungarian folk-lore, the first book of its kind. In aesthetics he was a follower of Hegel, and in his character sketches of authors he anticipated Hyppolyte Taine, for like him he endeavoured to discover that fundamental quality ["qualité maitresse"] of an author from which his remaining characteristics were derived.

The best work on aesthetics was by AUGUSTUS GREGUSS (1825-1882), a University professor. His life and work were the mirror of the refinement of his mind. He wrote an excellent book on the ballad, dealing especially with the sources of Scottish ballads and also, of those of Arany. He defined the ballad very pithily as a tragedy told in song. Greguss consecrated his life to the task of raising the taste of the nation by teaching men to love the beautiful and the good, which he declared were not different elements, but merely different rays from the same sun.

PAUL GYULAY (born 1826), Hungary's chief critic, is a very interesting figure. He was born at Kolozsvár and is now living in Budapest as an editor and retired University professor. He is a polemical writer and is opposed to luke-warm compromise. Many have been angry with him but all esteem him. His importance is perhaps best indicated by the fact that nearly all the generally accepted literary estimates of to-day are derived from him, although many of his opinions when first expressed seemed paradoxical.

Gyulay introduced perfect sincerity into criticism. He holds such a high opinion of the importance of truth and of the functions of criticism that he is always veracious and sometimes merciless. His convictions are so strong that he is ready to be their martyr. While many of his contemporaries regarded the eminent leader General Arthur Görgey, who was compelled to capitulate at Világos in 1849, as a traitor, Gyulay defended him, and on the other hand, he attacked the idols of the people, Kossuth and Jókai, or at least assailed their weak points. In an age when all men, even the proudest, bow their knee to the great monarch, public opinion, he often seeks not popularity but almost unpopularity. He is always ready to expose a writer's vanity or shallowness. A modest man himself, he is shocked at the charlatanism and the bragging self-esteem of some of his contem-poraries. He has always been the champion of good traditions against the too vehement reformers who would introduce foreign elements into Hungarian literature, and yet when the " orthologists " endeavoured to annihilate the results of the language reform, it was Gyulay who for a decade defended the valuable fruit of Kazinczy's labours. His critical acuteness is especially revealed when he is examining the composition of a lyric poem, the element of terror in a tragedy and the reality of the characters in a work of fiction. But this genius for criticism has its defects. Sometimes Gyulay is too biting and carries on his polemics for its own sake and not merely for the sake of truth. He is a consummate master of prose style. His chief works are an admirable and profound essay on Katona's *Bánk bán*, and *Vörösmarty's Biography*, in which he gives a wonderful description of the whole period. Among his orations and in his essays the best are those in which he spoke of his great friend Arany. In his short stories he does not excel in inventive power but in truthful characterisation, in style and in the realistic atmosphere with which he is able to surround an event. His best short story is *The Old Mansion's Last Tenant*, describing the gradual decay of an ancient estate as well as of its owner.

Gyulay is also distinguished as a lyric poet. His style is simple and concise, without much passion. An element of reflection moderates or represses his sentiments, but these restrained feelings serve to reveal his strength. In some poems the critic is manifest and we detect here and there a note of bitterness. A peculiar quality of his subjective poetry is the rapid alternation of irony and emotion. One of the best known of his poems tells of an incident in the war for freedom.

DEAR CAPTAIN MINE.

" Oh Captain mine, oh Captain see ! "
" What is it, lad, that aileth thee ? "
" Look ! on your cloak a crimson patch ! "
" Nay, heed it not, 'tis but a scratch."

" Oh Captain, turn aside I pray,
The way is steep, your footsteps stay."
" I stumbled o'er a stone, perchance,
Fix bayonets, men, and all advance ! "

The Honveds forward press ; not so,
The Captain wounded by the foe ;
" Onward, my lads," he cries again,
And falls in death amid the slain.

The oldest Hungarian Chronicles which have come down to us date from the thirteenth century and were written in Latin. The best known is the Chronicle of King Béla's *Anonymous Scribe*, which tells of the conquest of the country by the Hungarians in some detail but with little vivacity. The age and authorship of the book have been much discussed, for the writer does not state his name but merely describes himself as the scribe or notary of King Béla, and as there were four kings of that name we are in doubt as to which of them is meant. It is proved that the unknown scribe lived under Béla IV. (died 1270), or, at the earliest, under Béla III (died 1196).

The first history in which a sense of style may be detected was the Chronicle written in Hungarian by GASPAR HELTAI in 1575, the deeds of Matthias Corvinus being remarkably well told. Heltai's materials were largely drawn from the Latin work of the Italian humanist Bonfini, who lived at the Court of Matthias.

The best Hungarian historian of the eighteenth century was MICHAEL CSEREI (died 1756), who wrote the history of Transylvania from 1661 to 1712 in a vivid style, and with a somewhat moralising tendency.

The first of the more modern school of Hungarian historians was STEPHEN KATONA (died 1811). He worked with astounding diligence and a keen critical sense for original sources and produced a history in forty-two bulky volumes, telling the story of Hungary from the earliest times. All subsequent historians have used this work as the foundation for their own.

It was BENEDICT VIRÁG (1752–1830), however, the distinguished writer of odes, who first wrote a history of Hungary in a refined and artistic style. He began, about the beginning of the nineteenth century, to write a popular work entitled *Centuries of Hungarian History*, but he did not get further than the Battle of Mohács.

It is curious that the two most important concise histories of Hungary were written by two exiled historians, both living in Switzerland, after the revolution. One of these was the bishop MICHAEL HORVÁTH (1809-1878), who was Minister for Public Instruction in 1848-9, and who when exiled went to reside in Zurich.

The other was LADISLAS SZALAY (1813-1864) whose work deals chiefly with the juridical aspect of Hungarian affairs.

FRANCIS SALAMON (1825-1892), a professor at the University of Budapest was perhaps the most pithy of the historians. He produced some good work in the way of literary essays before taking up history. His chief book treats of Hungary under Turkish rule, during the sixteenth and seventeenth centuries, describing her administration, legislature, and economic condition. Salamon's strength lay in his ability to reconstruct in his imagination a series of important events with the aid of a few small details. Sometimes, it is true, the details did not provide a sufficient basis for his conclusions, but he was very ingenious in deducing the ancient methods of Hungarian warfare from a slight knowledge of the tactics that were employed.

At the request of the chief magistrate of the capital he wrote a *History of Budapest* down to the end of the Middle Ages. He showed, in a very interesting way how the part which Budapest was to play in Hungarian history was determined by its geological formation and geographical position.

Excepting history, the pursuit of no branch of knowledge has been attended with so much national sentiment as philology, and the reason is not hard to see. The nation lives in its language, so it becomes a national task to investigate it scientifically, the more especially since the Hungarian tongue does not belong to the Indo-Germanic group which is studied by the great Western nations. The greatest Hungarian philologist, and perhaps the most original genius in the Hungarian scientific world, was NICHOLAS RÉVAY (1750–1807), who was also a poet of the classical school. He first applied the methods of comparative philology to the problems of the Hungarian language, at a time when those methods were hardly known to the scholars of other nations. His principal work was in Latin ; *Elaboratior Grammatica Hungarica*, 1806.

We must, however, regard PAUL HUNFALVY (1810–1891), the eminent student of ancient Hungarian history and philology, and JOSEPH BUDENZ (1836–1892), who was of German origin and a professor in the University of Budapest, as the real founders of systematic comparative philology in Hungary.

During the last quarter of the nineteenth century the study of philology received a great impetus from a crusade against the extravagances of the language reform. The enthusiastic leader of this movement was GABRIEL SZARVAS (1832–1895), a brilliant controversialist and etymological scholar. The works of two other distinguished philologists, ALEXANDER KŐRŐSI CSOMA (1787–1842) and ARMINIUS VÁMBÉRY (1832–) were for the most part first published in English.

Csoma was one of the most remarkable and interesting personalities not merely in the Hungarian scientific world but in all Europe. Schopenhauer used to call him "the excellent Csoma," for he was fond of him on account of his investigations into Buddhism. Csoma was of Székely race and was led by his patriotism to become a scholar. In 1819 he left his country for the purpose of discovering the original home of the Hungarians. He passed the ruins of Babylon, traversed Persia and Afghanistan, usually travelling in disguise, and in 1822 arrived in Thibet, where, with the aid of the British Government, he lived for nine years in great simplicity and obscurity, braving the deadly climate animated by devotion to his cause, struggling with poverty, working day and night, and refusing great sums of money rather than abandon his task. Such was his life while studying the Thibetan language. His Thibetan grammar and dictionary were the first works on this subject in Europe. This self-sacrificing scholar lies buried in Darjeeling, facing the Himalaya mountains. Above his tomb is a white marble monument erected by the Asiatic Society, with a rose-bush and weeping willow bending over it.

Another famous Oriental scholar, Arminius Vámbéry, travelled in Asia for years dressed as a Dervish, facing innumerable dangers. He is now living in Budapest as a retired University professor. The account of his travels created a great sensation when it was published in 1865.

In his book called *The Origin of the Hungarians,* he opposed the theory that the Hungarians were related to the Ugrians, and maintained that they were of Turkish origin.

By the side of Gyulay must be placed his three friends who followed a similar line : Joseph Lévay, Charles Szász, and Ladislas Arany, the son of the great poet.

JOSEPH LÉVAY (born in 1825), the eminent translator of Robert Burns, is characterised in his original poetry by a reflective calmness and sobriety. Every line manifests infinite care. Thoughts of crystalline purity in forms of crystalline symmetry constitute his poetry. His *Vintage Day* is one of the most charming of idylls. The poet, in a distant land, is thinking of the home of his parents. It is a great day to-day, that of the vintage. The happy family is seated at dinner in the shade of a large pear-tree. The lips of his two little sisters are redder than ever withthe juice of the sweet purple grapes. In the course of a playful dispute one of them begins to sulk, and declares that she does not want any dinner. While the father breaks the neck of a wine flagon, one of the labourers fires his gun into the air as a salute, and the woman and children cry out though more amused than startled. The father bids the labourer draw near and offers him a glass of wine, though he may guess from the way in which the labourer's hat is tilted on his head that this is not the first glass he has tasted to-day. The hills re-echo with laughter and the songs of merry labourers. Only upon the mother's brow is there a cloud, as she thinks of one who is far away.

CHARLES SZÁSZ (1829–1906) is the third member of the little group, and a real poet, though not of the first rank. His best poems are perhaps those which he wrote after the death of his young wife, who was a talented poetess. Szász became very active as a translator, and his translations include several of Shakespeare's plays and of Tennyson's poems. His numerous prose works are chiefly devoted to the spreading amongst others of his own great knowledge of literature.

The fourth of the group was LADISLAS ARANY (1844–1898), the son of John Arany. He was a satirical epic poet, but he soon gave up writing poetry, perhaps because he did not find his talent strong enough to inspire men in a prosaic age, or perhaps he may have been oppressed by the greatness of his father's memory. His chief work, *The Mirage Pursuer*, was published anonymously, and he refused to allow a second edition to appear, although the first was rapidly sold out. In composition it reminds us of Pushkin's *Onyegin*, but in language of John Arany. The hero is a well-drawn specimen of a type that was common in the sixties, a sort of Hungarian Don Quixote. He is a good fellow, and loves his country sincerely, but has many faults. His enthusiasm is like a fire of twigs which blazes up in a moment and quickly expires. He loves to build castles in the air, but lacks persistence. He goes abroad, fights for Italian liberty under Garibaldi, then rambles about Europe and at length returns to Hungary. Here in his patriotic fervour he seeks to initiate a variety of reforms, but he soon comes to see the selfish interest that often hides behind the mask of patriotism, and that politics often means merely business, and so his desire for reform evaporates. His career is still more marred by the circumstance that once, when excited by the revelry at a banquet, he offended a lady whom he had loved as a girl.

Ladislas Arany was the type of a true Hungarian gentleman. Though widely cultured and acquainted with many lands, he retained a fervent love for his race, and that sentiment inspired his best poems.

In contrast with the little circle whose guiding star was John Arany, stood two pessimistic lyric poets, who, ignoring the traditions of Hungarian lyrical poetry, followed an eccentric line of their own. They were John Vajda and Gyula Reviczky, who died young.

JOHN VAJDA (1827–1897) was a passionate writer who loved to be unique. In 1848–9 he was an officer in the

Honvéd or national army. Later on he was compelled
by the Austrians as a punishment to serve in their army
as a private soldier, and in that capacity he spent a year
in Lombardy, which was then in the hands of the
Austrians. On returning home he lived in Budapest as
an author and editor, friendless, discontented and immersed in fantastical dreams. His soul thirsted for the
extraordinary and the grand, and he shunned commonplace people. " Our age," he said bitterly, " is the conspiracy of organised mediocrity against genius." In
poetry he sought for the great, the profound, the surprising. As a young man he fell in love with a dancer
named Gina, who was famous for her beauty, and who
became for him the symbol of an unattainable ideal.
This ideal, who, by the way, was another man's mistress,
he met again thirty years later, and the meeting inspired
his finest poem, *After Thirty Years*, in which life's tragedy
is expressed with great pathos.

"And so we have met once more," he says, "our last
meeting this side of the grave. When once I am dead
you will know what I am to you, eternal love enshrined
in song. Heaven has betrothed us to one another. You
who have loved so many, and I who have loved but you
alone, here we stand and take one long last look at one
another."

"Their looks expressed the grief not of those who had
lost Eden, but of those who had never gained it."

"Thus the moon seems to repose on a lofty cloud,
when the storm has been lulled to rest, and to gaze sadly
down upon the night, but without passion; she hears the
infinite silence of the forest, like the silence of the tomb,
while from the trees big heavy teardrops fall noiselessly
upon the dead leaves which strew the ground beneath."

19

The other pessimistic poet was GYULA REVICZKY (1855–1889). His short life was a continual struggle with disease and poverty. Like Schopenhauer and Heine, he gave expression to two contrasting tempers, now resignation and a conviction of the world's vanity, and now, a keen desire to live. In his poem, *The Death of Pan*, the two feelings are mingled. Down in the waist of a ship there is boisterous revelry, and we hear the sound of music and drinking and dancing. Suddenly a voice calls to the helmsman, " Thamus ! " but the helmsman does not heed the summons. Again comes the cry "Thamus ! " and he leaves the helm, mounts the upper deck and looks around, but as far as eye can reach there is no living thing. He is about to descend again, when his name is called for the third time, and on his startled ear there fall the words : " When thou reachest the headland, cry aloud, ' The great Pan is dead.' " The helmsman obeys and cries, " The great Pan is dead," whereupon he hears the sound of sobbing among the trees and hills, sighs are borne upon the breeze, and all Nature is filled with the sound of wailing. The reign of the Pagan gods is over, the great Pan is dead, and a voice cries : " Pan and his merry tribe have gone, but the one God remains, not in stones and trees, but in the heart. Hitherto the world has belonged to the proud and happy, but henceforth those who suffer shall own the earth. There shall be a sweetness even in tears, and though the forest is silent, the sad will find in it peace." And then, far off, near the horizon, there appears in the sky the Cross, bathed in the red light of the morning.

While most of the poets in the fifties and sixties found their model in Arany, the chief follower of Petőfi in lyric song was the ardent and fervently patriotic KÁLMÁN T'TH (1831–1881).

No task is more difficult for the historian or critic than to estimate his contemporaries rightly. From what point is he to gain a true perspective, for even to take a photograph he must stand at a certain distance from his subject ? How can his judgment have the necessary objectivity and how is he to overcome the distorting influence of social relations ? But although it is difficult for a man to judge his contemporaries individually, it is easier and even more important to characterise the general tendency of modern literature.

Literature cannot boast to-day such giant-like figures as Vörösmarty, Petőfi and Arany. The golden age of Hungarian literature has been followed by a period of comparative mediocrity, and the great talent and lofty inspiration which marked the time of the national revival (1825–1849) are lacking, but as in all such periods, the last of the late classics became the model for succeeding writers. This was Arany, whose style exercised an unbounded influence, though in the matter of the technique of versification there has been a decided advance upon that attained during the great age.

A conspicuous feature of modern literature is the absence of the popular element. Hungarian poetry reached its greatest height in the sublimation of the popular poetry. Petőfi, Tompa and Arany were rooted in the soil of the popular tales and ballads, but it would seem as if that soil were exhausted, at least for the time being. The popular play does not seem to be received either, and literature scarcely turns its eyes to the past at all. In both epic and dramatic poetry modern society occupies the field more and more exclusively. The heroic epic, cultivated by Vörösmarty and Arany, has entirely gone out of fashion. Dramatists, with the exception of a few talented men like

Eugene Rákosi and Louis Dóczi, the author of the comedy *The Kiss*, who do not come within the limits of this book, prefer to deal with so-called social problems which are not really of sufficient importance to deserve literary treatment.

The influence of journalism is steadily increasing, and as journalism is favourable to the *feuilleton*, that species of literature has been prolific in short stories and sketches. There are two masters of the *feuilleton*, of whom it is necessary to say a few words. They are Kálmán Mikszáth and Francis Herczeg.

KÁLMÁN MIKSZÁTH (born 1849) is Jókai's greatest follower. He has not the brilliant imagination and poetic idealism of Jókai, but he is vivid, witty and original. His best work, *The Good People of Palócz,** is a volume of short stories, all drawn from the life of the people and some of them written with thrilling tragic power.

Mikszáth's humour gains its depth and charm from his power of detecting the attractive and poetical even in the simplest circumstances of life. The story of *St. Peter's Umbrella* begins by telling that the inhabitants of a lonely little mountain village had never seen an umbrella, and that when on one occasion they discovered a large red one they thought it was a gift of St. Peter. Upon this foundation he builds up a charming story. He has also written a very successful satirical novel entitled *The New Zrinyiász.* Nicholas Zrinyi, the hero of Szigetvár, rises from his grave to find himself amidst the altered conditions of modern Hungary. There is great surprise and embarrassment everywhere. The character of each

* The Palócz race was descended from the Kumanians, but has been amalgamated with the Hungarians for centuries. Mikszáth himself is of Palócz origin.

statesman and party is revealed in the kind of reception given to the great general. The author is alluding to recent events, when with bitter irony he tells how Zrinyi gets into debt and accepts the post of bank manager to some Jewish bankers, who set a great value upon ancient Hungarian names.

The most witty novelist who has appeared since the death of Arany is FRANCIS HERCZEG (born 1863). He has written dramas as well as novels, but is at his best in the short story. The character of his talent may be briefly described by saying that he is an ironical observer of mankind. He has a keen scent for the foibles of men and women, especially of the latter, but he does not regard these weaknesses with either indignation or indifference ; he looks at them from a point of view of some elevation and is not blind to their humorous side. He sets before us with remarkable truth the types to be met in our streets every day. His characters seem to live before our eyes, so real and living are the features with which he has invested them. His inventiveness and fancy are not so great as those of Jókai, but his powers of observation, his excellent taste and *spirituel* attitude towards life, assure him a distinguished place, not only amongst Hungarian authors. Herczeg is sparing of words, *sobre* as the French would say. In his short stories, full of irony, we see the poetical spirit of a modern man of the world. He is an idealist without illusions.

Perhaps the Bohemian world of journalists has never been so truly painted as in Herczeg's novel, *András and Andor*, which is full of satirical observations.

Besides stories dealing with modern town life, like *The Gyurkovics Girls*, in which the characters seem to be living persons of our acquaintance, so vividly are they drawn, Herczeg has also written a historical novel, *The Pagans*. Its subject is the revolt of the Pagan Magyars against Christianity in the eleventh century. The author strives to enter into the thoughts of primitive natures. His hero is a young Hungarian noble who is a favourite with the Bishop St. Gerard. The young man yearns for the free life of the plains, leaves the monastery, and places himself at the head of the party of rebellion.

Herczeg is equally fortunate as a writer of historical dramas. *Brigadier Ocskay* depicts the times of the great leader Francis Rákóczy, and in *Byzantium* there is portrayed to us, in pithy sentences, the corruption and fall of Constantinople.

JOSEPH KISS (born in 1843) belongs to the school created by Arany. His name became known by his ballads. Kiss, who is a Jew, treats of a Jewish subject in his ballad, *Judith Simon*. From the house of Simon small coffins are carried every year into the graveyard ; every year an infant child dies. Despair drives the mother, Judith Simon, to go to the wise Rabbi to ask his advice. " Would you preserve your child *now ?* " asks the Rabbi. " You did not care to have a child when your first born was given to you. Where is your first child ? " Judith confesses that she killed her first child because its father had deserted her. The Rabbi commands her to deny herself the happiness of a mother's kiss ; she shall not kiss her daughter until her wedding-day. This will be the atonement for her crime. Judith fulfils the command. In vain the child asks for one kiss while she lies suffering on her bed ; the mother does not yield to her prayer. The father, roused to anger, drives the heartless mother from his house. After many years they celebrated the daughter's wedding. From the crowd which had come to see the beautiful and happy bride a poor beggar-woman rushes up to the bride and presses a kiss on her lips. She is pale and cold and dying. It is the mother who has atoned for her former deed. Among existing authors who write on æsthetics, the first in importance is certainly ZSOLT BEÖTHY (born in 1848). He is the author of a history of Hungarian literature; and also of a work analysing the tragic element in literature. It deals with the literatures of all nations.

Now that we have come to an end of our survey of Hungarian literature it will be well to cast a glance over the ground we have travelled. We have seen that Hungary's efforts for its own preservation have been the main spring of its literature, efforts rendered more necessary by her history, geographical situation and ethnical relations. Therefore patriotism enters more into Hungarian than into other literatures. It is the instinct of national self-preservation which we see in Count Széchenyi, though transfigured by the statesman's genius, and which has always caused politics to bulk so largely in the life of the people and has affected the form of literature by giving it a pre-eminently rhetorical character.

To determine the value of Hungarian literature we must consider its history and its amount. It was a thousand years ago that the Hungarians entered Europe and founded a state, which reached its greatest extent and power some six centuries later, when King Matthias occupied Vienna. Afterwards, the greater part of the country fell under the Turkish yoke, and when the Turks were finally driven out, Hungary had fewer inhabitants than London has now.

The language of Parliament and of the courts of justice was Latin, while German was spoken in the towns. These unfavourable circumstances must all be taken into account when seeking to form a right judgment of the country's literary activity, and if we do so, we may regard the prose output as normal ; so much we might fairly expect under the circumstances, but no more. The country has had some good prose writers, though it cannot boast a Bacon or a Macaulay. Among novelists Jókai is pre-eminent ; his rich imagination and inventiveness, and his genius for story-telling, render his novels fascinating even in translation. When, however, we come to consider Hungarian poetry, the case is different. In this respect Hungary has been richly dowered, for her poetry has been both more abundant and more brilliant than could have been expected. Alexander Petőfi was one of the bright stars in the firmament of literature ; the inspired Vörösmarty would be a distinguished figure even amidst the world's grandest poets, and Arany was an accomplished master of style and language. Just as during great political crises there have arisen gifted statesmen, so the national revival in the nineteenth century gave birth to great poets, and the works of these poets are entitled to a place amongst the literary treasures of the human race.

BIBLIOGRAPHY

THE first English work which dealt adequately with Hungarian literature was that of John Bowring: "Poetry of the Magyars, preceded
by a sketch of the language and literature of Hungary and Transylvania." London: 1830.

Bowring's work was based largely upon a book by Schedel
(Francis Toldy): "Handbuch der ungarischen Poesie," 1828.

Bowring also translated about eighty of Petőfi's poems: "Translations from Alexander Petőfi," by Sir John Bowring, LL.D., F.R.S.
London, 1866.

Gems from Petőfi and other Hungarian Poets, translated, with a
memoir of the former and a review of Hungary's poetical literature,
by W. N. Loew, New York, 1881 (enlarged and revised as: "Magyar
Poetry, 1899.") 8vo.

Mr. E. D. Butler wrote a concise account of Hungarian Literature
in the "Encyclopædia Britannica."

Dr. Emil Reich wrote a work under the title "Hungarian Literature
—London," 1898.

The most detailed account of Hungarian literature among the
non-Hungarian books written on this subject is J. Schwicker's
"Geschichte der ungarischen Literatur. Leipzig, 1889."

A bibliography of Hungarian literature up to 1711 was published
by Szabo (Régi magyar Kónyvtör) Vol. i. Kónyvtör. Manual
of printed Hungarian works, Vol. 2 (1885). Manual of the works
published in Hungary but not in the Hungarian language. Vol. 3
(by Szabo and Hellebrandt). 1896-1898. Manual of the works
of Hungarian authors published abroad but not in Hungarian
(1480-1711).

A bibliography of the works that appeared after 1711 was published
by G. Petrik (Bibliographia Hungariae, 1712-1860). Budapest,
1886, 1890-92, 1897.

INDEX

Redwood Library.

SELECTIONS FROM THE RULES.

1. Three volumes may be taken at a time and only three on one share. Two unbound numbers of a monthly and three numbers of a weekly publication are counted as a volume.

2. Books other than 7-day and 14-day ones may be kept out 28 days. *Books cannot be renewed or transferred.*

3. Books overdue are subject to a fine of one cent a day for fourteen days, *and five cents a day for each day thereafter.*

4. Neglect to pay the fine will debar from the use of the Library.

5. No book is to be lent out of the house of the person to whom it is charged.

6. Any person who shall soil (deface) or damage or lose a book belonging to the Library shall be liable to such fine as the Directors may impose; or shall pay the value of the book or of the set, if it be a part of a set, as the Directors may elect All scribbling or any marking or writing whatever, folding or turning down the leaves, as well as cutting or tearing any matter from a book belonging to the Library, will be considered defacement and damage.